DATE OF RETURN
UNLESS RECALLED BY LIBRARY

PLEASE TAKE GOOD CARE OF THIS BOOK

Child and Youth Migration

Child and Youth Migration

Mobility-in-Migration in an Era of Globalization

Edited by

Angela Veale
University College Cork, Ireland

and

Giorgia Donà
University of East London, UK

First published 2014 by
PALGRAVE MACMILLAN

Palgrave Macmillan in the UK is an imprint of Macmillan Publishers Limited, registered in England, company number 785998, of Houndmills, Basingstoke, Hampshire RG21 6XS.

Palgrave Macmillan in the US is a division of St Martin's Press LLC, 175 Fifth Avenue, New York, NY 10010.

Palgrave Macmillan is the global academic imprint of the above companies and has companies and representatives throughout the world.

Palgrave® and Macmillan® are registered trademarks in the United States, the United Kingdom, Europe and other countries

ISBN: 978–1–137–28066–4

This book is printed on paper suitable for recycling and made from fully managed and sustained forest sources. Logging, pulping and manufacturing processes are expected to conform to the environmental regulations of the country of origin.

A catalogue record for this book is available from the British Library.

A catalog record for this book is available from the Library of Congress.

Contents

List of Figures and Tables

Figures

Tables

Acknowledgments

We thank our colleagues in the School of Applied Psychology University College Cork and in the School of Law and Social Sciences at the University of East London. We also thank our contributors and reviewers and hope that they are as pleased as we are to see the book in print. Special thanks to Roshini Kempadoo for permission to use her photograph for the book cover. Thanks to Andrew James and the editorial team at Palgrave Macmillan. We would like to express appreciation to our families and friends for their interest in and support of this project. In particular, Angela Veale would like to extend a special thanks to Jeff Gonet, Pat and Sheila Veale, Conor Doolin and Leeann Lane, and also to Maria Dempsey, Samantha Dockray and Allen White. Giorgia Donà wishes to extend special thanks to Efthiha Voutira, Alice Bloch, Liz Egan, Lorena Marcassa, Anna Gobbo, Natale Possamai, Meri Gava and Carlo Donà, and to Matteo and Irene Donà, for including her in their imaginary journeys.

Notes on Contributors

Camilla Andres is an anthropologist and research assistant at School of Applied Psychology, University College, Cork. Her research interests include dynamics of relating within transnational families.

Fina Carpena-Mendez is Assistant Professor of Anthropology at Oregon State University. Her research interests include childhood and youth in late capitalism; neoliberalism, postdevelopment and migration; transnational families and emergent forms of life; learning, experience and embodiment in a globalized world.

Giorgia Donà is Professor of Forced Migration and Refugee Studies in the School of Law and Social Sciences at the University of East London and a Fellow of the Higher Education Academy. Her research focuses on forced migration and refugee movements, child protection and migration; psychosocial interventions and participatory methodologies, with a geographical focus on Central America, East Africa and Europe.

Neil Howard is Marie Curie research fellow at the Robert Schuman Centre for Advanced Studies, European University Institute. His work falls principally between the fields of political economy and political anthropology. He is particularly interested in the discourses, policies and institutional practices that frame, construct and ultimately depoliticize labor migration. He has published several articles related to the politics of human trafficking.

Rajith W. D. Lakshman is a research officer at the Institute of Development Studies (IDS), University of Sussex, as well as a research fellow at Middlesex University, London, both in the UK. Previously he was a senior lecturer in Economics affiliated with the University of Colombo, Sri Lanka. Rajith received his PhD from the University of Melbourne. Although topics related to forced migration (conflict, development and disaster-induced displacement) have dominated his work, he has focused more recently on regular forms of migration, primarily within the context of Sri Lanka.

Sunethra Perera is a senior lecturer in Demography attached to the University of Colombo, Sri Lanka. She receive her PhD from the University of Mahidol, Thailand, for her work on international contract labor migration and the children left behind in Sri Lanka. Sunethra holds a number of postgraduate qualifications on Population Studies and Economic Development. She has extensive experience in analyzing survey and census data on migration, mainly in Sri Lanka but also in other countries. She has written extensively on subjects of internal and international migration.

Samantha Punch is Professor of Sociology in the School of Applied Social Science at Stirling University. She is currently researching young people's livelihoods and migration in rural Bolivia and Argentina, and the sustainable use of aquatic resources and rural livelihoods in China, Vietnam and India. Her previous research includes children's experiences of sibling relationships and birth order in Scotland, and food practices, power and identity in residential children's homes in Scotland. She is coauthor of *Global Perspectives on Rural Childhood and Youth: Young Rural Lives* (2010, with Ruth Panelli and Elsbeth Robson), and *Children and Young People's Relationships: Learning across Majority and Minority Worlds* (2013, with Kay Tisdall).

Elodie Razy is Assistant Professor of Anthropology at the University of Liège, Belgium. Her teaching interests include the anthropology of children and childhood and the anthropology of migration. She published a book on early childhood in 2007 (*Naître et Devenir: Anthropologie de la Petite Enfance en Pays Soninké [Mali]*). She has also written several papers on children and migration and coedited two journal issues on the theme in 2011.

Reverend Pinnawala Sangasumana is a senior lecturer and the head of the Department of Geography at the University of Sri Jayewardenepura, Sri Lanka. He was awarded a PhD for his qualitative study on conceptualizing conflict-induced internal displacement in Sri Lanka (a split-site degree with the University of Sri Jayewardenepura and Uppsala University). His research interest in forced migration, including conflict displacement, derives from his long-time experience in teaching and research in Human Geography.

Dorte Thorsen is a postdoc fellow in the Anthropology Department, University of Sussex, and is currently starting a research project exploring how West African youth migrants working in the urban informal economy in the Maghreb envisage their near and distant future. She has done ethnographic research with children and youth who migrate from the Bisa region in southeastern Burkina Faso to Ouagadougou and Abidjan, and with their rural families in some 20 villages. Her research theorizes decision-making processes linked with young migrants' performance of identities, urban labor relations and the enactment of relatedness. She is the coauthor (with Iman Hashim) of *Child Migration in Africa* and has contributed articles to *Hommes et Migrations, Forum for Development Studies* and *Journal for Comparative Family Studies*.

Angela Veale is a lecturer in Applied Psychology, University College Cork, Ireland. Her research and publications focus on children and families in postconflict contexts in Africa, psychosocial interventions, psychological perspectives on migration and globalization, creative research methodologies and child psychotherapy. Her most recent publications include Veale et al. (2013) 'Participation as Principle and Tool in Social Reintegration: Young Mothers Formerly Associated with Armed Groups in Sierra Leone, Liberia and Northern Uganda', *Journal of Aggression, Maltreatment and Trauma*, 22(8), 829–848; Veale et al. (2013) 'Children of Young Mothers Formerly Associated with Armed Forces or Groups in Sierra Leone, Liberia and Northern Uganda' in O'Riordan, J., Horgan, D. and Martin, S. (eds). *Early Childhoods in the Global South*.

Diana Yeh is a senior lecturer in Sociology, University of Winchester. She was awarded the Sociological Review Fellowship in 2011. Her publications include the book *The Happy Hsiungs: Performing China and the Struggle for Modernity* and articles in journals such as *Ethnic and Racial Studies* and *Critical Quarterly*.

1
Complex Migrations, Migrant Child and Family Life Trajectories and Globalization

Angela Veale and Giorgia Donà

Introduction

Migration across multiple borders is a defining feature of the time in which we live, and children are central to this contemporary migration phenomenon (Bhabha 2013). Children migrate as members of migrant families and on their own. They are born of historically migrant families and may in their turn become migrants themselves. Children of migrants are often highly mobile, exchanging homes locally and internationally (Mand 2010; Olwig 2012). Adolescent migrants imagine their future lives as characterized by mobility (Veale and Kennedy 2011). Migration, whether personally experienced, part of one's life history or imagined into the future, has become a central dimension of the lived experiences of many children and young people globally.

While the number of studies on children's and young people's migration is increasing (Coe et al. 2011; Ensor and Gozdziak 2010; Hashim and Thorsen 2011; Ní Laoire et al. 2011; Parreñas 2005; Tyrrell et al. 2013), there are still very few such studies when considered in the context of the number of books on migration in general. This edited collection offers an innovative contribution to this emerging literature in a number of respects. Firstly, the chapters make visible new dynamics of child mobility-in-migration as migrant children and youth engage in multidirectional, multitemporal movements in response to changing global opportunities and constraints. We see that, in the lives of children and young people, migration and mobility intersect so that migration is not an end state, but rather is one form of movement in lives characterized by different forms of mobility: local, international; embodied, virtual; real, imaginative (Hannam, Sheller and Urry 2006; Gale 2009; Urry 2007). The novel aspect of this book is that it captures journeys by migrant children and youth that are short- and long term, near and distant, circular, onward and return, often with uncertain outcomes leaving open the possibility – even the likelihood – of further mobility into the future. It also conveys the experiences of 'left-behind' children, separated from their parent by migration, in circumstances in which restrictive migratory regimes in the receiving country make family reunification difficult if not impossible.

Secondly, the chapters contribute to positioning this complex mobility-in-migration within individual, intergenerational and collective migratory lifespan trajectories. A number of contributors capture the developmental transitions of children in historical or never migrant communities who traveled out, became migrant parents, and whose own children's lives are lived in different relationships to migration. In some cases, second-generation children of migrants are not themselves migrants, but they live highly mobile lives shaped by parental migration, ethno-national ties and global youth culture. The chapters also capture child migrants embedded in family and community relationships whether living together or negotiating intimacy at a distance, as family members individually and collectively pursue their objectives through migration.

Thirdly, the position of migrant children in relationship to globalization is explored. Stiglitz (2002) defines globalization as the closer integration of countries brought about by the liberalization of markets and technological change, but notes that goods, services, capital and knowledge flow more freely than people. New research is studying globally mobile children of the elite, such as children of professional migrant parents (Nette and Hayden 2007). By contrast, the chapters in this collection capture the lives of children and youth at the margins of globalization. The Human Development Report (United Nations Development Programme 2013) finds that migration patterns are changing with more South-to-South migration, nearly 80 percent of which takes place between bordering countries. Yet child and youth mobility within this migratory flow is largely invisible. This gap in the literature is addressed by a number of contributors. Furthermore, transnational families have been identified as an outcome of globalization (Dreby 2010; Parreñas 2005), and this is evident in this collection, but the book also captures a broader engagement of children and youth with globalization processes related to work and consumption, which remain underexplored.

Fourthly, the book makes a methodological contribution by bringing together research that draws on multisited and/or multitemporal and virtual methodologies as researchers follow their research subjects over time and space. Drawing together empirical research from Africa, Latin America, the United States, Asia and Europe, the collective impact is more than the sum of the individual chapters as the book extends its analytic reach to explore new migration trajectories as migrant parents and children respond to changing global opportunities in the South/North and constraints in the global North. It captures the ways in which children and youth engage with global systems, state policies and migration processes to advance their individual and collective life projects. This makes visible commonalities in their position that transcend local contexts to give insight into child and youth mobility and migratory processes in a globalizing system (Donà and Veale 2011). The following sections explore these themes in further detail.

Mobility-in-migration, children and youth

Children and young people are growing up in an increasingly mobile world (Barker et al. 2009; Urry 2007; Vertovec 2007a). This book draws attention to the complex, multidirectional, dynamic nature of children's mobility within global migratory processes. The chapters use multisited, multitemporal methodologies that capture an emergent complexity to cross-border migrations in which children and young people move for different purposes, distances and time periods within broader migration trajectories. The migration of a parent sparks a change of household for children who remain behind. Children born to migrant parents in a country of settlement 'return home' for short-term visits and move back and forth between countries of origin and settlement. Adolescents cross borders of their own volition seeking work or to earn money that can enable them to meet their intergenerational family obligations or to participate in a global consumer economy. They move to, fro and onwards as economic pressures mount due to global economic change. Children of migrants move locally to participate in activities with ethnic co-peers, make circular 'home' visits and engage virtually as 'global diaspora'. Across the different chapters, by following and seeking to understand this movement, we learn something new about how children, youth and families within migratory communities are engaging with global change.

The traditional migration story of an earlier generation of migrants that moved for work and settled long term in new host societies generated a research agenda that was dominated by a need to understand the impact of living as a member of a migrant ethnic minority in a majority host society. Research sought to understand the lives of child migrants and children born to immigrants in terms of ethnic identity (Phinney 1990), sociocultural adaptation (Berry et al. 2006), school adjustment (Fuligni 1998) and psychological or behavioral adjustment problems (Choi 2002; Fandrem et al. 2009; Oppedal et al. 2004). Post settlement, children's lives were assumed to be static. For a new generation of migrant children, youth and families, this old paradigm no longer fits the realities of their lives. Adult migration patterns are changing, giving way to 'new mobilities' (Baycan and Nijamp 2012) such as serial migration in which migrants move from one country they consider as 'home' for periods of time to another (Ossman 2004, 2013), seasonal or circular migration (Vertovec 2007b), transnational migration (Glick Schiller 2003) and return migration (Muggeridge and Donà 2006; King and Christou 2011; King et al. 2011). Within this new literature, the migration of children and young people is generally subsumed within adult migration or construed as an exceptional phenomenon (Donà 2006), including child trafficking (O'Connell Davidson 2011), asylum-seeking children (Lane and Tribe 2006) and unaccompanied minors (Bhabha 2004). New scholarly work is addressing childhood and new migrations (Whitehead and Hashim 2005). Ní Laoire (2011) explored the experiences of children moving within family groups as return migrants to Ireland and notions of 'homecoming'. Ní Laoire et al. (2011) identified a phenomenon of the 'in and out' serial migration of the children within middle-class professional Latin American families who move from one European country to another. Evidence of child mobility within migration is surfacing in the literature. Ní Laoire et al. (2011) noted the internal mobility experienced by asylum-seeker children in Ireland as they moved within the asylum system, the residential system and also between Irish towns. Coe et al. (2011) argues that children commonly experienced 'everyday ruptures' due to family mobility and draws continuity between previous eras marked by rural to urban internal migration and present-day international migration. Mand (2010) noted that British-born Bangladeshi migrant children were highly mobile between the two countries, moving for holidays, special occasions and longer stays of up to a year, and this facilitated families to remain interconnected and interdependent. Similarly, Olwig (2012) argues that, in the Caribbean, child mobility between households locally and transnationally facilitates adult migration, and that moves can be short-or long-term in duration and initiated by adults or by children. Furthermore, girls who move to live with caregivers are expected to contribute to domestic chores; as they approach adulthood, many move to seek work as migrant domestic workers, a progression that she argues is 'an extension and transformation of child migration' (Olwig 2012: 933). We argue that there is something fundamental about these child and youth mobilities within migration trajectories that are presently invisible and undertheorized that tells us something new about the experiences of migrant children and also about changing, complex migration in response to global economic and social change. A core aim of this volume is to contribute at an empirical level to knowledge about the intersection between children, migration and mobilities by highlighting underresearched child and youth short-term and micro-movements within major migration fluxes that occur in response to migration and global change. We refer to this as mobility-in-migration or complex migration.

Migration generally refers to large-scale movements of people from points of departures – usually understood as countries of origin – and points of arrival, receiving countries. It traditionally refers to long-term movements. Globalization, defined as the proliferation of cross-border flows and transnational networks, has changed our understanding of migration, as the new technologies of communication and transport connected to globalization allow frequent and multidirectional flows of people, ideas and cultural practices from a 'settler' model to also incorporate a temporary or transnational model, which captures the experiences of migrants who move on a temporary basis to host countries and still maintain relations with their countries of origin (Castles 2002).

The concept of mobility is broader than that of migration in that mobility encompasses 'both the large-scale movements of people, objects, capital and information across the world, as well as the more local processes of daily transportation, movement through public spaces and the travel of material things within everyday life' (Hannam et al. 2006: 1). In their editorial introduction to the first issue of the journal *Mobilities*, Hannam et al. (2006) set the agenda for mobility research, which, in addition to virtual and information technologies, spatial mobilities and materialities, includes migration, travel and tourism. The mobility literature, therefore, is concerned with all forms of mobility, ranging from daily routine movements around the home and neighborhood to long-distance movement and virtual mobility, and the ways in which transport, travel and communication functions in people's lives (Hannam, Sheller and Urry 2006; Urry 2007). It is about people moving back and forth, the dynamic nature of mobilities.

In this book, we use the term 'migration' to refer to large-scale, long-term movements, and the term 'mobility' to capture small-scale, short-term and dynamic movements of people as a practice of everyday life. While we understand that migration can be understood as one type of mobility, our goal is to highlight the connections between emerging forms of mobilities and conventional forms of migration. Recently, the concept of the mobility-migration nexus has been used to bring to the fore these connections (Hashim and Thorsen 2011). This edited book aims to advance this connection by examining specific ways in which the two concepts connect in the lives of children and young people.

The chapters in this volume draw attention to how children and young people use different types of mobilities-in-migration, that is, mobilities within their migration trajectories, for different purposes in response to changing economic, social and cultural circumstances over time and across different places. Punch (Chapter 2) describes the mobilities of Bolivian migrant youth to Argentina whom she first encountered in their rural communities when they were between the ages of 3 and 17 years, and followed for ten years as they began their migration journeys and diversified their work and mobility patterns in response to the Argentinean economic crisis of 2001. She captures an intersection of globalization, mobility and developmental transitions from childhood to young adulthood and young parenthood. Her chapter makes visible different types of mobilities in a migratory 'arc/career': outmigration, circular migration, return migration, internal migration and the lifespan and intergenerational complexities that have to be negotiated over time. Thorsen (Chapter 4) highlights mobility-in-migration among adolescents who have left their village to work in the capital of Burkino Faso or in Abidjan, the economic capital of Côte d'Ivoire, including internal and return migration and also social and cultural mobility, which the author captures in the consumption patterns and styles of dress that mimic global youth (hip hop) culture. Carpena-Méndez (Chapter 3) explores Nahua youth's circular migration between Puebla, Mexico and Philadelphia, following children of migrants as they began their migratory trajectories and become migrant parents themselves. Razy (Chapter 9) examines Soninke child circular migration in historically migrant communities between France and Mali and how families use child mobility to manage collective and intergenerational agendas of child training, and fulfill economic and social obligations in an intergenerational 'migratory debt' cycle. In contrast to studies of transnational families that focus on the social relationships that link societies of origin and settlement (Basch et al. 1994), this chapter draws attention to the function of child mobility itself for children, for families and for the social reproduction of the group. Circular mobility is embedded in the lives of the adults, and the author conveys a sense of children's lives lived in 'in-between' spaces. Collectively, these contributors make visible how interdependent internal and cross-border mobilities of children and young people are part of a dynamic, responsive adaption to demands sparked by economic crisis and change.

A focus on mobility-in-migration also draws attention to the relationship between dynamics of mobility and immobility, between migrants and nonmigrants, and between official and unofficial movements. An emerging trend in migration literature is greater attention to two forms of movement, official and unofficial. There are those who move legally and in time may be conferred with rights of family reunification – a mechanism that is increasingly used to secure the international mobility of children. Then there are those who move regardless, whose mobility criminalizes them, as they become 'economic refugees', 'bogus asylum seekers' or 'illegals'. Kubal (2012) argues that a growing number of those on the move exist in a state of semilegality, or what Menjivar (2006) refers to as liminal legality, on a continuum between previously defined binary poles of documented–undocumented. Veale and Andres (Chapter 7) explore the perspective of left-behind children of Nigerian migrant parent(s) in Ireland and their siblings born to their migrant parent(s) in Ireland. Children express their sense of physical immobility/imaginative mobility as their lives and those of their migrant parents are lived within the structuring context of Irish immigration laws.

Finally, an emerging theme in this book is the coexistence of material and virtual mobilities, a research theme that is still in its infancy. Yeh (Chapter 5) examines the mobility of children of migrants and Oriental youth cultures in urban Britain as she traces changing mobility patterns, from the migration and settlement patterns of the parental generation to the physical, virtual, transnational and aspirational mobility of the next generation and South-to-North global cultural flows. Donà (Chapter 6) looks at changing cohorts of Rwandan children over a 20-year period within and outside of Rwanda and shows that different mobilities (physical and virtual; local and international; short- and long-term) characterize the different generations. Both chapters show how mobility, youth culture and globalization intersect.

In short, this book highlights underresearched forms of child mobility within migration: seasonal back-and-forth movement that becomes longer stays away because of more stringent migratory regimes or less remuneration for work, or lots of smaller movements, town-to-town, region-to-region, within an overall migratory arc. 'Complex migrations' is a term that captures circular migration, return migration and local migration, in other words ongoing, multidirectional movements. What they tell us altogether is that they are happening at an increased speed, that they should be given more visibility and that they should be interconnected in the child migrant literature.

Childhood and migration: intersecting developmental/ mobility trajectories

We invited contributions for this book from researchers who are engaged in multisited, multitemporal child-centered research that explores children, new mobilities, migration and globalization. The children whose lives are the focus of this book include independent child migrants, child migrants in family groups, children of transnational migrant parents, forced migrant children and children of the diaspora. All chapters take a child-centered perspective, that is, they position children and those who began their migratory journeys as children central to their analysis.

This methodological approach highlights the intersection between developmental lifespan and migration trajectories, and also between individual and transgenerational and historic migration trajectories in communities undergoing rapid change. In contrast to literature that focuses on first- and second-generation migrants (Birman and Trickett 2001; Haller et al. 2011), the chapters in this book draw links between historical waves. They position an understanding of what it means to be a child in a lifespan, multisited and contextual perspective. Through movement, children and young people are learners and carriers of culture between one location and another; they forge intergenerational linkages between parents and obligations to grandparents (see also Whitehead et al. 2007); and their mobility and presence are a cause and an outcome of changing local/global conditions.

Children and young people undergo individuation as they move and make consumerist choices not only to express their migrant selves but also engage in the intergenerational ties, obligations and interdependencies that traditionally link generations. Children and young people are protagonists in historically migrant communities as children of migrants who give birth to a new generation of children who undergo varied, multidirectional forms of mobility, including becoming migrants and migrant parents themselves. Across the different chapters of this book, we sense a transgenerational, temporal connection whereby children and young people grow up as migrants, become mobile, and go 'global' as participants in a global youth culture while retaining connections with siblings, parents and communities back home. They give birth to children of their own in a migratory context, and in this way, life goes on. This moves us beyond static and universalist notions of 'child' as a chronological, age-bound social category, to capture migration as a sociocultural process structuring developmental transitions from childhood to young adulthood. This is similar to Mills et al. (2005) observation that transitions to adulthood in the world of work and establishing families are undergoing significant change in response to globalization, but the book also situates these transitions within intergenerational and in some cases, historical flows.

Across chapters, we experience children as active participants in migration-infused communities. Children witness the to-ing and fro-ing of young migrants dressed in the style of clothes favored by global youth; children directly experience or observe how migrant parents mediate love and care by sending money for education and food but also to purchase mobile phones and televisions that connect them materially, symbolically and imaginatively to a global consumerist community (Paek and Pan 2004). They communicate with migrant friends and family through text, mobile phone, Skype and Facebook, and feel connected to a world 'abroad'. They become linked to virtual networks with those who move. They imagine their future selves as globally mobile. In such ways, children appropriate through actively observing and 'listening-in' – what Rogoff (2003) refers to as 'intent participation' – different forms of contemporary mobility before they ever become mobile themselves. Contemporary mobilities of objects, of the imagination, of virtual and communicative travel (Urry 2007) are active in their material and 'interior' world as a form of situated learning about mobility, migration and global lives.

As Morrow (2009) points out, in a globalizing world, the interconnections and interdependencies of childhood and adulthood need to be elaborated. The developmental transition from childhood to adulthood occurs as individuals change roles and relationships in their community's structure (Rogoff 2003). Central to this is how the 'adult world' structures such developmental opportunities. While access to and total years spent in education have increased in developing countries (UNDP 2013), mass youth unemployment is increasing in the global South and North (International Labour Organisation 2013). Children and adolescents seek to participate in a global youth culture (Cole and Durham 2008), but more than this, adolescents in particular seek access to the resources, mirrored from 'adult' global culture, that confer independence, status and respect. Fewer job opportunities make it difficult for youth to access these material markers of adult status. De Hass (2010) has noted that enhanced consumerist demand for cheap foreign-produced goods fuels a 'culture of migration'. Through the eyes of children and youth, a more nuanced picture emerges that shows how neoliberal economic policies have resulted in an absence of valued, economically viable routes to adulthood status. As Thorsen (Chapter 4) shows, adolescents move in order to participate in a consumption-oriented, cash-based economy, which highlights the intersection between adolescent development, globalization, migration, work, consumption and self-representation. Howard (Chapter 10) highlights the tension that exists in the interconnections between childhood and adulthood in his analysis of rural Benin adolescents who migrate to cash-based economies in Nigerian mines to seek the resources to become a businessman or to marry, in short, to make the developmental transition from 'boy' to 'man'. But these adult-'oriented' initiatives bring their lives into conflict with a relatively new discourse of 'child trafficking'.

A strength of this book is that, as it delves into the particularities of children's and young people's lives in relationship to migration, we sense greater or more constrained degrees of child agency, or what Klocker (2007) refers to as 'thick' and 'thin' agency. Contexts in which adolescents move for work or consumption (see Punch, Howard, Carpena-Méndez, and Thorsen, this volume) or to partake in consumerist, global cultural flows, such as the international 'Oriental' party circle of the international student global elite (Yeh, Chapter 5), could be conceived as capturing 'thick' agency, the capacity to act within a broad range of options. Girls sent from France to Mali for marriage, as explored in Razy's chapter, or left-behind children of migrant parents (Lakshman, Perera and Sangasumana, Chapter 8; Veale and Andres, Chapter 7) could be argued to experience 'thinner' agency, that is, to act within very restricted contexts with few viable alternatives. It is tempting to view one group (adolescents, migrant laborers, international students) as resilient and adaptive, and the other group (girls sent for marriage, left-behind children of transnational parents) as victims of cultural or global legal regimes. Yet this is not what the chapters do. Contributors present neither a utopian nor dystopian view of childhood. Rather, the collective richly contextualized ethnographic descriptions of children's and young people's lives over space and time capture a dynamic and situated agency that becomes activated and manifest at the point of moving-as-life-response to changing circumstances *within a life-course trajectory*. Carpena-Méndez (Chapter 3) captures changing positions of optimism, realism, disillusionment and creative adaptation as young Mexican migrants become aware of their positioning within global political economic forces. Yeh (Chapter 5) shows how young British-Born Chinese (BBCs) use mobility to support identity and social belonging through meeting co-ethnics, but over time also become aware of their exclusion from another mobile youth culture, the night-life spaces of globally elite Oriental international students. The agency of participants is subject to global political and economic forces that control the production and consumption of culture and difference. Across a number of chapters, we see children's and young migrants' emotional and volitional experience of agency as bounded opportunity. Contributors avoid arguing for a recognition of the limitations of agency (Boehm et al. 2011) or falling into a common narrative theme in the child research literature of agency as a self-willed, volitional, resilient individual for whom it-all-comes-right-in-the-end. They leave the reader with a sense of a conscious, responsive agent who negotiates his/her position in an ongoing way in a highly unequal and unpredictable world. Children's development and mobility is more often situated within a family life-course trajectory and captures a *relational agency* emergent in child/family practices.

At the margins of globalization

In its simplistic sense, globalization refers to the widening, deepening and speeding up of global interconnections (Held et al. 1999). The term captures the process of integration arising from the interchange of worldviews, products, ideas and other aspects of culture (Al-Rodhan et al. 2006) as well as the compression of the world and the intensification of the consciousness of the world as a whole (Robertson 1992).

Migration and globalization are closely connected, yet the migration of people is often ignored in the literature on globalization. Children are also often excluded from our conceptualization of the world and research on globalization (Kaufman and Rizzini 2002). For Helton, 'globalization is often understood to refer to the transnational movement of goods, services, and capital while movement of people is frequently neglected as an important aspect of globalization. However, the mixing and un-mixing of populations will fundamentally shape individual lives and communal identities in the new century' (2002: 7–8). Globalization has altered migration patters: more sending, receiving and transit countries are involved in population movements than in the past; migration takes place more rapidly; more women are migrating on their own than in the past; and migrants use a broader range of migration routes (Castles and Loughna 2005).

Recent literature on the movement of people as part of global migratory processes has been framed within a migration-development nexus (Baycan and Nijamp 2012) or a migration-security nexus (Sørensen

2012). Both of these approaches focus on adult migration. Yet, the multidirectional movement of children constitutes another change in migration patterns that are connected to globalization, and there is a need to mainstream it as a significant component of globalization. As discussed above, children and young people are part of global migration circuits as members of transnational families (Parreñas 2005) and as undocumented independent migrants who cross borders in search of work (Hashim and Thorsen 2011) in a globalized neoliberal system.

Overall, this collection of papers explores how being a child or adolescent migrant functions in a globalizing world. This book is distinctive in that it brings together the separate fields of childhood studies, migration research and globalization, which have long been discussed as distinct and discrete areas.

This book strengthens the links between children, migration and globalization in three ways.

Firstly, it highlights child and youth mobility-in-migration as one of the changing manifestations of globalization. Differently from the traditional understanding of migration from South to North/West or from developing countries to developed ones, the book shows that there are varied child and youth migratory trajectories: North–South (France–Mali) and South–North (Mexico–United States; Rwanda–UK and Belgium); East–East (Sri Lanka to the Middle East) and South–South (Bolivia–Argentina; Benin–Nigeria; Rwanda–Togo); internal (within the United Kingdom; within Rwanda; within Bolivia); intracontinental (Bolivia–Argentina; Benin–Mali–Burkina Faso, Cote D'Ivoire; Rwanda–Togo), and transcontinental (Africa–Europe; Latin America–United States). There is a sense of dynamic interaction between growing up and moving and broader contextual changes due to globalization. Increased connections exist among child and young migrants and their siblings, parents, relatives, friends and communities who live in near and distant places.

Secondly, global discourses, economics and policies impact on child migrant lived experiences. While some of these young people are victims of global neoliberal economies, they also show that they can engage with globalization as consumers and buyers of global products in Burkina Faso and Bolivia, as shown respectively by Thorsen and Punch, this volume. Work and consumption are part of growing up in the era of globalization. The ability to work and to buy signals the transition from being dependent children to becoming independent adults and successful migrants. Migration increases the opportunities to become consumers of global goods, and through consumerism, children and young migrants gain higher status in their communities of origin. Globalization then occurs on a continuum with the local, national and regional and global interactions (Held et al. 1999). At one end of the continuum lie social and economic relations and networks that are organized on a local and/ or national basis; at the other end lie social and economic relations and networks that crystallize on the wider scale of regional and global interactions (Held et al. 1999).

Finally, migrant children and young people engage with processes of globalization by becoming recipients and promoters of global youth cultures, as shown by Yeh (Chapter 5). Their position as simultaneously young people and migrants gives rise to complex forms of hybrid cultures and identities that motivate them to engage with global youth culture (Bennett and Khan-Harris 2004). Independently of where they are, migrant children and young people connect physically, socially and mentally to the rest of the world, and develop a consciousness of the world as a whole (Robertson 1992). Through real or imagined/aspirational migration, many children and young people connect in social, relational and psychological ways to the world as a whole. They carry globalization 'in their mind'.

The chapters, however, also highlight a tension between inclusive and exclusive forms of globalization. As shown above, most of the children and young people move at the margins of conventional centers of globalization of the North/developed world. Their mobilities take place to and from the peripheries of the globalizing world in Africa, Asia and Latin America. Even when they move to the North/West, some of them inhabit the margins, as shown, for instance, by Carpena-Méndez's young undocumented Mexican migrants in the United States (Chapter 3) or Razy's marginalized Malians in France (Chapter 9). There is tension between the aspirations and initiatives of these children and young people to take advantage of the benefits of globalization through migration, and the structural constraints that prevent them from being fully part of globalization. Independently of where they are spatially, they are not outsiders or excluded from globalization, but rather they seem to find themselves positioned at the margins of globalization.

Methodological innovations: multisited, multitemporal methodologies

Research involving children growing up within complex migrations requires complex methodologies. It challenges researchers to respond by also moving, following them across time and space. Marcus (1995) marked a point of departure in ethnographic studies from single-site locations to multisited locations. This book captures a new transition point whereby researchers have to adapt and, similar to their subjects, engage in circular, serial, onward and virtual world research methodologies that mirror the complexity of lives as lived by this mobile-migrant generation. We asked contributors to engage with their research in terms of multisited and multitemporal aspects. In this respect, this book overall offers an innovative approach to understanding migration that intersects with individual and family life-course trajectories. Most chapters are multisited and/or multitemporal, and all used mixed methods. This methodological approach within individual chapters makes it possible to capture the ways in which children in different relationships to migration change and adapt to different circumstances over time. Multisited and multitemporal research enables a more holistic understanding of the complexities of migrant processes. Collectively, chapters in this edited collection show that in spite of the different national and local contexts, the lives of children and young people are embedded in migratory circuits and mobile worlds. Across different national and regional contexts, differently from other books that focus on a specific migrant group (Parreñas 2005) or regional context (Hashim and Thorsen 2011; Ní Laoire et al. 2011), the overall methodological approach of the book captures the 'global' dynamism of complex migration. We see the scale and diversity of these changes and movements, which are internal, interregional and transcontinental, and also the interconnections, that is, how places are connected and how children 'connect' to places.

It can be seen that individual contributors spent time not only in the field(s) but also in bringing their material, collected over a long period of time and in different settings, together in the space of a single chapter. Capturing complexity requires a significant investment in terms of finances to support fieldwork in different places at different times, time, effort and energy.

Virtual methodologies are an important emerging multisited and 'transtemporal' means of conducting research. Web-based technology is used by youth to mobilize and to meet up for recreation and political purposes. Yeh is both a participant and observer in migrant youth online forums. Donà examines web-based social practices of Rwandan diaspora youth and how they connect to homeland, organize political rallies and create transnational ties.

The following chapters

In Chapter 2, Punch explores the consequences of the financial crash in Argentina in 2002, sparked by neoliberal globalization, for young Bolivians who migrated there seasonally each year. She illustrates how processes of globalization impact upon youth transitions in unpredictable and unforeseen ways, in particular on young people's work, relationships and patterns of migration from rural Bolivia to Argentina. She highlights the diversity with which they manage crises over time by adapting their working patterns, restricting their consumption practices, adjusting their work–life balance and renegotiating family interdependencies.

In Chapter 3, Carpena-Méndez uses multitemporal ethnographic field-work in rural Puebla (Mexico) and in Philadelphia (United States) to examine how teenagers and young people self-organized in *bandas*, (peer groups) and were able to take the initiative in transnational migration and sustain processes of circular migration and the transnational life of their communities over time. In so doing, they have reconfigured the economic, social and ethnic practices and landscapes in their sending communities in rural Mexico and receiving urban contexts in the United States.

In Chapter 4, Thorsen focuses on adolescent boys who have left their rural homes to work and earn money in the capital, Ouagadougou, or in neighboring Côte d'Ivoire. She argues that African children are rarely associated with consumerism and globalization in international discourses on children's migration and work. She examines how globalism plays an important role in enabling adolescent migrants with small incomes to engage in consumption of products and styles that they associate with globalization, despite their difficulties of navigating exploitative labor markets while balancing their interests as members of transnational communities.

In Chapter 5, Yeh draws on research on emerging 'Oriental' youth cultures in urban Britain to examine new forms of mobility among children of migrants. She explores how their mobilities are shaped by family migrations and how developmental shifts from childhood to youth intersect with migration trajectories. She considers the ways in which these young people's mobility transcends pathways shaped by familial and ethno-national ties and relates specifically to a youth culture that is shared with other 'Oriental' migrant youth, which draws attention to the broader processes of the transnational migrations of other young people, processes of racialization and the globalization of culture.

In Chapter 6, Donà examines children's and young people's mobilities that take place during conflict and forced migration. Research that began in Rwanda is combined with multisited ethnography with diasporic Rwandans living in Africa and Europe and netnography of Rwandan mobilities in virtual space. She argues that, in glocal contexts, mobilities fulfill multiple functions: they are a survival strategy for children and young people, a driving force to achieve one's aspirations, a means to explore identity issues, and a way to strengthen social ties. They are mobile in material and in virtual spaces where ye-(young electronic) diasporas are promoters, audiences and actors of glocal movements.

In Chapter 7, Veale and Andres highlight the challenges facing children in Nigerian transnational families, in particular siblings separated through migration, based on multisited fieldwork in Ireland and in Nigeria. A core theme is the opportunities and tensions that are created through the global imaginings of left-behind children of life in 'the West', as their awareness of the daily life of their migrant parent(s) and siblings is mediated by the media and the pressures of global consumption. The left-behind child feels not only the loss of the parent but also the loss of being separated from the opportunities afforded by the West. Globalization, or the meaning and significance of Europe, infuses communication and decision making. The juxtaposition of reality and ideas about places far away complicates family life as children both in Ireland and Nigeria struggle to manage the challenge of living with both local and global culture.

In Chapter 8, Lakshman, Perera and Sangasumana examine the educational outcomes of Sri Lankan children left behind by international migrant parents. Drawing on a Sri Lankan household survey and interviews with left-behind children, caregivers and migration policymakers, the findings show that children of international migrant parents fare less well educationally compared to other children. This chapter makes an important contribution to the literature by analyzing the impact of the gender of the migrant parent on child educational outcomes. In mother-migrant households, children are more likely to drop out of school. We see how gendered globalized labor opportunities for women, in low-paid caring and domestic work in Gulf states, has consequences in the lives of their children.

In Chapter 9, Razy utilizes multisited ethnography to explore different forms of mobility of transnational migrant children between France and the Soninke Homeland, Mali. She describes how movement takes two main forms: the short holiday stay and the long stay in Mali. Forms of mobility differ according to age and gender. Through this analysis, the chapter draws attention to the function of child mobility for children, for families and for the social reproduction of the group. Children forge intergenerational linkages between parents, and their obligations to grandparents and their mobility functions as a fulfillment of a 'migratory debt' to the collective homeland.

In Chapter 10, Howard examines anti-child trafficking discourse and policy in Benin and then contrasts this discourse and policy with interview data gathered from adolescent labor migrants in Abeokuta, Nigeria.

A tension emerges between discourses of child protection and anti-child trafficking and the lived experiences of Nigerian youth migrants and their communities. This chapter offers a critical exploration of what happens at the nexus of adolescent migration and anti-child trafficking policy.

In Chapter 11, Donà and Veale conclude by drawing together some core themes, gaps and directions for future research.

Conclusion

This book contributes to an underexamined dimension of global change: the link between children and youth, large-scale migration and individual small-scale mobility in a globalizing world. It captures child and youth migrant life trajectories within intergenerationally situated, historical migrant flows and changing global patterns. It highlights the situated, bounded, relational agency as children and youth move in response to changing family needs, economic circumstances and global opportunities. It captures the inclusionary and exclusionary dynamics of globalization in the lives of children and a developing awareness among child and young migrants of their position and relationship to these dynamics. Collectively, the case studies that are presented here offer insight into the lives of children and young people around the globe and bring visibility to developmental and social evolutionary change in the lives of children, their families and communities as they engage with changing global conditions.

References

Al-Rodhan, R., Nayef, F., and Stoudmann, G. (2006) *Definitions of Globalization: A Comprehensive Overview and a Proposed Definition* (Geneva: Geneva Centre for Security Policy).

Barker, J., Kraftl, P., Horton, J., and Tucker, F. (2009) 'The Road Less Travelled: New Directions in Children's Mobility', *Mobilities*, 4(1), 1–10.

Basch, L., Glick Schiller, N., and Szanton-Blanc, C. (1994) *Nations Unbound: Transnational Projects and the Deterroritorialized Nation-State* (New York: Gordon and Breach).

Baycan, T., and Nijamp, P. (2012) 'The Migration-Development Nexus: New perspectives and challenges' in R. Capella and T. Ponce Dentinho (eds) *Globalization Trends and Regional Development* (Cheltenham: Edward Elgar).

Bennett, A., and Kahn-Harris, K. (eds) (2004) *After Subculture: Critical Studies in Contemporary Youth Culture* (Basingstoke: Palgrave Macmillan).

Berry, J., Phinney, J. S., Sam, D. L., and Vedder, P. (eds) (2006) *Immigrant Youth in Cultural Transition: Acculturation, Identity and Adaptation across National Contexts* (Mahwah, NJ: Lawrence Erlbaum Associates).

18   *Angela Veale and Giorgia Donà*

Bhabha, J. (2004) 'Seeking Asylum Alone: Treatment of Separated and Trafficked Children in Need of Refugee Protection', *International Migration*, 42(1), 141–148.

Bhabha, J. (2013). 'Children, Migration, and Human Rights', *The Encyclopedia of Global Human Migration*. DOI: 10.1002/9781444351071.wbeghm119.

Birman, D., and Trickett, E. J. (2001) 'Cultural Transitions in First-generation Immigrants: Acculturation of Soviet Jewish Refugee Adolescents and Parents', *Journal of Cross-Cultural Psychology*, 32(4), 1–19.

Boehm, D., Hess, J. M., Coe, C., Rae-Espinoza, H., and Reynolds, R. R. (2011) 'Introduction: Children, Youth, and the Everyday Ruptures of Migration' in C. Coe, R. Reynolds, D. Boehm, J. Hess, and H. Rae-Expinoza (eds) *Everyday Ruptures: Children, Youth and Migration in Global Perspective* (Nashville, TN: Vanderbilt University Press).

Castles, S. (2002) 'Migration and Community Formation under Conditions of Globalization', *International Migration Review*, 36(4), 1143–1168.

Castles, S. and Loughna, S. (2005) 'Trends in Asylum Migration to Industrialized Countries, 1990–2001', in G. J. Borjas and J. Crisp (eds) *Poverty, International Migration and Asylum* (London: Palgrave in association with the UN University), 39–69).

Choi, H. (2002) 'Understanding Adolescent Depression in Ethnocultural Context', *Advances in Nursing Science*, 25, 71–85.

Coe, C., Boehm, D., Hess, J., Espinoza, H., and Reynolds, R. (eds) (2011) *Everyday Ruptures: Children and Migration in Global Perspective* (Nashville, TN: Vanderbilt University Press).

Cole, J., and Durham, D. (eds) (2008) *Figuring the Future: Youth and Temporality in a Global Era* (Santa Fe, NM: American Research Press).

Donà G. (2006) 'Changing Migration Patterns and Responses in the Context of Child and Youth Forced Migration', *International Journal of Migration, Health and Social Care*, 2(2), 2–6.

Donà, G. and Veale, A. (2011) 'Divergent Discourses, Children and Forced Migration', *Journal of Ethnic and Migration Studies*, 37(8), 1273–1289.

Dreby, J. (2010) *Divided by Borders: Mexican Migrants and Their Children* (Oakland, CA: University of California Press).

Ensor, M. O. and Gozdziak, E. M. (eds) (2010) *Children and Migration: At the Crossroads of Resiliency and Migration* (London: Palgrave Macmillan).

Fandrem, H., Sam, D., and Roland, E. (2009) 'Depressive Symptoms among Native and Immigrant Adolescents in Norway: The Role of Gender and Urbanization', *Social Indicators Research*, 92(1), 91–109.

Fuligni, A. (1998) 'The Adjustment of Children from Immigrant Families', *Current Directions in Psychological Research*, 7, 99–103.

Gale, T. (2009) 'Urban Beachers, Virtual Worlds and "The End of Tourism" ', *Mobilities*, 4(1), 119–138.

Glick Schiller, N. (2003) 'The Centrality of Ethnography in the Study of Transnational Migration: Seeing the Wetland instead of the Swamp' in N. Foner (ed.) *American Arrivals: Anthropology Engages the New Immigration* (Sante Fe, NM: School of American Research Press), 99–128.

Haller, W., Portes, A., and Lynch, S. M. (2011) 'Dreams Fulfilled, Dreams Shattered: Determinants of Segmented Assimilation in the Second Generation', *Social Forces*, 89(3), 733–762.

Hannam, K., Sheller, M., and Urry, J. (2006) 'Editorial: Mobilities, Immobilities and Moorings', *Mobilities*, 1(1), 1–22.

Hashim, I., and Thorsen, D. (2011) *Child Migration in Africa* (London: Zed Books).

De Hass, H. (2010) 'Migration and Development: A Theoretical Perspective', *International Migration Review*, 44(1), 227–264.

Held, D., McGrew, A., Goldblatt, D., and Perraton, J. (1999) *Global Transformations: Politics, Economics and Culture* (Cambridge: Polity Press).

Helton, A. C. (2002) *The Price of Indifference: Refugee and Humanitarian Action in the New Century* (Oxford: Oxford University Press).

International Labour Organisation (2013) *Global Employment Trends for Youth: A Generation at Risk* (Geneva: ILO). <http://www.ilo.org/wcmsp5/groups/public/---dgreports/---dcomm/documents/publication/wcms_212899.pdf> Accessed August 20, 2013.

Kaufman, N. H., and Rizzini, I. (eds) (2002) *Globalization and Children: Exploring Potentials for Enhancing Opportunities in the Lives of Children and Youth* (New York: Kluwer Academic).

King, R., and Christou, A. (2011) 'Of Counter-Diaspora and Reverse Transnationalism: Return Mobilities to and from the Ancestral Homeland', *Mobilities*, 6, 451–406.

King, R., Christou, A., and Aherg, J. (2011) '"Diverse Mobilities": Second Generation Greek-Germans Engage with Homeland as Children and as Adults', *Mobilities*, 6, 483–501.

Klocker, N. (2007) 'An Example of "Thin" Agency: Child Domestic Workers in Tanzania' in R. Panelli, S. Punch, and E. Robson (eds) *Global Perspectives on Rural Childhood and Youth: Young Rural Lives* (New York: Routledge), 83–94.

Kubal, A. (2012) 'Conceptualizing Semi-legality in Migration Research', *Working Papers 58*, (Oxford: International Migration Institute, University of Oxford).

Lane, P. and Tribe, R. (2006) 'Unequal Care: An Introduction to Understanding UK Policy and Its Impact on Asylum-Seeking Children', *International Journal of Migration, Health and Social Care*, 2(2), 7–14.

Mand, K. (2010) ' "I've got two houses. One in Bangladesh and one in London ... everybody has": Home, Locality and Belonging(s)', *Childhood*, 17(2), 273–287.

Marcus, G. E. (1995) 'Ethnography in/of the World System: The Emergence of Multi-sited Ethnography', *Annual Review of Anthropology*, 24, 95–117.

Menjivar, C. (2006) 'Liminal Legality: Salvadoran and Guatemalan Immigrants' Lives in the United States', *American Journal of Sociology*, 111(4), 999–1037.

Mills, M., Blossfeld, H., and Klijzing, E. (2005) 'Becoming an Adult in Uncertain Times' in H. Blossfeld, E. Klijzing, M. Mills, and K. Kurz (eds) *Globalization, Uncertainty and Youth in Society* (London: Routledge), 423–441.

Morrow, V. (2009) Editorial. 'The Global Financial Crisis and Children's Happiness: A Time for Re-visioning', *Childhood*, 16(3), 293–298.

Muggeridge, H., and Doná, G. (2006) 'Back Home? Refugees' Experiences of the First Visit Back to Their Country of Origin', *Journal of Refugee Studies*, 19(4), 415–432.

Nette, J., and Hayden, M. (2007) 'Globally Mobile Children: The Sense of Belonging', *Educational Studies*, 33(4), 435–444.

Ní Laoire, C. (2011) 'Narratives of "Innocent Irish Childhoods": Return Migration and Intergenerational Family Dynamics', *Journal of Ethnic and Migration Studies*, 37(8), 1253–1271.

Ní Laoire, C., Carpena-Méndez, F., Tyrrell, N., and White, A. (2011) *Childhood and Migration in Europe: Portraits of Mobility, Identity and Belonging in Contemporary Ireland* (Farnham, Surrey: Ashgate).

O'Connell Davidson, J. (2011) 'Moving Children? Child Trafficking, Child Migration and Child Rights', *Critical Social Policy*, 31(3), 454–477.

Olwig, K. (2012) 'The Care Chain, Children's Mobility and the Caribbean Migration Tradition', *Journal of Ethnic and Migration Studies*, 38(6), 933–952.

Oppedal, B., Roysamb, E., and Sam, D. (2004) 'The Effect of Acculturation and Social Support on Change in Mental Health among Young Immigrants', *International Journal of Behavioral Sciences*, 28, 481–494.

Ossman, S. (2004) 'Studies in Serial Migration', *International Migration*, 42(4), 111–121.

Ossman, S. (2013) *Moving Matters: Paths of Serial Migration* (Stanford, CA: Stanford University Press).

Paek, H., and Pan, Z. (2004) 'Spreading Global Consumerism: Effects of Mass Media and Advertising on Consumeristic Values in China', *Mass Communication and Society*, 7(4), 491–515.

Parreñas, R. (2005) *Children of Global Migration: Transnational Families and Gendered Woes* (Stanford, CA: Stanford University Press).

Phinney, J. (1990) 'Ethnic Identity in Adolescents and Adults: Review of Research', *Psychological Bulletin*, 108(3) 499–514.

Robertson, R. (1992) *Globalization: Social Theory and Global Culture*, reprint. ed. (London: Sage).

Rogoff, B. (2003) *The Cultural Nature of Human Development* (Oxford: Oxford University Press).

Sørensen, N. (2012) 'Revisiting the Migration-Development Nexus: From Social Networks and Remittances to Markers for Migration Control', *International Migration*, 50(3), 61–76.

Stiglitz, J. (2002) *Globalization and Its Discontents* (New York: Norton).

Tyrrell, N., Whilte, A., Ní Laoire, C., and Carpena-Méndez, F. (2013) *Transnational Migration and Childhood* (London: Routledge).

United Nations Development Program (2013) *Human Development Report: The Rise of the South*. (Geneva: UNDP).

Urry, J. (2007) *Mobilities*. (Cambridge: Polity Press).

Veale, A. and Kennedy, E. (2011) 'Indian Young People Negotiating Transnational Identities' in M. Darmody, N. Tyrrell, and S. Song (eds) *The Changing Faces of Ireland* (Rotterdam: Sense), 53–77.

Vertovec, S. (2007a) 'Super-diversity and Its Implications', *Ethnic and Racial Studies*, 30(6), 1024–1054.

Vertovec, S. (2007b) 'Circular Migration: The Way Forward in Global Policy?' *Working Paper No. 4.* (International Migration Institute, University of Oxford).

Whitehead, A., and Hashim, I. (2005) 'Children and Migration', *Background Paper for DFID Migration Team* (Brighton: DRC on Migration, Globalisation and Poverty, University of Sussex).

Whitehead, A., Hashim, I., and Iversen, V. (2007) *Child Migration, Child Agency and Inter-Generational Relations in Africa and South Asia* (Brighton: Sussex Centre for Migration Research on Migration, Globalization and Poverty, University of Sussex).

2
Young Migrant Trajectories from Bolivia to Argentina: Changes and Continuities in an Era of Globalization

Samantha Punch

Introduction

In recent years, there has been an increased interest in migration during the life course stages of childhood and youth (for example, de Lima et al. 2012; Gardner 2012; Hashim and Thorsen 2011; White et al. 2011). Migration offers a range of opportunities and constraints for children and young people. The advantages may include regular work, higher wages, ability to send remittances home, opportunity to travel, acquisition of new skills and possibly higher social status back home (Punch 2007; Thorsen 2006). The disadvantages tend to involve difficulties in leaving home for the first time, particularly at a young age, status as an outsider, long working hours, poor working conditions and family ties that may constrain the nature of their migration. Such benefits and limitations are likely to vary according to young people's age, gender, birth order, family ties and peer and sibling relationships (Punch 2010). Furthermore, migration frequently encompasses both continuity and change (McHugh 2000) as young migrants negotiate their new livelihoods and relationships while often retaining links with their families and community of origin. Hence, it is pertinent to consider migration in relation to children and young people, particularly as migration is often intertwined with life course trajectories as children move from childhood, through youth and toward adulthood. While these are not linear, nor fixed, pathways, multiple youth transitions (in relation to work, education, housing, parenthood) illustrate the importance of considering childhood and youth as dynamic life course stages, rather than being related to specific age categories. The chapter makes visible different types of mobilities in a migratory 'arc/career': outmigration, circular migration, return migration, internal migration and the lifespan and intergenerational complexities that have to be negotiated over time. There is something fundamental about these child and youth mobilities within migration trajectories that are presently invisible and undertheorized that tells us something new about the experiences of migrant children and also about changing, complex migration in response to global economic and social change. The chapter contributes at an empirical level to knowledge about the intersection between children, migration and mobilities by highlighting underresearched child and youth short-term and micro-movements within major migration fluxes that occur in response to migration and global change, and that the editors conceptualize as mobility-in-migration or complex migration.

There are key linkages between migration transitions and youth transitions as, across both majority world and minority world contexts, young people are grappling with uncertain futures while moving back and forth between different spaces as they strive to form their own household and develop new relationships alongside continuing to maintain interdependent relations with their parents and siblings (see also Mills and Blossfeld 2005). Globally, many young people migrate in search of work, and their migrant youth transitions are likely to encompass flexibility and fluidity, as well as be heavily curtailed and constrained (de Lima et al. 2012). Skeldon (2012) argues that such transitional processes involve change over both time and space, and he reminds us to consider the interconnections of related transitions that link to migration while also urging us to place these in the wider economic, social, political and historical context. The aim of this chapter, based on a case study of young Bolivians who migrated to work in Argentina, is to illustrate how these migrant and youth transitions are also negotiated both within and across generations, involving a dynamic mix of opportunities and constraints associated with migration, work and relationships in a structurally restricted environment of economic crisis.

This chapter illustrates that young migrant trajectories are not only influenced by internal and local factors, such as children's relationships and household needs, but are also shaped by global economic processes. This chapter captures an intersection of migration, globalization and developmental transitions from childhood to young adulthood and young parenthood. It demonstrates how neoliberal globalization can impact upon young people's migration in unpredictable and unforeseen ways. While some young people are victims of global neoliberal economies, they also show that they can engage with globalization as consumers and buyers of global products. Work and consumption are part of growing up in the era of globalization. Argentina (the migrant destination country) had embraced a neoliberal economic approach that centered around the values of a global economy: free market, free trade and the unrestricted flow of capital. Scholte highlights the relationship between neoliberalism and globalization:

> From a neoliberal perspective, globalization is an economically driven process that should proceed on first principles of private property and uninhibited market forces. ... With a combination of privatization, liberalization and deregulation, globalization should bring maximum prosperity ... neoliberal doctrine has exerted a powerful hold on governing circles during the past quarter-century of accelerated globalization. (Scholte 2005: 1)

However, neoliberal globalization was not sustainable for the Argentinean economy, which collapsed in 2001–2002, leading to extreme economic hardship and social chaos. This regional crisis was linked to globalization as it had emerged out of Argentina's striving for greater equality and development within the global economy, but it was based on fragile foundations that eventually crumbled. Many aspects of globalization, such as 'deregulation, the growth of transnational corporations, the competition for skilled labor, growing income inequality, and the opening of emerging economies are introducing new risks, opportunities, and networks' (Goldin and Reinert 2012: 160) that are linked to processes of migration. Such economic and social factors, which are global in nature, have led to the contemporary period being referred to as an 'age of migration' (Castles and Miller 2009), in which development, globalization and inequality are intertwined (see Baycan and Nijkamp 2012; Martell 2010).

This chapter explores the changes in individual youth migration trajectories from Bolivia to Argentina over a ten-year period, and examines these as a range of coping strategies in response to globalizing economic processes. It is based on a longitudinal and multisited ethnographic study with young Bolivian migrants who were working on agricultural plantations mainly in the north of Argentina. It begins with a brief description of the methods, the context of migration and the financial collapse of Argentina. The chapter then explores the knock-on effect of this economic crisis for the young Bolivians who migrated there seasonally each year. It discusses the ways in which young migrants adapted their migrant strategies in the light of this global economic change. As Boehm et al. remind us, it is important to 'look at the nuances of global migrations, the breaks and disruptions but also the continuities of daily life' (2011: 6). Hence, this chapter considers both the changes and continuities that have impacted upon young people's patterns of migration from rural Bolivia to Argentina.

Methodology

This chapter is based on a follow-up study from my doctoral research on rural Bolivian childhoods that was conducted from July 1993 to July 1995, and July to December 1996 (Punch 2001, 2002). Ten years later, I undertook further ethnographic fieldwork from April to July 2006 (Punch 2012a, 2012b) in order to trace the children who were 3 to 17 years old when I first met them. The aim was to explore the constraints and opportunities they had faced as they developed their livelihoods. The follow-up study was mainly based on participant observation and semistructured interviews in both rural Bolivia and two migrant destinations in Argentina. Migration was a specific strand that I pursued in the follow-up study as, when I returned to Bolivia in 2006, I discovered that only 5 of the 32 primary school children who had participated in my doctoral research still remained in the community. The others had all migrated to either the nearby town of Tarija or to neighboring Argentina. Consequently I visited the agricultural plantations of Salta and Jujuy in the north of Argentina in June 2006, and the agricultural plantations south of Buenos Aires in July 2006 in order to track down some of the participants from the original research. As part of the previous doctoral study I had also made two trips to the northern agricultural plantations in Argentina to interview migrants during July 1994 and June 1995.

The qualitative data generated during the follow-up study in 2006 included interviews with five young female migrants and eight young male migrants in Argentina, as well as five returned young migrants (three girls and two boys) in Bolivia, all of whom I had known ten years previously and all of whom had experienced the Argentinean economic crisis in 2001 (see Table 2.1). These respondents were chosen for the focus of this chapter as they had all begun migrating prior to the economic crash. Hence, my interviews with them explored their migratory experiences before, during and after the crisis, up until I met them again in 2006. When I had last seen them in 1994–1996, seven of them had already begun migrating and eleven were still at school in rural Bolivia.

Thus these follow-up migration interviews were conducted with young adults aged 18–29, but a key part of the interview was their reflections on the impact of the economic crisis on their migrant trajectories when they were 13–24 years old respectively. The names of the community in Bolivia and the respondents have all been changed in order to maintain anonymity and confidentiality. A pseudonym ending in the letter 'a' is female, and all the other pseudonyms are male.

Conducting longitudinal, multisited research enabled a more holistic understanding of the complexities of migrant processes, by providing insights into the social, cultural and economic contexts at both the sender and the destination communities. In this respect, the chapter offers an innovative approach to understanding how migration intersects with individual and family life course trajectories. Multisited and/ or multitemporal methodologies made it possible to observe the ways in which children in different relationships to migration change and adapt to different circumstances. These approaches show the 'global' dynamism of complex migration. This facilitated a greater understanding of the 'push' and 'pull' factors associated with migration in both the home and the destination countries. Furthermore, given that I knew the young people and their families over a long period, it was perhaps easier for them to open up to me about the relational aspects and emotional costs attached to migration (see also Boehm et al. 2011). When I interviewed the migrants at the destination in Argentina, they were able to talk in detail about their siblings and parents back home as they knew I was familiar with their broader relationships. The longer-term and multisited perspective enabled me to explore the range of positives and negatives attached to young people's changing aspirations and opportunities over the life course (see also Hashim and Thorsen 2011). It was particularly useful to know what the children's premigrant lives were like back home in order to comprehend the relative advantages and disadvantages of their migrant lifestyles in the host country.

Most research on migration is a snapshot in time, which means it is difficult to capture the ways in which migrant patterns may change and adapt to different circumstances over time. The longitudinal dimension of the research allowed me to explore the dynamic ways in which globalization impacted their migrant pathways, highlighting processes of transition and changing mobility patterns. It not only gave me an insight into youth transitions over time but also an understanding of the changing nature of their relationships and the ways in which these impact on processes of migration (for a more detailed discussion of the strengths and challenges of longitudinal, multisited ethnography, see Punch 2012a, 2012b).

Table 2.1 Characteristics of interview sample regarding the economic crisis in Argentina

Name	Age and location at first contact	Migrant status in 1996	Age and location in 2006	Migrant status in 2006
Rosaura	9 – Bolivia	Nonmigrant	21 – Bolivia	Return migrant
Rebecca	15 – N. Argentina	Migrant	26 – Bolivia	Return migrant
Alcira	16 – N. Argentina	Migrant	27 – Bolivia	Return migrant
Beto	17 – N. Argentina	Migrant	28 – Bolivia	Circular migrant
Gonzalo	13 – Bolivia	Nonmigrant	25 – Bolivia	Return migrant
Melisa	7 – Bolivia	Nonmigrant	19 – N.Argentina	Migrant
Marianela	7 – Bolivia	Nonmigrant	20 – S.Argentina	Migrant
Ana Rosa	10 – Bolivia	Nonmigrant	22 – N.Argentina	Migrant
Natalia	13 – Bolivia	Nonmigrant	24 – N.Argentina	Migrant
Nilsa	15 – N.Argentina	Migrant	26 – N. Argentina	Migrant
Alfredo	5 – Bolivia	Nonmigrant	18 – N.Argentina	Migrant
David	8 – Bolivia	Nonmigrant	19 – N. Argentina	Migrant
Carlos	10 – Bolivia	Nonmigrant	21 – N. Argentina	Migrant
Santiago	9 – Bolivia	Nonmigrant	22 – N.Argentina	Migrant
Julián	13 – Bolivia	Nonmigrant	25 – N.Argentina	Migrant
Ramiro	15 – N.Argentina	Migrant	27 – S.Argentina	Migrant
Pepe	16 – N.Argentina	Migrant	27 – N.Argentina	Migrant
Domingo	17 – N.Argentina	Migrant	29 – N.Argentina	Migrant

Migration from Rural Bolivia to Argentina

The research at the sending community in rural Bolivia took place in Churquiales, in the region of Tarija. At the time of the follow-up study in 2006, there were only six years of education available at the primary school, and despite some recent developments, many households continued to lack basic services such as running water, telephone line, toilets and electricity. The rural community engaged in subsistence farming (potatoes, maize and a limited selection of fruit and vegetables), with small surpluses sold in local and regional markets. The majority of the family plots of land were not sufficient to enable all the children to inherit enough to subsist. Hence, once children finished primary school, they were usually expected to seek alternative livelihoods, at least for a while, until some land became available. The amount of paid work for young people or adults was minimal. Most of the work was seasonal, occurring mainly during the planting and harvesting seasons, and irregular, because much of the land did not have irrigation. During the dry season from May to October there were virtually no opportunities for paid work. Thus, the main strategy for young people to cope with the lack of access to land and limited economic opportunities was to migrate in search of work in Tarija town, 55 km away, or across the border in Argentina:

> There are no jobs for work ... then everyone begins to go, and one also has to just go, then everyone with their bags, their bags and they're off. (Santiago, 22, La Colonia, Argentina, 2006)

> There's more work there [in Argentina] ... I'm now almost used to coming and going. (Beto, 28, circular migrant, Churquiales, Bolivia, 2006)

Most boys and some girls went to the agricultural plantations in Salta and Jujuy in the north of Argentina (approximately 100 km away). They tended to begin migrating for work around 15 years old, a year or two after they left primary school, rather than choosing to migrate to continue their secondary schooling, as migrant work was perceived to be more beneficial (Punch 2002). It was largely low-skilled seasonal work, involving the planting and harvesting of tomatoes, peppers and other vegetables. Some girls sought work as domestic maids either in Tarija or in Argentina. Thus migration also benefitted those who stayed behind by reducing competition for limited resources and land.

Migration to Argentina was not new to this community, but over recent decades more and more young people were turning to migration given the lack of work opportunities at home. The history of migration from the region resulted in migrant ties through family and community links to the north of Argentina, which facilitated further migration (see also Martell 2010: 108). As Goldin and Reinert suggest, 'Migration both relies on networks and creates and reinforces them' (2012: 180). Such established social networks also facilitate cross-border mobility as well as offer support and employment opportunities at the destination, thereby enhancing the benefits and mitigating some of the risks associated with migration (Baycan and Nijkamp 2012).

However, the wage differentials between Bolivia and Argentina had changed dramatically since I first met the research participants in 1993–1996. Throughout the 1990s up until 2001 when the Argentinean economy collapsed, the daily wage for agricultural or domestic labor was five times higher in Argentina compared with Churquiales in Bolivia. This was partly because in 1991, in an attempt to stop inflation, the government decreed that the Argentinean peso had the same value as one US dollar (López Levy 2004). Since earning capacity was so much greater in Argentina, migration was a useful seasonal and temporary transition that enabled young people to work regularly and have the chance to save for their future, which for some included buying their own plot of land or building a house. All of the migrants interviewed during this follow-up study had experienced the higher agricultural wages in Argentina before the economic crash in 2001. They used to migrate seasonally for about 7 to 8 months, working long hours with only a half-day free on Sundays. The other 4 to 5 months during the summer, they would be back home in Churquiales, spending their Argentinean earnings on clothes and going to intercommunity football matches on Sundays, which usually involved a long socializing and drinking session afterwards, as well as going to other social events and regular parties:

> We used to work, earn 2,000 dollars and what did we do? Went to Bolivia to indulge in the lazy life. We spent it all.... We enjoyed ourselves until it ran out, then we would go again in search of more work. (Ramiro, 27, Mar del Plata, Argentina, 2006)

> Before [the migrant earnings] went a long way here... they didn't control it, they just spent it, they just knew that they could afford it. (Beto, 28, circular migrant, Churquiales, Bolivia, 2006)

Prior to 2001, the young migrants would return to their community and consider themselves on holiday, to have a rest. While they did contribute to their household labor during this time, it was largely a social world of leisure in Churquiales, which contrasted with an economic world of work in Argentina (Punch 2007). However, this lifestyle suddenly changed in late 2001 when the conversion of the Argentinean peso to $1was no longer sustainable as debt and unemployment had been increasing dramatically. The fixed exchange rate of one peso to $1 had been feigning stability for years in a country that was rapidly facing an economic meltdown. In the 1990s, 'Inflation was down, foreign investment was up, and privatization was ubiquitous' (López Levy 2004: 55), but by 2001 unemployment accounted for more than 20 percent of the economically active population and underemployment was also over 20 percent. Thus, the effects of unregulated, neoliberal globalization resulted in the economic crisis of 2002: '[P]rivatization led to a high-cost economy.... This, plus an overvalued currency and trade liberalization led to a surge of imports that destroyed swathes of Argentine industry and an increasing trade deficit' (Green 2003: 14). The government lost control over the economy and had to take drastic measures. In January 2002, the state forced the savings of individuals that were in dollars in bank accounts, to be converted to pesos at a rate set by the government. This resulted in a sudden massive drop in the value of people's savings.

The economic collapse of Argentina led to a high increase in inflation as well as social unrest with looting and street demonstrations as people struggled to understand the turmoil: 'After the January 2002 devaluation, Buenos Aires went from being the most expensive capital in Latin America to the fourth cheapest in the world' (López Levy 2004: 13). This social and economic crisis resulted in many negative consequences for the large numbers of Bolivian migrant workers. Instead of earning five times more than they would receive in Bolivia for similar work as had happened prior to the financial collapse, in 2002 Bolivian and Argentinean agricultural wages were equal and the cost of living had risen sharply:

> Foodstuff rose a lot. What happened is that one day it was one price, the next day another price. Money dropped in value, immediately money lost its worth. (Carlos, 21, Fraile, Argentina, 2006)

Only gradually did wages begin to rise again from 2004, and by 2006 Bolivians were earning twice as much in Argentina compared with back home, but this was still three times less than what they had been used to. As Parrado states in relation to financial crises in Mexico: 'Unstable employment conditions, rapid declines in personal and family incomes, depletion of accumulated savings, and sudden increases in the cost of living rapidly trigger new survival strategies' (2005: 329). The remainder of this chapter explores how the young Bolivian migrants reacted and adapted to the economic crisis in Argentina that had been the result of global processes of neoliberal economic restructuring.

Adapting to economic change: the migrants who stayed in Argentina

The young migrants in Argentina and the return migrants I interviewed in Bolivia had responded in a variety of ways to Argentina's financial crash. Many described their initial reaction as one of shock, as they had not seen it coming:

> We didn't know, nobody knew ... no one knew that the peso was going to drop in value. It was one day to the next because there wasn't even time for people to change it into dollars. (Alcira, 27, return migrant, Churquiales, Bolivia, 2006)

It was surprising to discover that many young people had continued to migrate throughout the crisis, even though their earning power had dropped considerably. The wages had actually remained the same, but the peso was no longer worth $1, so the exchange rate was greatly reduced, even dropping to the equivalent of one boliviano (one fifth of a US dollar). The young migrants who chose to stay in Argentina explained that even during the crisis, when wage levels were comparable to those in Bolivia, the Argentinean plantations provided them with regular employment compared to the irregular and uncertain paid work back home:

> For a long time people were in a bad way, you know, but then after, after a while they went back. No one can get work here ... just for a day, sometimes twice a week one is able to get a day's work, but after that there's no work ... it's hard. (Beto, 28, circular migrant, Churquiales, Bolivia, 2006)

Thus, as Martell (2010) reminds us, although wage differentials are an important driving force for migrants, there are other economic factors, such as employment opportunities, and social factors, such as social networks, which are also relevant to the decision to migrate. However, those who decided to continue to migrate after the economic crisis had to change their work–life balance as it was no longer feasible to sustain approximately four months of relaxing social life in Bolivia alongside only eight months of hard migrant work in Argentina. During the first year of the crisis, most of those who decided to stay in Argentina ended up not going back to Bolivia at all during the summer period. Prior to the crisis in 2001, when their wages had a high-value equivalent of US dollars, the summers in Bolivia used to be an important time of freedom and consumption for young people, which enhanced their status and identity as a migrant (see also Goldin and Reinert 2012). As a result of the crisis, their reduced ability to consume had an impact on their youth cultures, which were heavily curtailed compared with previous years of earning high migrant wages. Thus, similar to the experiences of some young migrants in West Africa, their decreased earning power affected 'their ability to build up symbolic capital through gift-giving and investments in their village or at the destination, as well as their engagement in social and cultural activities' (Hashim and Thorsen 2011: 126). This led to new forms of migrant identity (see Martell 2010), which did not reflect the social status of the consuming migrant prior to the crisis (Punch 2007). Previously, young migrants returned with material goods and socialized with their peers during periods back home, but after the crisis, visits were limited and migrant identities were linked more directly to their economic and hard-working status rather than to a more social, consumer identity.

Instead of returning to Bolivia to rest during the summer, once the harvest season was completed in the northern plantations they moved further south in Argentina, seeking work in different climatic zones that produced later harvests: 'Afterwards, once the harvest is finished here, then people go to another place to work' (Ana Rosa, 22, Fraile, Argentina, 2006). Thus, in an attempt to boost the lower value of their wages, they combined their seasonal migrant work in the north with other opportunities they found by travelling southwards. For example, some young migrants would earn a regular monthly wage for their work in the north, but turned to piecework (a *tantero*), being paid per crate harvested for several months as they moved between different harvests. Others learned new skills, such as how to package the produce (an *embalador*), which involved working unsociable hours, often through the night, and needing to be on call whenever a buyer was available:

> The landowners always harvest during the day, so at night you have to pack the produce and you have to stay up until dawn. And that's why, when suddenly the tomatoes are ripe, you only get one hour's sleep at night, day and night you have to be at the job. Of course you earn well too. ... It's not work that's fixed in one place, this packaging work is almost two months. ... Then it finishes, then you have to move to another place, and from there to another place ... like that, mini seasons, mini seasons, wherever the work is. (Julián, 25, La Colonia, Argentina, 2006)

Working as a packager and as a pieceworker tended to require extremely long hours, but migrants were more likely to end up earning more than an average agricultural daily wage:

> For contract work you don't earn much, because he [the employer] sets the price, 'I'm going to pay you so much a month', he says and that's it. It's not like that when you go by yourself, then you have to go around looking for work and ... piecework, that's how you earn more. (Alcira, 27, return migrant, Churquiales, Bolivia, 2006)

Therefore, for some migrants, working patterns intensified during the economic crisis as they took on multiple roles (see also Mills et al. 2005), working several seasons instead of one or combining different types of agricultural work. By expanding both the spatial and temporal dimensions of their migratory practices, they were able to outweigh the costs associated with their diminished wages. However, their increased spatial mobility at the destination was alongside decreased cross-border mobility as well as decreased social mobility as they returned less frequently and were now less able to consume and engage in a more relaxed lifestyle during the summer months back home. Thus, as Hashim and Thorsen (2011) argue, there are both positive and negative elements attached to the mobilities of migrants that can be curtailed and facilitated by their environments.

Some who were already working in the south of Argentina with more regular monthly work were also too scared to return to Bolivia for a long break in case their employer would not hold their job for them. Competition for work increased, and those in a regular position could not risk losing it, whereas previously there had been plentiful employment opportunities on the plantations. Even several years after the crisis in 2006, young migrants would only return for one or two weeks to visit family during a brief break, staying on to work for longer periods or seeking work in other locations in Argentina for the other few months. Some continued to choose not to return at all some years because they felt that the long journey and the money spent on travel was not worth it for just two weeks' holiday:

> Ah, you go from here [Argentina] to there [Bolivia], and in an instant you've run out of money, and that's it! (Melisa, 19, Acherales, Argentina, 2006)

> I had a job, so I couldn't really go back there for very long. There, the main thing is going out and playing football, and the money rapidly runs out...and then you have to pack your bags to go off again. (Julián, 25, La Colonia, Argentina, 2006)

Another strategy that two of the migrants I spoke to decided to pursue, was to move from working on the southern agricultural plantations near Buenos Aires up to the north of Argentina. As Goldin and Reinert (2012: 182) suggest, by moving to an area with a high density of migrants, they lower some of the risks and uncertainty associated with migration, and this was particularly the case during the financial crisis:

> I came to work up here because it was closer to home, if I go to visit them. (Santiago, 22, La Colonia, Argentina, 2006)

> [To] go back home from Buenos Aires, the fare is expensive now. You almost have to have about 400 pesos for a return trip. Instead

from here to go to Tarija, you can get home from here with 50 pesos. (Carlos, 21, Fraile, Argentina, 2006)

While the south offered higher daily wages, the cost of living was more expensive, and the much greater distance to Bolivia meant a high cost for transport if they wanted to return home. This was viable before the crisis, when they were earning well and returning home for several months, but not after 2001. Thus, moving to live and work up north instead meant a shorter distance and lower costs when going back to visit family. As Martell (2010: 109) points out, 'proximity enables migration', and this is particularly the case when wage differentials are not as beneficial and migrants are keen to retain links with their home community. Interestingly, many texts on migration and globalization emphasize the benefits of communication technologies for maintaining contact with families back home (such as Coe et al. 2011; de Lima et al. 2012), but in this case study of Bolivian migrants, their rural community lacks electricity, telephone landlines and mobile phone reception, which means that communication back home is limited mainly to letters or verbal news via other migrants. This illustrates the reality of the digital divide and global disparities in access to email, the Internet and mobile phones (Kaufman et al. 2002). Thus, the stronger migratory ties between northern Argentina and southern Bolivia have resulted in social capital for young migrants, enabling them to remain connected via their face-to-face social networks. These networks are also important for maintaining family ties at a distance (Gardner 2012) as they are used for sending remittances to family back home when someone in the host country returns to the community in Bolivia.

Furthermore, by working in the north, it was even feasible to cross the border to buy cheaper goods and clothes in Bermejo, the border town in Bolivia. This was more necessary after 2001, given that goods had become very expensive because of inflation in Argentina and that migrants were not always returning home each year. Another advantage of moving north to places such as Fraile or La Colonia was that these were popular migrant destinations as Bolivians had been working there on the sugar plantations since the first half of the twentieth century (Reboratti 1976; Whiteford 1975). Such areas had more Bolivians living there than Argentineans, and the Bolivian migrant communities in the northwest of Argentina offered a stronger social network compared with southern regions: 'Here there are many people you know who come, here in La Colonia you can find loads of acquaintances' (Santiago, 22, La Colonia, Argentina, 2006). This also became more important in a context in which migrants were no longer returning home for prolonged periods during the summer months. Most migrants tend to work six days or six and a half days a week, so knowing that on their (half) day off they can play football or socialize with their friends is some comfort. Prior to the crisis, they were able to tolerate extremely long working hours in more isolated locations when they knew they would enjoy the long summer months back home, but after 2001, some preferred to change their migrant destination in order to cope with the expanded patterns of work and the curtailed social life.

Some of the more successful migrants who had been able to engage in more risky migrant strategies, such as by renting land, reconsidered their approach. Renting land is very expensive but if the crop produces well and the market prices are good, extremely high profits can be secured. However, if the harvest fails because of poor climatic conditions or if most harvests in the region are productive and the markets flood with similar produce and the price drops, then the losses can be substantial. For example, some migrants spoke about grouping together to rent land and earning enough in one year to buy a truck among them. Unfortunately, the following year the price was low, and the truck had to be sold. After the economic crisis, some who had previously rented land decided to return to more stable, less risky, monthly paid work. Their earning potential was likely to be lower in the long run, but in the context of volatile market prices, this was a rational decision.

A key change that all the migrants commented on was that consumption practices had to be adapted in order to adjust to the huge reduction in the exchange rate and the high levels of inflation. During the crisis, this even meant eating less as well as eating cheaper foodstuffs, as Gonzalo explains:

> It was on telly that prices were going to rise, but no one imagined that they were going to go up to such a high price, just like that from one week to the next, everything changed, everything. Now let's say for example: we used to buy a kilo of bread at 80 cents [of a peso] a kilo, that's what they would give you a bag of bread for, it was enough to eat. Afterwards the kilo cost five pesos....Things were really expensive. Then we had to eat less. (Gonzalo, 25, return migrant, Churquiales, Bolivia, 2006)

He was living with relatives who were settled in Argentina, and instead of eating meat every day they would only eat it once a week and in smaller portions. However, even before the crisis most migrants would not have eaten meat regularly anyway as they tended to prefer to save their migrant earnings to spend back in Bolivia during their long holidays. For many, immediately after the economic crash, working was about survival rather than an opportunity to save and buy consumer goods: '[I]f we work we eat, if we don't work we don't eat' (Rosaura, 21, return migrant, Churquiales, Bolivia, 2006).

After 2001, the high levels of conspicuous consumption back home in Bolivia could no longer be indulged in. The young migrants had to adapt by spending much less on clothes, trainers and stereos. They gave smaller gifts to parents and siblings, bringing back more essential food items for the household rather than nonessential clothes. Their savings from long periods of hard migrant labor were dramatically reduced, and remittances sent back to their family in Bolivia were less regular and smaller amounts.

In rural Bolivia, like other parts of the majority world (see Hashim and Thorsen 2011; Parrado 2005) relations of interdependence between parents and children, and between siblings are important over the life course, as family networks help protect individuals against economic instability and social risks (Mills and Blossfeld 2005). In a majority world society with no welfare benefits, like rural Bolivia, young people have a strong sense of family responsibilities, including caring for their parents when they are old. Murphy-Berman and Kaufman (2002: 23) refer to cultures of relatedness, based on collectivist values, in which 'children ideally should be raised so they will remain loyal and connected to the family over their lifetime.... These caring duties are firm obligations, not personal choices'. However, in rural Bolivia such obligations are negotiable in practice, particularly as they tend to be worked out with siblings, often influenced by birth-order position (Punch 2001). Hence, I have developed the concept of *negotiated and constrained interdependencies* as a term that reflects how young people in the majority world are constrained by various structures and cultural expectations of family responsibilities, yet also assert their agency within such limitations as they balance both household and individual needs (Punch 2002). These negotiated and constrained household interdependencies exist both within and across the generations. As Morrow (2012) argues, this 'intergenerational mutuality' is a common feature of many majority world childhoods in which young people balance social risks and strive to fulfill moral responsibilities toward their household while pursuing individual aspirations (see also Thorsen 2006).

Household roles and responsibilities had to be renegotiated in response to the economic crash in Argentina. Given that many young migrants decided to stay in Argentina throughout the crisis, this impacted their families back home. Many of their older parents relied on them to come back for 3 to 4 summer months, which is also the rainy season, when most help is needed on the household's land in Bolivia, particularly during the planting and harvesting periods. Some migrant siblings grouped together to send some remittances to their aging parents so that they were able to afford to pay for day laborers to help them during this period. Three brothers in Argentina who did not go home in 2001–2002, asked their sister who was working as a domestic maid in the town of Tarija in Bolivia to return to help their parents for that agricultural season. This meant that she had to give up her job for several months, but she was happy to be able to help at that difficult time:

> I wanted to be more with my dad, with my mum and help them there a bit. I was happy to have had that time. ... There I was in the house, I helped them to sow, to cook. That time none of my brothers went back. (Marianela, 20, Mar de Plata, Argentina, 2006)

This example illustrates the new forms of mobilities (internal to the country of origin and circular) that emerge in response to migration processes that have been affected by global change. Her brothers experienced greater mobility within Argentina as they sought extended periods of work further south, but this led to restricted mobility in relation to returning home to Bolivia. In contrast, she was able to temporarily leave her migrant domestic work and go back home, reflecting shifting patterns of coming and going in the context of migration.

In another household, the older siblings had all migrated, and they pressured the youngest sibling left at home not to migrate until the crisis had passed, given that they were unable to return during those two years: 'There has always got to be one who stays behind' (David, 19, La Colonia, Argentina, 2006). This highlights the importance of birth order in shaping the opportunities and limitations regarding young people's trajectories of work and migration (see also Punch 2001). Thus, given the prevalence of migration from rural Bolivia, patterns of negotiated and constrained interdependencies between family members shifted and adjusted, particularly during the first few years of the Argentinean crisis.

Coping strategies: the migrants who returned to Bolivia

Some young migrants did not migrate for a year or two when the crisis was at its worst: 'Of course, that's why at that time many people didn't come from Bolivia' (Pepe, 27, La Colonia, Argentina, 2006). Pepe is refer-ring to the fact that for some young people, the crisis meant starting to migrate at a later age than they might have without the crisis (at 17 to 18 years old instead of 15 to 16), and for others it meant returning to Bolivia and not going the following year. The majority of those who returned were those with young families, as living expenses were much cheaper in Churquiales. As Goldin and Reinert point out, it is easier for those who are young and single to take more risks in response to wage differentials between countries, but harder for those with young families and greater obligations (2012: 179). Rebecca, her husband, Pepe, and their young child returned for five years, but as they were still young, they did not own their own land to sow in Churquiales. Consequently, they sharecropped with an older couple in the community who provided the land, the seed, the tools and the fertilizer, while Rebecca and Pepe did all the work. The harvest was then split 70 percent to the older couple who had given all the material inputs and 30 percent for them-selves as the laborers. After five years, Pepe began migrating again, but this time leaving Rebecca and their child back in Bolivia, given that the exchange rate was still much lower than it had been when all three of them migrated together.

It was a relatively common strategy for young families to return to Bolivia while just the father of the household continued to migrate. As Alcira explains,

> At that time I didn't go, I stayed of course. I stayed because then, then it was so expensive, so my husband couldn't take us...we couldn't afford it. (27, Return migrant, Churquiales, Bolivia, 2006)

Luckily, they had recently just built themselves a house on a corner of his father's land in Churquiales. They had used $3000 of their savings from their migrant work prior to the crisis to build the house and furnish it. Fortunately, they only had $2000 of savings left in the bank when the economic crash happened, which meant that they lost over three-quarters of it:

> Luckily, just that year I came back here to build my house...that's where I invested it [savings]. Ah, I was lucky...it [the crash] caught me with a small amount of money, it was around 2,000 dollars. And then afterwards, it was like...it wasn't even, it didn't even reach 500...500 I had left, it was incredible! (Beto, 28, circular migrant, Churquiales, Bolivia, 2006)

During the crisis, several young families found it cheaper and easier for the wife and children to return to Bolivia, while the husband continued to work seasonally in Argentina. This is also because as a migrant family they would need a room at the agricultural plantations where the family could stay together: '[W]ith family, the landowners almost don't really want you' (Julián, 25, La Colonia, Argentina, 2006). As Sayad (2004) argues, it is nearly always more difficult for an entire family to migrate. For the young Bolivians, by migrating alone it was easier to secure agricultural work, as an individual man could then share accommodations with other migrant workers. He would also be more flexible and mobile in order to seek piecework or work as a packager moving between different harvests. In addition, after 2001, the rise in inflation meant the cost of living was too much to easily cover the expenses of a wife and children. Thus, while keeping the family together can be beneficial for the young male migrant in that his wife will shop, cook for him and do the washing, this was not viable for many during the crisis. However, sending his wife and children back to Bolivia was not without difficulties either, as she would then have to manage working some land to provide for their subsistence needs while also caring for the children.

Once the worst of the crisis was over, for some families it was not always an easy decision whether to continue with just the husband migrating or to try to resume migrating as a family unit. At times there could be tensions between what the young husband and wife each preferred, as Nilsa observes:

> He doesn't want me to stay there [in Bolivia] and he comes here, he wants me to be here, cooking, helping him. I like it back there…I don't know if it's because my mum and dad are there…that must be why I can't get used to it here. (Nilsa, 26, Acherales, Argentina, 2006)

Thus, young people would have to negotiate and renegotiate their migrant preferences with their new partners as well as with their families of birth as they moved through the life course. The longitudinal research demonstrates how global economic processes can impact on levels of both out- and return migration (see also Katz 2004).

Conclusion

The chapter has showed the different types of mobilities in a migratory 'arc/career': outmigration, circular migration, return migration, internal migration, and the lifespan and intergenerational complexities that have to be negotiated over time. It has highlighted the emergent complexity of mobility-in-migration in response to global economic and social changes. Differently from the traditional understanding of migration from south to north/west or from developing countries to developed ones, the chapter has shown that there are varied child and youth migratory trajectories.

By using a longitudinal and multisited ethnographic case study, this chapter has offered an innovative approach to the examination of globalization, migration and changes in family dynamics. In particular, it has considered the global financial crisis in Argentina as part of the effects of neoliberalization and global restructuring, and explored the impacts of these processes on young Bolivian migrants. It has illustrated the benefits of considering the life course trajectory interwoven with the migration/mobility trajectory of young migrants. The chapter has shown the intersection between developmental lifespan and migration trajectories, and also between individual and transgenerational and historic migration trajectories in communities undergoing rapid change. The impacts of the Argentinean economic crash indicate how migrant conditions can change dramatically and globalization can increase the vulnerabilities of migrants (see also Bastia 2011). Exploring the changes in migration to Argentina over a ten-year period enabled me to understand the range of coping strategies that young people and their families developed to get through the economic crisis. Given that many young migrants take pathways that are flexible and opportunistic, longitudinal research into how their migrant trajectories change over time and over the life course can be insightful. This chapter has illustrated the diversity with which young people manage shocks or crises over time by adapting their working patterns, restricting their consumption practices, reducing their social life and adjusting their work–life balance, changing employment locations and renegotiating family interdependencies. Thus, importantly, this chapter contributes to the limited but growing micro-level studies that show how globalization impacts the life course and family relations of individuals (see also Boehm et al. 2011; Mills et al. 2005). As migration and mobility are dynamic processes that are increasing globally, micro-level empirical studies are required to reveal the complexity and diversity of the links between international migration, development and global change (Baycan and Nijkamp 2012).

An interesting finding from many of the young Bolivian migrants was that very few had any specific plans for the future:

> How would it be to go and live in Churquiales? The thing is that back there, there is a lack of work, there almost isn't any. You have to sow a variety of things, look after the animals. ... My husband says that

when he retires, we're going to go and live in Bolivia he says, I don't know. ... It's 'cos there life is cheaper than here, here is more expensive. (Natalia, 24, Fraile, Argentina, 2006)

I'm going to see, perhaps I'll settle here ... or I'll go somewhere else, I've yet to really think about it. (David, 19, La Colonia, Argentina, 2006)

When I asked them where they thought they would be living and working in five years' time, they had no definite views. Their livelihoods tended to be marked with uncertainty and unpredictability (see also Amit and Dyck 2012; Hansen 2005; Waage 2006), yet they also seemed able to react fairly spontaneously to emerging opportunities and constraints (see also Panelli et al. 2007). The longitudinal aspect of the research revealed that, despite the lack of planning in their lives, the young people demonstrated an ability to adapt to and cope with a variety of contingencies (see also Langevang 2008). Their ability to move and be mobile (see also Porter et al. 2010; Thorsen 2006) meant that their migrant lifestyles were dynamic and flexible, and their specific migrant destination was often linked to changing circumstances at different scales, such as the new relationships they formed or global economic processes.

The findings of this chapter are not dissimilar to those of Parrado, who examined youth transitions in Mexico during periods of financial crisis. He found that there was a greater reliance on family interdependencies and support, recognizing 'the importance of *household* and couple survival strategies for understanding individual responses to the forces of globalization and uncertainty in Mexico' (2005: 346). The economic crisis in Argentina that was sparked by neoliberal globalization had ramifications for the social and economic life of young Bolivian migrants. It curtailed their consumption practices and mobility back and forth across the border, but increased the mobility for young, single migrants within the destination of Argentina. The chapter supports the views of Goldin and Reinert (2012: 183) that it is those who are 'young and without children of their own that bear the uncertainty of migration', as most of the young couples with a child returned to Bolivia during the crisis because it was too expensive to meet the costs of living together as a family unit in Argentina. The young, single migrants demonstrated their ability to be mobile and adapt to changing circumstances, developing social relationships to travel further afield and increasing their earning power by extending their spatial and temporal contexts of migrant work. Hence, although this chapter focuses on major migrations inside and across borders, it also provides examples of underresearched mobilities, including shorter journeys for visits or summer holidays and internal movements within the host country. Thus new forms of mobilities, including cross-national, internal and circular, as well as micro-migrations are seen to emerge, which interlink with family dynamics as young migrants continue to negotiate and grapple with their intergenerational and intragenerational interdependencies with household members back home.

Acknowledgments

Grateful thanks to all the participants in this research and to the British Academy for a small grant, award number SG-41890, which covered the fieldwork expenses. Thanks also to the editors and anonymous reviewers whose feedback enabled me to improve this chapter.

References

Amit, V., and Dyck, N. (2012) *Young Men in Uncertain Times* (Oxford: Berghahn Books).

Bastia, T. (2011) 'Migration as Protest? Negotiating Gender, Class and Ethnicity in Urban Bolivia', *Environment and Planning A*, 43(7), 1514–1529.

Baycan, T., and Nijkamp, P. (2012) 'The Migration-development Nexus: New Perspectives and Challenges' in R. Capello and T. Dentinho (eds) *Globalization Trends and Regional Development* (Cheltenham: Edward Elgar Publishing), 181–210.

Boehm, D., Hess, J., Coe, C., Rae-Espinoza, H., and Reynolds, R. (2011) 'Children, Youth, and the Everyday Ruptures of Migration' in C. Coe, R. Reynolds, D. Boehm, J. Hess, and H. Rae-Espinoza (eds) *Everyday Ruptures: Children, Youth, and Migration in Global Perspective* (Nashville: Vanderbilt University Press), 1–22.

Castles, S., and Miller, M. (2009) *The Age of Migration: International Population Movements in the Modern World*, 4th ed. (Basingstoke: Palgrave).

Coe, C., Reynolds, R., Boehm, D., Hess, J., and Rae-Espinoza, H. (eds) (2011) *Everyday Ruptures: Children, Youth, and Migration in Global Perspective* (Nashville: Vanderbilt University Press).

De Lima, P., Punch, S., and Whitehead, A. (2012) 'Exploring Children's Experiences of Migration: Movement and Family Relationships', *Briefing 61* (Edinburgh: Centre for Research on Families and Relationships). https://www.era.lib.ed.ac.uk/bitstream/1842/6555/1/briefing%2061.pdf. Accessed April 15, 2014.

Gardner, K. (2012) 'Transnational Migration and the Study of Children', *Journal of Ethnic and Migration Studies, Special Issue on Children's Transnational Migration*, 38(6), 889–912.

Goldin, I., and Reinert, K. (2012) *Globalization for Development: Meeting New Challenges* (Oxford: Oxford University Press).

Green, D. (2003) *Silent Revolution: The Rise and Crisis of Market Economics in Latin America* (London: Latin America Bureau).

Hansen, K. T. (2005) 'Getting Stuck in the Compound: Some Odds against Social Adulthood in Lusaka, Zambia', *Africa Today*, 51(4), 3–16.

Hashim, I., and Thorsen, D. (2011) *Children's Independent Migration in Africa* (London: Nordic African Institute, Uppsala and ZED Books).

Katz, C. (2004) *Growing Up Global: Economic Restructuring and Children's Everyday Lives* (Minneapolis, MN: University of Minnesota Press).

Kaufman, N., Rizzini, I., Wilson, K., and Bush, M. (2002) 'The Impact of Global Economic, Political, and Social Transformations on the Lives of Children' in N. Kaufman and I. Rizzini (eds) *Globalization and Children: Exploring Potentials for Enhancing Opportunities in the Lives of Children and Youth* (New York: Kluwer Academic/Plenum Publishers), 3–18.

Langevang, T. (2008) 'We Are Managing!: Uncertain Paths to Respectable Adulthoods in Accra, Ghana', *Geoforum*, 39(6), 2039–2047.

López Levy, M. (2004) *We Are Millions: Neo-Liberalism and New Forms of Political Action in Argentina* (London: Latin America Bureau).

Martell, L. (2010) *The Sociology of Globalization* (Cambridge: Polity Press).

McHugh, K. (2000) 'Inside, Outside, Upside Down, Backward, Forward, Round and Round: A Case for Ethnographic Studies in Migration', *Progress in Human Geography*, 24(1), 71–89.

Mills, M., and Blossfeld, H. (2005) 'Globalization, Uncertainty and the Early Life Course. A Theoretical Framework' in H. Blossfeld, E. Klijzing, M. Mills, and K. Kurz (eds) *Globalization, Uncertainty and Youth in Society* (London: Routledge), 1–24.

Mills, M., Blossfeld, H., and Klijzing, E. (2005) 'Becoming an Adult in Uncertain Times' in H. Blossfeld, E. Klijzing, M. Mills, and K. Kurz (eds) *Globalization, Uncertainty and Youth in Society* (London: Routledge), 423–441.

Morrow, V. (2012) 'Troubling Transitions? Young People's Experiences of Growing Up in Poverty in Rural Andhra Pradesh, India', *Journal of Youth Studies*, 16(1), 86–100.

Murphy-Berman, V., and Kaufman, N. (2002) 'Globalization in Cross-cultural Perspective' in N. Kaufman and I. Rizzini (eds) *Globalization and Children: Exploring Potentials for Enhancing Opportunities in the Lives of Children and Youth* (New York: Kluwer Academic/Plenum Publishers), 19–30.

Panelli, R., Punch, S., and Robson, E. (eds) (2007) *Global Perspectives on Rural Childhood and Youth: Young Rural Lives* (*London*: Routledge).

Parrado, E. (2005) 'Transition to Adulthood in Mexico' in H. Blossfeld, E. Klijzing, M. Mills, and K. Kurz (eds) *Globalization, Uncertainty and Youth in Society* (London: Routledge), 327–348.

Porter, G., Hampshire, K., Mashiri, M., Dube, S., and Maponya, G. (2010) 'Youthscapes and Escapes in Rural Africa: Education, Mobility and Livelihood Trajectories for Young People in Eastern Cape, South Africa', *Journal of International Development*, 22, 1090–1101.

Punch, S. (2001) 'Household Division of Labour: Generation, Gender, Age, Birth Order and Sibling Composition', *Work, Employment and Society*, 15(4), 803–823.

Punch, S. (2002) 'Youth Transitions and Interdependent Adult-child Relations in Rural Bolivia', *Journal of Rural Studies*, 18(2), 123–133.

Punch, S. (2007) 'Negotiating Migrant Identities: Young People in Bolivia and Argentina', *Children's Geographies*, 5(1), 95–112.

Punch, S. (2010) 'Moving for a Better Life: To Stay or to Go?' in D. Kassem, L. Murphy, and E. Taylor (eds) *Key Issues in Childhood and Youth Studies* (London: Routledge), 202–215.

Punch, S. (2012a) 'Hidden Struggles of Fieldwork: Exploring the Role and Use of Field Diaries', *Emotion, Space and Society*, 5, 86–93.

Punch, S. (2012b) 'Studying Transnational Migration: A Longitudinal and Multi-sited Ethnographic Approach', *Journal of Migration and Ethnic Studies*, 38(6), 1007–1023.

Reboratti, C. (1976) 'Migración Estacional en el Noroeste Argentino y su Repercusión en la Estructura Agraria', *Demografía y Economía*, 10(2), 235–253.

Sayad, A. (2004) *The Suffering of the Immigrant* (Cambridge: Polity Press).

Scholte, J. A. (2005) *The Sources of Neoliberal Globalization, Overarching Concerns: Program Paper No. 8.*, United Nations Research Institute for Social Development.

Skeldon, R. (2012) 'Migration Transitions Revisited: Their Continued Relevance for the Development of Migration Theory,' *Population, Space and Place*, 18(2), 154–166.

Thorsen, D. (2006) 'Child Migrants in Transit: Strategies to Assert New Identities in Rural Burkina Faso' in C. Christiansen, M. Utas, and H. E. Vigh (eds) *Navigating Youth, Generating Adulthood: Social Becoming in an African Context* (Uppsala :The Nordic Africa Institute), 88–114.

Waage, T. (2006) 'Coping with Unpredictability: "Preparing for Life" in Ngaoundéré, Cameroon' in C. Christiansen, M. Utas, and H. E. Vigh (eds) *Navigating Youth, Generating Adulthood: Social Becoming in an African Context* (Uppsala: The Nordic Africa Institute), 61–87.

White, A., Ni Laoire, C., Tyrrell, N., and Carpena-Mendez, F. (2011) 'Children's Roles in Transnational Migration', *Special Issue on Transnational Migration and Childhood, Journal of Ethnic and Migration Studies*, 27(8), 1159–1170.

Whiteford, J. (1975) *Urbanization of Rural Proletarians: Bolivian Migrant Workers in Northwest Argentina* (Ann Arbor, MI: University Microfilms International).

3
Transnational/Indigenous Youth: Learning, Feeling and Being in Globalized Contexts

Fina Carpena-Méndez

Introduction

The neoliberal restructuring of the Mexican state and the project of North American integration have worked to uproot indigenous and rural populations from their local subsistence economies and to incorporate them into the unprecedented growth of the service sector in the United States. In the context of a wide constellation of policy changes under neoliberal regimes, Mexican indigenous rural communities without previous experience of transnational migration were rapidly incorporated into transnational migratory circuits during the last decade of the twentieth century. New conceptual developments have attempted to comprehend the workings of contemporary migration phenomena in the context of neoliberalism. Rapid and massive transnational migration movements without networks of support constructed over several generations, which is understood as 'accelerated migration' (Binford 2000, 2003a, 2004), and the growing commercialization of international migration or the 'migration industry' (Gammeltoft-Hansen and Sørensen 2013) characterize the migratory patterns and networks that have emerged under neoliberal globalism.

What is overlooked when considering how questions of contemporary migration might be explored is the fact that adolescents and young people have often taken the lead in new migratory processes. The cultural and social resources that youth have drawn upon to lead and sustain these circular migratory processes, and the effects that their lived experiences as immigrants in the United States have had on their self-understandings and their perceptions of possible futures back in their Mexican rural villages are not well known. In this chapter, I argue that

an examination of the changing daily experiences of Mexican indigenous children and the formation of youth subjectivities in new migrant-
sending communities reveals the crucial connections between emerging
forms of rurality without agriculture, the unaccompanied migration of
indigenous youth to Philadelphia and the restructuring of urban spaces
and citizenship in global North cities.

The chapter draws from over a decade of multitemporal fieldwork with
Nahua children and youth from the state of Puebla, Mexico, from 2002,
tracing their ongoing circularity across the border, their experiences in
Philadelphia and for some, their return migration in 2011.[1] It documents their experiences of growing up in new migrant-sending communities that have been recently incorporated into transnational migration
circuits, taking the lead in the migration process to Philadelphia, and
analyzes the significance of their experiences as immigrants in the
United States. It captures changing mobilities within migratory careers
of outmigration, circular migration and return migration to rural
communities back in Mexico. In so doing, it uncovers the importance of
bandas (self-organized youth groups) in initiating and sustaining back-
and-forth mobilities-in-migration. The story that emerged in my fieldwork, one that documents how youth took the lead in transnational
migration in an indigenous community without previous experience
in international migration, the reorganization of children's practices
in the sending community, the reformulation of migrant youth self-
understandings in Philadelphia, and their experiences of return migration, is one that I replicate in the structure of this chapter.

From indigenous village to a transnational community: youth taking the lead in migration and the children left behind sustaining the everyday

Mexican rural areas are undergoing major accelerated transformations.
There is a great deal of uncertainty about the future of rural communities. Under the new rules of trade liberalization, the new legal framework for the progressive privatization of *ejido*[2] lands, and the withdrawal
of state subsidies for small-scale producers, local subsistence economies are being progressively dismantled. The latest historical round
of modernizing globalization has taken place through the implementation of neoliberal policies working in synergy to uproot rural youth
from subsistence activities and to produce new sociabilities and altered
subjectivities by incorporating indigenous youth into the global market
of production and consumption.

My fieldwork took place in the community of San Matias,[3] which was monolingual in Nahuatl until the 1970s, when young people were drawn to Mexico City's expanding labor market for intermittent periods of time. Girls were employed mainly as domestics and boys in construction, in *tortillerias* or as street sellers. Networks of kinship relationships and economic cooperation were extended between the peasant village and the capital's shantytowns, facilitating migrant reception in the city and the periodic return to the village for peak moments of the agricultural cycle, rituals and celebrations. The generation that came of age during the 1970s (middle-aged adults at the time of my fieldwork) recall experiencing quotidian violence in marginal neighborhoods on the capital's fringes, social discrimination for speaking an indigenous language, racist insults at work and public spaces, and the shame of having to learn Spanish to interact not only with middle-class European descendants and *mestizo* employers but also with other indigenous people with longer histories of rural–urban migration who would establish an ethnoracial hierarchy of Indianness. Ironically, these same ethnoracial hierarchies of Indianness have been encountered again decades later by the new generations of transnational migrant youth working with other indigenous and *mestizo* Mexican immigrants in Philadelphia and New York.

This circularity that characterized processes of internal rural–urban migration during the 1970s and 1980s generated the emergence of 'youth' as a new social category and subject position in indigenous communities. It is this subject position from which at the end of the 1990s economic restructuring under neoliberal regimes produced the conditions for young people to take the lead in transnational migration by drawing on forms of self-organization in *bandas*. I have described elsewhere (Carpena-Méndez 2007) how *pandillerismo* or 'being *banda*' (youth gang practices) became the forms of 'being young' (understood as a social category indicative of a modern self that had no equivalent in Nahua age categories as a specific and distinct stage in the life course) that Nahua youth imitated and experimented with in urban marginal areas. Becoming *banda* was experienced as both a form of overcoming the Indian identity of their parents and adjusting and coping with the conditions of life in the streets of the shantytowns. In the late 1980s, *pandillas,* or youth *bandas*, spread through the rural landscape of central Mexico, introduced by the back-and-forth processes of youth labor migration.

Like other institutions and practices alien to indigenous villages, youth gangs were absorbed and integrated into the social organization of their communities. Since the 1980s, *bandas* in this rural area have been territorialized by *barrios* and affiliation to preexisting village divisions based on kinship and *compadrazgo* (co-godparenthood) networks. Being *banda* is to display urbanness, a strategy that Nahua youth employ to modernize the self. It is not, however, a radically different form of sociality from the ones of their grandparents and ancestors. *Pandillas* are territorial, and their membership depends on geographical divisions in kinship-composed barrios. Youth *bandas* identify themselves with a specific *barrio*, with the street corners of that *barrio* where they meet at night. When young people comment on the formation of their *bandas*, they often stress the historical continuity of village kinship and divisions based on political factions, which youth *bandas* reproduce.

There is also a perceived generational dimension of *pandillerismo* in this indigenous village. In the last 20 years, generations of village gangs have engaged with changes in media-based popular music and imaginaries, knitting them into their village social organization. Generations of *bandas* coexist in the same *barrio* and unite as a big organization in specific village celebrations. Children of different ages have their own street groups, which belong to the *barrio's banda*. In the past, *banda* members would leave street activities as they grew older and got married, but would continue to be part of the *barrio* gang at village celebrations; others would stay in the street gang as adults. Nowadays, *banda* members migrate to the north at age 14 or 16, and younger children remain or join the new gang generation of their village *barrio*. *Barrio* groups of youth are peer groups that provide friendship and support networks in migration to the city and across borders.

After the implementation of the North American Free Trade Agreement (NAFTA) in 1994, an accelerated migration to the United States started to take place. This involved a rapid outflow of migrants over a short period of time who could not rely on preexisting transnational networks that were constructed gradually over several generations to provide knowledge and sustain the process, as in other Mexican regions with long migratory histories. Boys and girls in their teens took the lead in emerging patterns of circular migration by using gang membership and practices as social capital to construct support networks in their passages to the north. Through patterns of circular undocumented migration lasting an average of two or three years, youth sought low-wage, unprotected jobs in New York and Philadelphia, mostly in restaurants and factories. When returning to the village, the first waves of migrant youth had the fantasy of building their own block house, open a little store, or even investing in a restaurant in a nearby town instead of working in the cornfields. They soon realized that in order to sustain an improved standard of living it is necessary to have a constant flow of remittances, and decided to return to the United States. Migrant returnees tended to spend their time *paseando en la calle* (hanging out in the street) until they had exhausted their savings and decided to go again to the north, thus initiating another migratory cycle.

The network of kin and *carnales* (ritual brotherhood) in the *banda* provide the connections and the type of information required for crossing the border, as well as the initial social and economic support in the United States. Teenagers' lives and migratory projects are increasingly dependent on the *banda*. Youth migratory cycles tend to reproduce gang generations. Groups of friends from the *barrio's* gang, who belong to the same generation, tend to migrate together with a 'coyote', who charges a fee to guide migrants across the border. When one generation or age cohort migrates, the younger remaining generation in the *barrio* takes the lead in the *banda's* activities. Being *banda* is a matter of belonging to an inherited network of social relations; that is, a specific construction of personhood through mutual dependence. One does not stop being part of the *banda* after crossing the border.

In the first years of youth migration to New York and Philadelphia, *banda* members on both sides of the border began to gather *cooperaciones*, or contributions, to finance *sonidos* (DJ concerts), which coincided with religious celebrations throughout the year and the festive cycle. These are events intended to reinforce togetherness and reciprocity and to construct belongingness, following the same moral and practical logic as the cargo system (a form of rural local governance in which people take turns at civil leadership). Indigenous youth are reviving and reshaping practices and ideologies from tradition, while at the same time working as a new transnational institution at both sides of the border, thus making possible reception in the United States and reinscription back in rural Mexico. Despite these unproductive investments, in less than a decade, this Nahua community was transformed from dirt-floored single-room *jacales* and dirt streets, where people would walk barefoot for two or three hours daily to get to their scattered fields, to a transnational community where youth's remittances have made it possible to pave streets, purchase trucks to avoid walking to the cornfields, open Internet cafes, and shoe and office products stores that cater for the needs of modern childhood.

In indigenous communities that are experiencing rapid processes of youth outmigration, there has been a broad transformation in the condition of children's lives and their imaginaries of childhood. Young migrant parents' narratives are informed by dominant neoliberal discursive formations that relate migration to self-improvement, self-entrepreneurship, consumption-based citizenship and belonging for rural and marginalized populations, and the provision of better educational opportunities and a better future for their children. Their hope is to send remittances back to their families to provide a decent childhood for their children, which is always understood as a modern nurtured and protected childhood mediated through the market and consumption. However, what young migrant parents and their children who are left behind experience on the different sides of national borders is often far from the imaginaries that first framed the migratory project. Although the Mexican state promotes the figures of migrants as heroes and agents of economic development, migrant parents living in the United States often struggle to provide financial support to the children left behind and their caregivers. Due to their subaltern economic integration in the context of the segmentation between protected and unprotected labor, they face difficulties in finding and simultaneously keeping several low-paid jobs, and experience racial and social discrimination. Plans to stay in the United States only two or three years and return to Mexico with the economic means to initiate a better life there are often altered, leading them to prolong their stay in the United States for several years without seeing or visiting their children whom they left behind. They also soon realize that poor migrants do not have the right to live in a family and that in many cases reuniting with their children in the United States will not be possible. Making use of new technologies of communication available to them, such as weekly phone conversations, they attempt to generate new forms of relatedness, affect and care for what has been conceptualized as 'transnational parenting' (Coe 2008; Dreby 2010; Parreñas 2001, 2005, 2008), at the core of which lies the substitution of daily physical contact and the sharing of habitual everyday activities and emotional support for material goods as a way to fulfill their parental responsibilities and to express love for their children.

Bitter disagreements and misunderstandings often arise in the households of the caregivers of the children who are left behind over the use and distribution of remittances and the allocation of labor demands to family members, including the children. These children must navigate the process of being incorporated into new households and develop ties of relatedness with the families that raise, nurture and provide them with daily care. This is an ambiguous social process that unfolds over time through participation and inclusion in everyday practices, and the sharing of housework and agricultural tasks.[4] A fostered child who is successfully integrated into a household has progressively developed a feeling of ease when sharing housework and other agricultural and domestic responsibilities, a sense of corporeal bond by co-sleeping and being fed, and has actively constructed affection for and a sense of indebtedness to her caregivers (Leinaweaver 2008; Walmsley 2008). Children who express resentment against their migrant parents are often those who experienced conflicts and difficulties becoming incorporated as members of their fostering households. In Nahua communities of central Mexico, 'family' is conceptualized as 'working together' and the exchange of *ayuda* (mutual help) among domestic groups within the same residential compound and between residencies (Good Eshelman 2005).

Receiving remittances often situates children in an ambiguous subject position in the process of integration into the household. Transnational migration relies on local fostering practices to care for the children who are left behind, but the cultural expectations on which these practices are based sometimes clash with the formation of a transnational family life. Reception of remittances creates new cultural expectations in both migrant parents and their children for an unproductive childhood, whereas local understandings and practices of relatedness compel children to actively participate in household and agricultural work in order to successfully integrate into a fostering household. Not all children left behind receive remittances, or receive them regularly, or receive enough to cover their needs (redefined by parental migration and children's access to consumer goods). Not all children who are left behind have the opportunity to attend school regularly, even if they live in households that do receive remittances. During the first years of youth outmigration, when households had difficulty pooling labor for agricultural tasks, children's work intensified. Many children left behind were overburdened with work and responsibility, juggling contradictory expectations from migrant parents, caregivers, peers and school. In households where there were not enough hands available due to outmigration, children missed school in peak moments of the agricultural cycle. Some children who are left behind express resentment not only against their parents but also their caretakers when they are asked to help or contribute with their work to the household economy, knowing that their caretakers are receiving remittances from their parents in the United States. In other cases, children assume the task that is given to them with interest and a sense of accomplishment for their contribution to the household while they are young, only to start realizing (with a certain regret and bitterness) when they reach adolescence that they are not receiving monetary compensation for their work. These feelings intensify when they see that they are working in the fields side by side with other community members who are hired for periods that require intense labor, like the harvest or the sowing. Thus the likelihood increases that they themselves will begin their own migratory journeys.

Being indigenous immigrants in Philadelphia: embodying neoliberalism, learning ethnicity

Although San Matias did not have previous experience of transnational migration, and most of the first waves of migrants were young people in their teens and early twenties, the circular movement of unaccompanied youth across the border constructed strong migration networks based on kinship and place-based relationships. Peer groups organized in *bandas* across borders have been crucial in facilitating migrant reception in the United States and reinscription back into rural Mexico given the impossibility that migrants encounter of both becoming legal residents and authorized workers, escaping poverty and subordination in the United States, and using remittances to generate alternative livelihoods that would allow them to imagine a future in rural Mexico. Transnational life has been experienced in the form of circular migration and hypermobility. Consequently, both rural communities in Mexico and new migrant reception areas in the urban US are being reshaped as unstable and transitory spaces by neoliberal states.

Nahua youth from new migrant-sending communities in Puebla have crafted a space for themselves in new contexts of migrant reception in the United States. In so doing, they have contributed to reworking labor, interethnic and social relations in the contexts of immigration, while at the same time their subjectivities and self-understandings have been profoundly reshaped by their experiences of immigration in the United States. The migratory project entails an imagined way out of a situation of deepened social inequality and economic uncertainty that often becomes a lived reality that has to be faced again in the context of migrant reception. New York and New Jersey became in the 1990s a new context of Mexican immigration, especially for many new migrant-sending areas in the state of Puebla (Smith 2006; Binford 2004). Patterns of investment and disinvestment in certain economic sectors and local economies have affected where new immigrants have located in the United States since the 1990s. They have sometimes displaced the descendants of earlier waves of immigration (Singer et al. 2008). This has been the case with Nahua youth, who have created their own labor niche in Philadelphia in the food services sector, displacing other ethnic groups with longer histories of immigration by accepting unprotected labor conditions and low salaries.

At the end of the 1990s, when Nahua youth from Puebla began to cross the border with the United States, they went first to new contexts of Mexican immigration such as New York and New Jersey. They worked in a diversity of jobs such as cleaning, factory work and restaurants (mainly in low-entry positions such as washing dishes and preparing salads). These first years and experiences as immigrants in the United States were characterized by experimentation with gender practices and forms of self-organizing among peer groups (including transnational communication and the organizing of *bandas'* activities back in rural Mexico), extreme social isolation within the broader local community and complete dedication to work (which precluded questions as to the meaning of their experiences as immigrants and workers), and ethnic conflict with Latinos and African-American youth gangs in public spaces. Young migrants' lives depended on the *banda*, for the initial economic investment to cross the border, to get a place to stay and a job upon arrival in the United States, and for day-to-day support and sense of belonging. Boys were the first to migrate, and some girls followed later, always summoned by and under the supervision of male kin. In some cases, girls would live in apartments with brothers, uncles or cousins. Other times girls lived with their peer group in the girls' *bandas*, following the same gendered division between boys and girls *bandas* and spaces in rural Mexico (Carpena-Méndez 2007). Nineteen-year-old Guadadalupe explained his first experience in the United States, when he was 16 years old:

> Everyone wanted to go to the North to see how it is. The friends on the other side pay from the border on, and we pay from here to the border. Then we gather the money for the crossing. The border is a sad thing because we are ill-treated.... When you have already crossed...you are sent to your kin there. I was sent to my friends of the *banda*. First. you have to repay the money that the friends in the *banda* loaned me. This is the first thing to do. My friends looked for a job for me. When you cannot speak English, minimum wage. All the time you are asked if you want to work part-time, but you say no, you want to make money, you want to work all day. I started to work in a pizzeria. There was only one girl who could speak Spanish, and I started to lean on her (*empecé a basarme en ella*). From there, I tried to excel myself (*intenté superarme*). I lived with my friends of the *banda* in a shared apartment with three rooms. We were twelve boys there, and we paid $100 each.... We were so many people.... When my sister who was 17 also arrived in Philadelphia, she asked

me if she could stay in the apartment. Look, I told her, there are pure guys here (*aquí hay puros chavos*), what are you going to do here? We cannot accept you here. And she went to live with her girlfriends of the [girls'] gang in New York.

The conceptualization of separate male and female *bandas*, even when they belong to the same neighborhood *banda*, reproduces their elders' gendered spatial and labor divisions. Yet, paradoxically, when boys and girls live together in the United States, they find it necessary to rework gender practices within the domestic space. Depending on their job schedule, domestic tasks (cleaning, cooking, buying groceries, and doing laundry) are assigned and rotated daily among all members, and all living expenses are equally shared. Because boys tend to have jobs as cooks – acquiring more sophisticated cooking skills and techniques – and girls as kitchen assistants, in the domestic spaces, boys are assigned cooking tasks more often than girls, altering embodied gender practices in the community of origin in rural Mexico. Lucia, for instance, who lived in Philadelphia for three years with her boyfriend and other members of his family and neighborhood, almost never cooked there, but upon returning to San Matias and moving in with her parents-in-law (following patrilocal residential rules), she continued to assume all the kitchen tasks in the household:

I had my assigned day to do the cleaning...but men in the house knew how to cook better because they worked as cooks, and it was easier that they did the cooking in the house too.... When they were not at home, either I cooked for myself or I did not eat.... But I was not frowned upon.... Because each person had their turn to cook, and it was not my turn.... But that was when I lived with the banda. (Lucia, 20 years old)

This experiential reworking of gender practices has a limited temporality associated with the organization of domesticity in the United States within the *banda*. When *banda* members leave the shared apartment to form their own nuclear families and have children in the United States, women tend to assume all domestic responsibilities, 'then, the woman is only for the house, for cleaning, laundry, cooking...and the man is the one who goes out to work, the same as in the village, because here we don't have support to raise our children', explains Marcela.

During the first year of my fieldwork in San Matias I witnessed many times little boys drawn to their mother's or other female members' tortilla-making practices around the *comal* (clay or metal griddle) with curiosity and amusement about what seemed an interesting activity to try and participate in. Every time a little boy attempted to take a piece of *masa* to make a tortilla, women would slap them on their hands saying, 'Are you a woman?' A recurring theme in my conversations with community elders was their perceived lack of culinary culture: 'We don't have a lot of food here, we just eat tortillas and chili, here we don't know how to cook...but our food is better than in the city; tortillas from the city do not nourish us enough, you have to eat a lot to feel full' (Pedro, 60-year-old man). This is in line with their internalized, discredited cultural legacies as Indians and their ongoing efforts to think well of themselves. When these children with whom I worked in San Matias reached youth and early adulthood as immigrants in the United States, they soon were able to master the culinary skills to rise from kitchen apprentices or assistants to chefs. San Matias is nowadays renowned as a transnational indigenous community from where some of the best chefs in Philadelphia come, where young people have a special talent, interest and inventiveness for the culinary arts. When they periodically return to rural Mexico, most of these young men assume daily agricultural responsibilities, leaving kitchen tasks to the women in the household. The perception is that the gendered division of labor in San Matias will not be altered unless the sociomaterial basis of daily life dramatically changes. That is, as long as handmade tortillas continue to be a staple, local cultural notions of femininity and the balance between female and masculine forces that underlie and sustain the social and natural universe, will compel that a man and a woman 'work for each other' in segregated gendered spheres (see Taggart 2007 for an analysis of the relationship between love and work in Nahua societies). This flexibility and accommodation of gender practices in different moments of the life course in the context of circular transnational migration is part of the effort migrants make to creatively adapt to new mobilities.

During the first migration cohorts to the United States, young people identified completely with the *banda* of which they were a member, and which provided belonging and protection. They did not have a real social existence except through the *banda*. Social life outside of the domestic and work spaces was limited to going to Latin dances once a week to break with routines and the boredom of endless labor. Their subjection to capitalist discipline, where work organizes one's time and colonizes one's entire existence (in the case of undocumented immigrants receiving poverty wages and constantly looking for additional part-time jobs to supplement their earnings), produced feelings of exhaustion and disorientation in many of the youth. Their narratives often reflected an emerging self-understanding of their lives as shaped by the limitations imposed by their undocumented status and their subaltern economic integration in the labor market: 'We are not free, in the US we don't have any freedom; we cannot drive, we cannot go anywhere, our lives are sheer work and more work. I realized poverty in Mexico is more beautiful because people live together more and help each other' (Rafael, 19 years old). In my fieldwork in Philadelphia, I encountered several cases of single young mothers from San Matias living on their own whose little children would spend most of the day alone in the apartment without any social interaction while their mothers were working. These children showed delayed language development and rarely enjoyed time outside of the apartment because their mothers just had one day a week in which they would not go to work (in order to buy groceries or do laundry), and they were too afraid of spending time in parks or recreational areas with their children for fear of deportation.

Within this experience of social isolation, the spaces of the Latin dances and work sites constituted primary contact zones with other ethnic groups. In these spaces, tensions between Mexican immigrants and African Americans and bilingual Latinos came to the fore in the reorganization of ethnoracial hierarchies and the competition for the jobs available locally in the unprecedented expansion of the informal economy under neoliberal regimes. Outside the small group of peers of the *banda*, migrant youth found all daily environments, public spaces and work sites, in the United States extremely hostile. Especially at the dances, youth from San Matias encountered an American-style gang culture that shapes ethnic conflict with Puerto Rican and African-American youth in a context of extreme social powerlessness in the urban US. When talking about their experiences of conflict with American gangs, youth from San Matias refer to them as 'real gangs' and to their own *bandas* (which draw from kinship and place-based networks and social organizations in rural Mexico and which emerged as a form of improving the self and providing mutual support in the process of rural–urban migration) as *banditas* or 'little gangs'. However, the clash between rural Mexican-style youth gang cultures and American gangs is not the only form of conflict in public spaces that San Matias youth experience in New York and Philadelphia. San Matias youth often confronted immigrant gangs from other neighboring villages and towns in rural Puebla. Every village in this region of the state of Puebla has its youth *bandas*, which have embodied past intervillage conflict and alliances, while currently being in a process of transnationalization. As gang activities reproduce regional divisions and alliances through networks of fictive kinship, San Matias gangs participate in dances and celebrations in other villages, either as allies or enemies. The transnationalization of rural *bandas* is simultaneously anchored in a double process of exportation and importation of gang practices across the border (Smith 2006). Rural Mexican youth and spaces become Americanized, and rural Mexicans open enclaves of Mexican regional and social relations in the United States. Joel (19 years old, 16 at the time of migration) from the Shalacas gang, explains his experience:

> In Philadelphia, there are 18 of us, from the Shalacas gang. On Sundays we used to play soccer, and Tuesdays we went to dance. At the beginning, everyone went straight home [after dancing]. But there were other guys from Tlaxcala who looked at us wrong ... and we had problems with them, fighting.... Alcohol gives us courage. Los Inquietos (the uneasy ones) from San Juan Tianguismanalco ... with them we did have problems because they are always drugged. They are really a gang! We had lots of fights even though there was a lot of security in the dance halls.

One young man (19 years old) moved from New York to Philadelphia to work in a restaurant, summoned by a friend and former coworker in New York. In less than a decade, through migrant youths' use of social networks to find employment, Philadelphia came to be the main destination for migrant youth from San Matias, who came to form one of the main Mexican immigrant communities in the city and be an important part of the workforce, and who transformed the restaurant sector and the ethnic and social landscape of South Philadelphia. In the context of the neoliberal restructuring of regional economies, the increased migration from rural areas in Mexico is deeply interconnected with the reconfiguration of local labor markets and the recomposition of labor forces in the United States. The availability of undocumented migrant workers is central to labor flexibility and the reorganization of work processes required in neoliberal economies. Undocumented workers are paid in cash (under the counter), which makes them vulnerable to assault by other gang members on their way home after they leave work, and are unlikely to receive benefits such as medical and unemployment insurance. Yet, despite – or perhaps as a consequence of – the structural impediments that undocumented migrants face in order to escape poverty in the context of immigration, many youth from San Matias over time have been able to carve out a space for themselves in the social worlds of immigration. On the one hand, labor self-recruiting through kinship and place-based migrant networks responds to the flexibility required by bosses and business owners to make a profit under neoliberalized local labor markets. On the other hand, Mexican immigrant ethics and self-understandings as 'hard workers' are part of the daily tactics developed for enhancing job security in a context of low-income, low-status and non-unionized jobs (Zavella 2011). The labor trajectory and self-representation of Hilario (22 years old, 16 when he first migrated) is characteristic of many other youth from San Matias who are living in Philadelphia:

I began to work as a dishwasher. I thought it would be something really difficult, impossible, to become a cook, because I could not speak English. Really impossible.... But then, I realized everything was very repetitive, they were always using and doing the same things.... And they were always saying the same. Then, I began to pay attention and to improve my English. And I began to climb kitchen positions. The first step was to make salads, which is something easy, and less hard than washing dishes whole day. What I really wanted was to eat. In the kitchen they would give you what you wanted to eat and let me cook my own food. And I would prepare my food in the way I liked it. I would experiment with it. And when I did not have anything to do, I would always offer to help out the cook. I was never seen standing still once. I was always doing something, cleaning, helping others...something that *gringos* never do (if they have nothing to do, they go out to chat). The boss paid attention to my attitude and thought that I wanted to learn, but in reality I was doing it not to be fired. I thought that if I do not work fast and hard, they would fire me. And that is what bosses like in comparison with the attitudes of blacks... One day the cook was ill and they asked me to cook, and I did it well. When the cook came back, we started to work together, two, three days, and I began to learn a lot. After some time, I made the boss fire the black guy making salads. I told him [the boss] I did not like him [the coworker] because he was not a hard-working guy. I kicked him out; I spoke really badly of him (*le eché mucha tierra*), and in his place I introduced my brother-in-law. Then I kicked out the other black who washed dishes, and I introduced my friend Agustin. The kitchen was already ours, and then I introduced my brother. He helped me. We were already four of us in the kitchen. Then, I introduced my sister to work as a waitress. Since my English was much better and I could communicate well, I was giving orders, managing everything myself.

And at that time I was very lucky that that restaurant was in all its splendor. There were as many customers as ants.... And we worked as dogs. I worked there for three years, and then I started to unfold my creativity, to take a look at cooking books, at the Internet, to try new recipes.... Over time, I moved to other different restaurants, and I could negotiate my salary, fend for myself.

Hilario and his work companions continuously negotiate and enforce the Mexican ethic of hard work on the job (through socialization processes of the newcomer),[5] reproducing racialized stereotypes of themselves and other ethnic groups and embodying neoliberal subjectivities as flexible workers, as a way to navigate the structural vulnerabilities to which their lives are subjected.

This Mexican immigrant work ethic, however, is not only an effect of the constitution of migrant selves under neoliberal discursive and labor regimes. It is also the backdrop against which exhaustion, illness, depression and accidents are an inextricable part of their daily living and working conditions in the United States, and from which an embodied consciousness of their position in the world eventually emerges in some of the youth. With this consciousness there is a search for renewed self-understandings and novel possibilities of a life back in their rural villages, a life that is already inextricably intertwined with the settlement processes that some youth have forged in Philadelphia.

The subaltern integration of indigenous immigrants from Mexico in a labor market has been affected by the global economic crisis (Cornelius et al. 2010). The hardening of migratory policies that followed the global economic downturn of 2008 has had an impact on family transnationalism and the return scenarios devised by migrants, simultaneously altering and accentuating processes of integration in Philadelphia. In the next section, I turn to the experiences of return migration since the global economic collapse and the alternative development projects that young migrants are creating in rural Mexico.

Return migration and alternative forms of development: sustaining transnational communities

Mexico is in the process of dismantling an agricultural system that has historically provided food security in rural regions. Since the 1990s, the neoliberal turn of the Mexican state has enabled the progressive withdrawal of credits and subsidies for subsistence farmers, after decades of deepening their dependence on the state for commercial fertilizer and pesticides. Simultaneously, new social programs such as *Oportunidades*, which target mothers and children, have been opening new spaces of state intervention and social control at the heart of intimate family relations and everyday enculturation practices, seeking to transform the very organization of childhood experiences in indigenous groups. The transnational migration of young people has been celebrated as local development in the form of remittances and the possibility of consumption, despite evidence that remittances have not been invested in new productive projects and that a materially improved lifestyle based on increased consumption has begot more migration (Binford 2003b). The new ruralities that have been emerging in the last decade are no longer synonymous with agrarian activities, and they indicate a deepened articulation of rural spaces to the global society through commodities and labor and service markets (Appendini and Torres-Mazuera 2008; Salas Quintanal et al. 2011). These emerging forms of rurality force us to rethink our conceptual borders, imposed over the rural and the urban, to consider new analytical tools that could uncover the significance of the distinctive forms of agency exercised by children and young people through mobility within moments of historical disruption, as key social actors responding in their own creative ways to the new round of development and modernization.

Moreover, in less than a decade of accelerated migration, it has become evident that the neoliberal model of development based on migrant remittances cannot be sustained, particularly because the economic recession of 2008 has made it increasingly difficult to continue crossing the border in labor migration cycles every two or three years. Nahua youth find themselves caught up in and having to cope with the increasing collapse of the neoliberal model of development. My fieldwork materials suggest that Nahua youth have continued to attempt to cross the border since the economic recession of 2008, although only highly skilled and accomplished cooks continue to be sought after in restaurants in Philadelphia. Deportations are increasingly happening at the workplace rather than at the border, and new processes of forced return migration due to deportation or loss of jobs have become evident in the last years.

The gambits that indigenous youth are envisaging to navigate this situation have turned their hope for their future back to their rural villages. Besides sending remittances for disc jockey concerts and the construction of block houses, contributions were gathered by youth working in Philadelphia to build a high school in their mountain village in order to extend the period of formal education beyond primary and secondary school with the hope of delaying the migration of adolescents. The murals in the school, painted by the village youth, were inspired by their life experiences over the last decade of growing up as children left behind with contradictory expectations placed on them by migrant parents, grandparents in need of children's labor to carry out agricultural tasks, the school and peer groups. They reflect on the misunderstandings between different generations that are divided by the border, and children's ambivalence toward the commercial gifts and toys they receive as a form of love as a substitute for daily intimate care. They emphasize the moral responsibility that the children who are left behind should have toward their migrant parents' sacrifice, to excel in their studies and to be appreciative of their economic support as a form of care and love. Written in both Spanish and Nahuatl, the school murals emphasize a renewed appreciation for their own cultural legacy, the beauty of the local landscape, and the sensory richness of rural life versus the limited freedom and the flatness of life as an undocumented worker in Philadelphia.

The durability and scope of transnational life is affected by macro-level factors (such as the efforts of the Mexican state to engage the Mexican diaspora to become part of Mexico's imagined political community), and the ability of migrants' children to continue engaging transnational practices (Smith 2006). Drawing from my fieldwork experience, I argue that the continuation of a transnational life depends not only on the nature of the incorporation process in the United States but also on the possibility of reinscription back into rural Mexico. The project of return migration, rather than being the end of the migratory project, is a central mechanism in the maintenance of transnational life. Return migration requires a strong economic investment and an active imagining of the creation of economically and socially sustainable possibilities. After a decade of lived experience of circular migration, it has become evident that migrant remittances are not sufficient to create alternative forms of sustainable livelihoods (through consumption or investment in stores and small business) and that most families have continued to engage in small-scale farming to sustain the household economy, as a strategy against food insecurity and to keep their lands productive in the context of land-grabbing by transnational corporations. Young migrant returnees are experimenting with new ways of keeping their cornfields productive while attempting novel forms of making a living with local knowledge and resources, hoping to stem the flow of youth outmigration. As shown in a previous section, during the last decade many Nahua youth became accomplished cooks in Philadelphia, while periodically coming back to their mountain communities and struggling to forge new forms of belonging to rural areas and social life through transnational youth organizations in parallel to the cargo system. They were rapidly promoted from kitchen positions like dishwashing to chefs who could negotiate their salary and circulate among upscale restaurants while making their own decisions about menus and labor organization. It is important to point out that this is not an isolated case, but a trend for a new community of rural Mexican immigrants in Philadelphia who have, in less than a decade, created their own niche in the labor market as cooks.

Working at the opposite ends of the global food system has provided indigenous youth with a renewed awareness of the interconnections between their world and the world of others, enabling them to reappropriate their culture after being subjected to the supreme form of symbolic domination and dispossession that is the migratory experience. Nahua youth on both sides of the border are struggling to keep their fields of *criollo* blue corn to produce *pinole* as a specialty product to be exported to the United States, marketing an entirely new *pinole*-based product to upscale organic restaurants and markets, and attempting to retain the money made in their own transnational communities. *Pinole* is blue corn flour made into a local traditional sweet beverage, not for everyday consumption, but as a treat for children on special occasions. *Pinole* is associated with treasured childhood memories of motherly care. Migrant youth who work as cooks in Philadelphia envisioned the possibility of inventing new recipes with *pinole* for products that could be imported to cater to the tastes and eating habits of Americans, such as *pinole* muffins, chips, ice cream and desserts. Nahua cooks in Philadelphia began to entice their bosses and clientele by introducing recipes made with *pinole* on the menus. Soon *pinole* products were also sold in weekly street markets and at cultural events. Some youth returned to rural Mexico to organize the families to produce blue corn for the transnational *pinole* project, while others worked on promoting the products in the United States and searching for the support of foundations to navigate all the certifications and legal procedures needed to import the product since most of the youth were undocumented immigrants.

Not being aware of the concept of organic produce, Nahua youth in Philadelphia soon figured out that that was how their grandparents produced corn and beans in the past. They recalled memories of childhood experiences in which playing and helping with agricultural tasks side by side with their grandparents could not be disentangled. Partly unconscious, embodied knowledge, internalized through a process of trial and error in which children would progressively become integrated participants in communities of practice (Lave and Wenger 1991, Wenger 2000), an experiential know-how that was never formalized through directed verbal instruction, began to be articulated in new ways with their conscious awareness and their self-understanding as bearers of precious knowledge. Thus, their renewed self-understanding countered the condition of the displaced existence of immigrants in our societies today (Sayad 2004). In the context of the recession, some Nahua youth are returning to Mexico to push alternative agendas that are grounded on other imaginaries. They are equipped with new sensory, embodied experiences of life in the United States, the possibility of remembering a different order of existence, new awareness of the interconnections between their world and the world of others, and a renewed self-understanding.

The process of return migration, however, is not without contradictions, struggles and conflicts between generations and among different factions in the community regarding the use of the land. Upon returning to Mexico, these Nahua youth who had memories of working in the fields as children, but who had been displaced from agricultural work during their teens, are experiencing deeply complex processes of translation and imbrications of knowledge. They are not simply turning to their grandparents as custodians of agricultural knowledge, but are engaging them in figuring out how to deal with the challenges brought by environmental degradation and the increasing unpredictability of climate change in the struggle to preserve community land. With the recent reform of the constitution that allows the privatization of *ejido* land, elders, however, are entrusted with the work of remembering who has rights to what land. The transnational organization of the productive project relied on the cross-border self-organizing of youth and their back-and-forth migratory cycles. Some migrant youth returned to the village to create a twin organization for the one created in Philadelphia and to coordinate the actions of both. They served as mediators and translators between their parents and grandparents and the multiple *técnicos*, engineers and university researchers who were called by the funding agency to guide and supervise the project.

When the transnational *pinole* project began, it was planned that it would include all the families in the village. Community conflicts arose, however, as soon as the youth leaders who initiated the project in Philadelphia began to turn over control of the production process to outside experts (such as agricultural engineers and transnational nongovernmental organizations [NGOs]), who were crucial to achieving certifications and solving the last phase of commercialization. Julio, one of the first organizers of the project in Philadelphia, and now a permanent returned migrant in rural Mexico explained:

> Here people have their own way of doing things … and we began to meddle in people's pride …. Our original project was to use local resources and knowledge, because here we know how to grow corn. … Our idea was to gather resources to be able to use what we already have here, but engineers started coming, lots of them…. They would say, make furrows like that so that water can be retained, let's compost, let's do such and such thing…. No … can you imagine the elders?…. [T]hat all these things are not going to work, that is what they said…. And they were right … because it takes time and sensitivity to adapt to each plot, each piece of land is different, different altitude, you have to go to the fields every day to know. (Julio, 17 when he first migrated to Philadelphia, now 24)

Of all the families who began participating in the project, only 13 are still involved; most of the families quit the project within the first three years. The *pinole* project was envisioned by the youth in Philadelphia as a social project aimed at a broad understanding of sustainability to include their traditional form of life. They could not foresee that a productive project to insert traditionally produced blue corn flour in the global market had to be managed as a project to create a business. In this business, children were not allowed to be actively involved in the production process because, by international standards, their participation would be considered a form of child labor. The clash between the practices imposed in order to produce organic blue corn according to the requirements of outside agencies and families' own ways of organizing agricultural production is also a clash between Western forms of knowledge production and native epistemologies. Something is being missed and unrecognized by the former about how the cultural transmission of agricultural and environmental knowledge happens and the active role children have in this process, that is, recognition that for the last decade, children left behind in their mountain villages by migrant parents and older siblings were burdened by greater responsibility at an earlier age to sustain agricultural work. By contributing their work, care and creativity, these children helped stitch together the ruptures of the everyday in a transitional society. It was this embodied knowledge during childhood experiences that facilitated migrant youths' dreams of sustainability, not only of their transnational community but of a form of life back in their mountain villages.

Conclusion

A new generation of rural Mexicans has been growing up in the context of the rapid dismantling of subsistence agriculture, accelerated transnational migration, deepening social inequality, and dependence on remittances to improve standards of living. Neoliberal globalism has created transitory and unstable spaces in which daily life has been reconfigured, and has produced new forms of risk and vulnerability for both the Mexican countryside and for the new contexts of Mexican immigration in the United States. Migration, therefore, has to be understood as a global social process, taking into account the effects on the everyday and the reconfiguration of the self in both new sending areas and cosmopolitan receiving contexts. This chapter has explored how children and young people have responded to these unstable and rapidly changing everyday realities in both sending and receiving contexts through back-and-forth mobility across the border.

The international migration of indigenous communities that until recently were engaged in subsistence agriculture has increasingly become a youth process. By drawing on forms of self-organization in *bandas*, young people were able to take the initiative in transnational migration and sustain processes of circular migration and the transnational life of their communities over time, reshaping the economic, social, and ethnic practices and landscapes in their sending communities in rural Mexico and receiving urban contexts in the United States. The cross-border self-organizing of youth and their back-and-forth migratory cycles, as well as the experiential learning about different worlds that comes from these new forms of mobility, allowed them to create an alternative transnational productive project in order to forge a future for themselves, becoming key sociopolitical actors in their communities.

Far from becoming passive economic dependents on remittances, the children growing up in migrant-sending communities contribute with their work, care and creativity to repairing family relationships and to sustaining agricultural practices. As the lives of children and migrant youth are affected by mobility and the experiences of others – migrant parents in the United States and peers of the transnational *banda* – on the other side of the border, they struggle to understand their place in this world and their own subjectivities. Their daily lives are fully embedded in complex learning processes that are shaped by their experiences of transculturality, mobility-in-migration, the management of different cultural repertoires and ethnic flexibility. Within this ethnographic gaze, children and young people's agency appears as key to the concurrent processes of reshaping and reproducing forms of life, embodying, contesting and reappropriating contradictory flows of knowledge and practices. We cannot understand contemporary forms of rurality and indigeneity in Mexico without considering children and youth as key subjects of historical transformation.

Notes

1. Fieldwork was conducted in 2002–2004 in rural Mexico, tracing the formation of indigenous youth *bandas*, their self-organizing and ongoing circularity across the border, with short follow-up visits to document youth's experiences in Philadelphia in 2006, 2008 and 2009, and of return migration to their rural communities in 2011. I have kept in contact with some of the youth with whom I first worked when they were adolescents in rural Mexico for almost a decade through regular phone and email conversations.
2. Land redistributed among peasant and indigenous communities after the Mexican Revolution and exploited communally. The new Agrarian Law of 1992 ended the process of land redistribution to open up *ejido* land to the market.
3. This is a pseudonym.
4. New kinship studies in the last two decades have emphasized how culturally situated forms of constructing relatedness through daily practices of coresidence, commensality, reciprocal exchange of labor and other numerous kinds of social obligations are constitutive of kin-making processes (Magazine 2013; Van Vleet 2008).
5. I borrow this concept from Zavella 2011.

References

Appendini, K., and Torres-Mazuera, G. (eds) (2008) *¿Ruralidad sin Agricultura?* (Mexico DF: El Colegio de México).

Binford, L. (2003a) 'Migración Acelerada entre Puebla y los Estados Unidos' in K. E. Masferrer, E. Díaz Brenis, and J. Mondaraón Melo (eds) *Etnografía del Estado de Puebla: Puebla Centro* (Puebla, Mexico: Gobierno del Estado de Puebla/ Secretaría de Cultura), 58–67.

Binford, L. (2003b) 'Migrant Remittances and (Under)Development in Mexico', *Critique of Anthropology*, 23(3), 305–336.

Binford, L. (2004) *La Economía Política de la Migración Acelerada: Siete Estudios de Caso.* (Puebla and Mexico City: Universidad Autónoma de Puebla y Consejo Nacional de Ciencia y Tecnología).

Binford, L., and D'Aubeterre, M. E. (eds) (2000) *Conflictos Migratorios Transnacionales y Respuestas Comunitarias* (Puebla, Mexico: Instituto de Ciencias Sociales y Humanidades-BUAP).

Carpena-Méndez, F. (2007) '"Our Lives Are Like a Sock Inside-out": Children's Work and Youth Identity in Neoliberal Rural Mexico' in R. Panelli, S. Punch, and E. Robson (eds) *Global Perspectives on Rural Childhood and Youth: Young rural lives* (London and New York: Routledge), 41–56.

Coe, C. (2008) 'The Structuring of Feeling in Ghanaian Transnational Families', *City and Society*, 20(2), 222–250.

Cornelius, W., Fitzgerald, D., Lewin Fischer, P., and Muse-Orlinoff, L. (eds) (2010). *Mexican Migration and the U.S. Economic Crisis: A Transnational Perspective* (San Diego, CA: Center for Comparative Immigration Studies, University of California, San Diego).

Dreby, J. (2010) *Divided by Borders: Mexican Migrants and Their Children* (Berkeley, Los Angeles, London: University of California Press).

Gammeltoft-Hansen, T., and Nyberg Sørensen, N. (eds) (2013) *The Migration Industry and the Commercialization of International Migration* (London and New York: Routledge).

Good Eshelman, C. (2005) ' "Trabajando Juntos Como Uno": Conceptos Nahuas del Grupo Doméstico y la Persona' in D. Robichaux (ed) *Familia y Parentesco en Mesoamérica: Unas Miradas Antropológicas* (Mexico City: Universidad Iberoamericana), 275–294.

Lave, J., and Wenger, E. (1991) *Situated Learning: Legitimate Peripheral Participation* (Cambridge, UK: Cambridge University Press).

Leinaweaver, J. (2008) *The Circulation of Children: Kinship, Adoption, and Morality in Andean Peru* (Durham, NC: Duke University Press).

Magazine, R. (2013) *The Village Is like a Wheel: Rethinking Cargos, Family, and Ethnicity in Highland Mexico* (Tucson: The University of Arizona Press).

Parreñas, R. S. (2001) 'Mothering from a Distance: Emotions, Gender, and Intergenerational Relations in Filipino Transnational Families', *Feminist Studies*, 27, 361–384.

Parreñas, R. S. (2005) 'Long Distance Intimacy: Class, Gender and Intergenerational Relations between Mothers and Children in Filipino Transnational Families', *Global Networks*, 5(4), 317–336.

Parreñas, R. S. (2008) *Children of Global Migration: Transnational Families and Gender Woes* (Stanford, CA: Stanford University Press).

Salas Quintanal, H., Rivermar Pérez, M. L., and Velasco Santos, P. (eds) (2011) *Nuevas Ruralidades: Expresiones de la Transformación Social en México* (Mexico, DF: Juan Pablos Editor).

Sayad, A. (2004) *The Suffering of the Immigrant* (Cambridge, UK: Polity Press).

Singer, A., Hardwick, S., and Brettell, C. (eds) (2008) *Twenty-First Century Gateways: Immigrant Incorporation in Suburban America* (Washington, DC: Brookings Institution Press).

Smith, R. (2006) *Mexican New York: Transnational Lives of New Immigrants* (Berkeley, Los Angeles, London: University of California Press).

Taggart, J. (2007) *Remembering Victoria: A Tragic Nahuat Love Story* (Austin, TX: University of Texas Press).

Van Vleet, K. (2008) *Performing Kinship: Narrative, Gender, and the Intimacies of Power in the Andes* (Austin: University of Texas Press).

Walmsley, E. (2008) 'Raised by Another Mother: Informal Fostering and Kinship Ambiguities in Northwest Ecuador', *Journal of Latin American and Caribbean Anthropology*, 13(1), 168–195.

Wenger, E. (2000) *Communities of Practice: Learning, Meaning, and Identity* (Cambridge, UK: Cambridge University Press).

Zavella, P. (2011) *I'm Neither Here nor There: Mexicans' Quotidian Struggles with Migration and Poverty* (Durham, NC, and London: Duke University Press).

4
Jeans, Bicycles and Mobile Phones: Adolescent Migrants' Material Consumption in Burkina Faso

Dorte Thorsen

Introduction

African children are rarely associated with globalization and the commercialization of childhood through consumerism, except for their participation in the global supply chain as child labor.[1] Accordingly, they are represented as a uniform category despite the fact that great inequalities in wealth and opportunity exist both across and within countries. International discourses on child protection in the global South tend to see those entering the world of paid work as being deprived of their childhood (Bourdillon 2006; Nieuwenhuys 2007). Such discourses advocate an essentially Eurocentric and middle-class type of childhood in which work is not readily accepted as a means of accumulating practical and social skills and know-how (Bourdillon forthcoming; Razy and Rodet 2011). With the aim of protecting children from hazardous and exploitative work, young people up to the age of 18 are categorized as children (cf. International Labor Office [ILO] Convention No. 182). The idea that adolescents can migrate to find work on their own initiative and for material reasons beyond meeting basic needs is overshadowed by representations of migrant children as forced migrants, victims of trafficking or exploitation (cf. Robson 2010; Human Rights Watch 2007; ILO 2001, 2010).

This chapter focuses on young migrants aged 14–24 years, who have left their village to work in Ouagadougou, the capital of Burkina Faso, or Abidjan, the economic capital of Côte d'Ivoire. It explores the relationship between work and consumption in adolescent migrants' lives and offers insights into the purchasing power of one of the most marginalized social categories in the city, and into the dynamics between material desires and adolescent migrants' navigation of the urban context. To grasp how social relations shape adolescent migrants' pathways, the chapter also explores the role of migration, work and consumption in creating, maintaining and breaking relationships. It highlights mobility-in-migration among adolescents who have left their village to find work in urban areas, including patterns of internal and return migration and also social and cultural mobility as captured by consumption patterns and styles of dress that mimic and reinterpret global youth (hip-hop) culture. The objective of the chapter is thus to take a fresh look at how we understand African migrant children and youth, and to use ethnographic facts to add new perspectives on the linkages between adolescence, different forms of mobilities embedded in migration, work consumption and globalization.

The ethnography of young rural-urban migrants from the Bisa region in southeastern Burkina Faso is based on a total of 12 months' fieldwork between 2005 and 2008, where I interviewed 120 young migrants in Ouagadougou and Abidjan, who had begun their migration before the age of 18 years. Moreover, I traced 15 migrants in multiple sites throughout the four years. To overcome time constraints imposed by employers and/or the need to earn for street-working adolescents, I developed a methodology of doing repeated interviews and informal conversations at workplaces, meeting points and where they lived, and also interviewed their families in the village of origin. Despite this time-consuming task of visiting their families in a considerable number of villages in the Bisa region at the expense of spending more time observing migrant children's lives in the cities, the value to the young migrants was enormous. Knowing their background and bringing them greetings and pictures of their family often created a better rapport and revealed twists and turns as their lives rolled out. In this case, multisited research offered insights into the way in which events in the city or back home impacted young migrants' reflections on how they best could achieve their dreams, and resulted in decisions that brought them back to the village, to new occupations or to new migration destinations. Moreover, my visits to their families revealed that most of the parents, or at least the fathers, had been migrants in the past, and that most families had members in several locations.

Material consumption among young people in Africa

Anthropologists have long grappled with theorizing consumption practices in the global South through the rhetoric of appropriation and creolization. This perspective has developed from the early theoriza-tion within anthropology of colonial subjects' emulation of the dress styles and behavior of European colonizers, and its subsequent critiques that Africans were not simply imitating but were, in fact, parodying Europeans to counter and unsettle the colonial project of civilizing the native (Ferguson 2006: 157–160). Contemporary scholarship that focuses on the consumption of Western clothing, music, cars and so forth argues that it may appear as imitation, but that in the process of adapting global styles to local social and cultural contexts, the meaning is remade and becomes imbued with local symbols and resistance to be excluded from global material flows (Hahn 2008; Hansen 2004b; Massey 1998).

Notwithstanding great inequalities between a relatively small elite and the majority of African people, the general features of consumption in Africa can, as noted by Hans Peter Hahn, be summed up in two points. First, people generally have few material possessions. Each object can be incorporated into the expression of personal or cultural identity, but it may also function as savings or a source of symbolic or material capital. Second, the globalization of trade has stimulated a rapid expansion in the acquisition of industrially produced goods over the past three decades, especially of enamel and plastic products, second-hand clothing and electronic equipment like radios and mobile phones (Hahn 2008: 19–20). New objects are not only acquired for their use value but also for the role they attain in the local symbolic system, which allows the consumer to construct a particular personal or social identity as long as it keeps within the limits of locally recognizable forms of consumption (Gell 1986). The opening of new markets in the global South, notably in China, India, Brazil and the United Arab Emirates, has impacted the price-setting of industrially produced products and made available affordable products for a larger range of people (Dobler 2008). In light of this development, it is important to examine the dynamic between purchasing power, income earning and working children's material desires.

While few, if any, Africanist scholars have focused on children as consumers, several have looked at youth's material consumption. Popular representations of youth as engaging carelessly in risky behavior and excessive consumption have been challenged persuasively by several scholars. Filip de Boeck, for example, looked at consumption practices among Zairian youth in the diamond fields of Angola in the 1990s, whose sumptuous spending on bottled beer, Western consumer goods and women had become a major marker of success. Such consump-tion, he argued, is firmly situated within the local idioms of wealth and status that are integrated into a wider notion of well-being, social and physical reproduction linked with farming, hunting and sexual reproduction. Moreover, these idioms are linked with witchcraft and the idea that quick wealth requires enormous sacrifices (de Boeck 1998). In this perspective, generous but ephemeral spending symbolizes an individual's investment in social relations. Another side of consumption, however, is the accumulation and display of goods. Investigating the decoration of women's rooms in northern Nigeria and their extravagant display of enamel and porcelain ware, Editha Platte draws attention to another perspective. She contends that women's consumption of decorative items is an extension of traditional displays of female wealth in earthen pots and decorated calabashes. The size of the collection bears witness of the woman's economic standing because she has savings on which she can fall back. The collection also shows the negotiation power of the network of women around her, since they haggle for the gifts she should be given at marriage. Through accumulating decorative items, young women thus communicate both their social standing and the extent of their social connections (Platte 2008). Within local idioms of wealth, the display of consumed goods demonstrates the benefits for young people of belonging to a group. While these studies point to different ways of adhering to the local articulation of wealth, it is important to examine how changing markets and consumer preferences may impact the meaning of consumption practices. Karen Tranberg Hansen's work in Zambia shows that the consumption of cosmopolitan Western clothing is gendered and, to some extent, also influenced by generation. Women who dress in miniskirts have driven popular and political discourses, which, in the course of time, have changed from being about morality and parents' control over their daughters to being explicitly about women's sexuality and men's prerogative to power through their control over women (Hansen 2004a). Adding critical perspectives on the notion of conspicuous consumption and historicizing changing consumption patterns and their reception, these studies are helpful in the analysis of the conjunction of adolescent migrants' embodiment of the successful migrant and their spending patterns.

Rural families in cultures of pervasive mobility

In the West African savannah, migration has been an important source of livelihood for several generations, and most households are multilocal and complex. Since colonialism, the region has functioned as a labor reserve for the coastal plantation economies of the Gold Coast and Côte d'Ivoire (Cordell et al. 1996; Pacere 2004). Today the diaspora in Côte d'Ivoire is by far the most numerous and, despite forced and voluntary repatriations during the civil war in 2002–2007, the most influential in Burkina Faso. Even though the urban population in Burkina Faso has tripled in the past 30 years, 81.7 percent of the population still lived in rural areas in 2005 (UNDP 2007); hence, rural households are likely to have supplied, and still supply, the mainstay of migrants.

Rural households consist of several sublayers associated with productive and reproductive units. In a longitudinal study of Kusasi households in northeastern Ghana, economic anthropologist Ann Whitehead drew attention to the separate economic spheres of men and women and of adults and children within a household. Households, she noted, have one collective farming unit led by the household head, and numerous individual farming or income-generating units managed by his dependents when they are not obliged to work on the household farm (Whitehead 1996). Central to Whitehead's argument is a complex intertwining of the separate economic spheres, which gives rise to both dependencies and interdependencies between women and men, young and old in a household. Dependencies are related to structural claims on labor and services, whereas interdependencies are voluntary contributions, for example, of meeting expenditures or requests for services when capable of doing so (Whitehead and Kabeer 2001). Depending on the demographic composition of the household, children are important sources of labor, especially for women who cannot command the labor of adult men (Bledsoe 1980; Roberts 1988; Whitehead 1984). The need for labor is intertwined with ensuring children's skill acquisition. Not entirely carved in stone, their learning is linked with common views on age and gender-appropriate work, their ability to master particular tasks, and different household members' views on what a child should and should not do (Abebe 2007; Katz 2004; Reynolds 1991).

Mobility shapes childhood and adolescence in different ways. Kinship ideologies and practices assign parental responsibilities for a child to several adults other than the biological parents. While children may sleep at a grandmother's house at the request of the elderly woman (Alber 2004; Vischer 1997), there is also a long tradition of fosterage within the kinship group for labor purposes, to ensure the well-being of a child or open new opportunities for education, whether in school or training in the cottage industry or marketplaces (Bass 1996; Bledsoe 1990; Goody 1982; Hashim 2007; Notermans 2004). In addition to physical mobility, the hope for social mobility through education may encourage children to spend their independent revenues on school-related expenses, whether they are migrants or not (Hashim 2011). However, the absence of older household members may also imply an increased need for children's labor on the household farms and interfere with their school education. Finally, the long history of migration in the savannah region means that children's work, schooling and/or formation away from the rural household is seen as a normal pathway for young people (Hashim and Thorsen 2011: 26–27).

In the Bisa region, the household head is in principle responsible for the main staples – millet, maize and rice – the family's health and the children's education, while the wife is responsible for providing sauce ingredients to make tasty, varied and healthy meals. She also buys clothes and shoes for her children. However, migration increases interdependencies within the household. With many men and a good number of women in their 20s being away on migration for shorter or longer periods of time, women – mothers and grandmothers – are important farmers in their own right. They grow a substantial proportion of the millet and rice needed for food security, health and educational costs (Thorsen 2002). From around the age of 11–12 years children are increasingly drawn into farm work, especially if they are not enrolled at school. Apart from working on the collective household farm and on their mother's or grandmother's farm, both boys and girls are encouraged to develop their own economic sphere and are given small plots of land and time to do so. Children thus participate in the household economy in significant ways. The organization of households implies that children from an early age learn about the separate economic spheres. Progressively they take up gendered responsibilities of doing certain types of work, engaging in certain income-generating activities, and gradually they buy clothes, shoes and other necessities themselves.

This engagement in independent economic activities is a driver to migrate, especially for adolescents who are not in school. As there are hardly any employment possibilities in the Bisa region and revenues from farming fluctuate tremendously from one year to the next, the older generations do not count on all their children remaining in the village, nor do they wish that children remain in a situation of deep and chronic poverty. However, cultural practices impede adolescent girls in migrating independently. They sometimes migrate with female kin or a married brother, but most marry around the age of 17 years and migrate as young wives. Adolescent boys, on the other hand, set off with older kin or with brothers and friends of a similar age, sometimes with a parent's approval, sometimes not (Thorsen 2009). My analysis in the following sections is of the relationship between boys' or young men's work and material consumption.

As there is a lack of both statistical and qualitative evidence of the demographic composition of rural households in the Bisa region and of the migration flows from this region, it is difficult to establish whether adolescents' migration is a new phenomenon. On the one hand, historian Isaie Dougnon documented that the British and French colonial administrations adopted policies related to the minimum age for employing migrants, at 14 and 16 years, respectively, to curtail the exploitation of young migrant workers (Dougnon 2002). This suggests that adolescents have been part of the migration flow for a long time and in sufficiently large numbers to represent a problem for the colonial administrations. On the other hand, the author's observations in rural and urban Bisa communities indicate that social change linked with school education, the development of the urban economy, new material desires and the establishment of migration as a path to social becoming entice adolescents in their early teens to migrate if they are not enrolled in school. Yet, the civil war in Côte d'Ivoire and a short-lived rise in cotton-farming in the Bisa region delayed the migration of young people or encouraged them to return to farm in the village at the beginning of the rainy season. In the mid-2000s there was no clear indication of a shift in migration flows.

Adolescents' migration: work and savings

Most of the boys interviewed justified their migration to the city or to neighboring Côte d'Ivoire with the wish to earn money since 'nothing worked in the village'. While this is a direct outcome of the lack of opportunities for young people in the Bisa region, comparable to the sense of marginalization among rural adolescents and youth in other regions of West Africa (cf. Agarwal et al. 1997; Awumbila and Ardayfio-Schandorf 2008; Castle and Diarra 2003; de Lange 2006; Hilson 2008; Imorou 2008), it is also an indication of how young people seek more autonomy and negotiate dependencies and interdependencies within the family through migration. Or that is the intention. The boys participating in this research set off from home after the harvest, that is, at the time of the year when they have few labor obligations to seniors in the household, and they alluded to old patterns of circular migration between rural and urban areas when maintaining they would return to farm the following season. However, most of them remained in the city for a longer period of time and thereby increased their ability to focus on their own accumulation of wealth since they did not have to work on the household farm. This choice was often sanctioned by their parents because, as pointed out by Whitehead et al., parents balance the need for a child's labor against the wish to ensure the child's welfare, the ability of the child to develop his or her individual economy and to maintain strong links with the child in the long term through a sense of mutual indebtedness (Whitehead et al. 2007: 23). The autonomy sought by adolescent Bisa boys should not necessarily be seen as a process of individualization. Even though they liberated themselves from working for their seniors, they were embedded in the community of migrants from their region, who, as we shall see, made inroads on their ability to earn and save.

The analysis of adolescent migrants' work in the urban informal economy of Ouagadougou and Abidjan reveals how notions of age-appropriate work, or perhaps rather age-appropriate remuneration, affected young migrants' ability to increase their autonomy. Established Bisa migrants frequently recruited young workers in their home region for their businesses. In both Ouagadougou and Abidjan, the youngest migrants became family labor in their relative's shop or restaurant or peddled food and beverages on the streets for their relative, whereas migrants in their early 20s usually did work that was paid by commission or received a monthly salary. This difference is linked with young migrants' ability to assert themselves as being of an age at which they contribute economically to the rural household and therefore should be given space to earn.

What is particularly interesting in this analysis, however, is that it draws attention to the negotiated nature of the transition from child to youth migrant, and how work, income and location shape this process. It highlights the intersection between developmental life-span and migration trajectories, and also between individual, transgenerational and historic migration trajectories in rural communities in West Africa. Despite the fact that workers in a family business are often labeled as unpaid labor in statistical surveys, adolescent Bisa migrants expected to be given a ticket and a gift in cash and/or kind when they were ready to return home, as is also known from elsewhere in West Africa (cf. Castle and Diarra 2003; Hashim 2007; Jacquemin 2012). Gifts offered in recompense for favors and services are part of the social and moral fabric of the household and a way of invoking interdependence, cohesion and solidarity. However, not all young migrants appreciate being tied into an urban household as a 'child'. Fifteen-year-old Boureima, who sold small sachets of drinking water for his aunt, chose to leave her house because she did not buy him a pair of jeans when he asked for them.[2] He had come to Ouagadougou to work, he claimed, and did not intend to wait several months for his compensation.[3] Malik, another 15-year-old migrant, had traveled to Abidjan with an established migrant from his village, in whose shop he worked for three years because he could not find other employment. Malik considered the migrant as a brother, and said that he only expected the usual remuneration of a gift and the return fare. However, when the brother increasingly squandered his business capital and the prospects of receiving a gift dwindled, Malik moved to another part of Abidjan to work in vegetable gardening for a brother from his immediate family. Now aged 18 years, he was paid for his work.[4]

The two boys' stories demonstrate that adolescents assess the likelihood of their gift's being commensurate with their work and sufficient to meet their desired consumption. In the case of default, they move on to other employers, kin or not. Underlying this economic rationality is also the wish for autonomy and for escaping adult control over their remuneration. They negotiate their relational age by seeking to prove that they are indeed wage earners. In both cases, location plays an important role: in Ouagadougou young migrants take matters in their own hands and find low-paid work by approaching potential employers on their own or engage in low-skill services like shoe shining. The wage level in Ouagadougou is much lower than in Abidjan. Here employment is hard to come by, however, without the assistance of an intermediary who vouches for the young migrant's ability and morality. Hence they depend on their relatives' and friends' evaluation of their ability to work in salaried employment. However, as they develop a social network over time, the length of time spent at a destination impacts the alternatives available to young migrants (Guichaoua 2006; Thorsen 2009).

High unemployment rates in Ouagadougou and Abidjan make it difficult for both rural and urban children and youth to find secure employment with a good wage. Children employed informally generally earn very small wages. As few of the adolescent Bisa migrants had been to school, they were barred from work that required literacy and numeracy. Additionally, few had the means to start up an independent trade, so they had to stick to low-paid jobs in small food businesses, domestic service and brick-making sites or do street peddling on a commission unless they offered small itinerant services. The niche occupation in Ouagadougou for adolescent boys from the Bisa region was shoe shining. In 2005, the starting wage for migrants aged 14–15 years was around 3000 CFA francs [5 euros[5]] for doing dishes in small roadside restaurants. Shoeshiners earned slightly more, but also spent a good part of their earnings on food. Those who had a couple of years' experience and helped cook and serve food earned 7000 CFA francs [11 euros]. Interviews showed that adolescents were subject to frequent pay reductions. Some were issued as a punishment for breaking crockery, wasting food or getting the change wrong in trade, but employers also reduced the wage and paid with one or two months' delay if the business slowed down, or else they did not pay at all. What set young migrants apart from urban children and youth was the necessity of finding income sources. Not only did they justify their migration to the city with the wish to earn money, they also needed money for food and, possibly, accommodation. The cost of living is lower in Ouagadougou than in Abidjan; nevertheless, it is harder to save up in Ouagadougou The youngest migrants interviewed lived with relatives or found employment where accommodation was part of the wage, but those in their late teens or early twenties shared cheap housing in the unplanned settlements. Boarding and lodging thus made inroads on their ability to save.

The process of gradually attaining the autonomy to develop their own economic activities places adolescents in limbo. Although adolescents see migration as a means to social mobility through creating space for accumulating different types of wealth, which then allows them to assert their age in relation to other members in the network of kin, older relatives exercise social control over this process through their evaluation of what an adolescent is capable of doing for work and through retaining control over the remuneration-as-a-gift. Escaping this control introduces another set of constraints related to the costs of living and vulnerabilities linked with contingencies in the urban informal economy, such as job loss, nonpayment and intense competition for customers in street-based activities. Adolescent migrants weigh different forms of remuneration against each other and seek to second-guess how the social control exercised by kin and social relations will impact on their ability to spend their earnings as they like. Obviously, this is a complex process, and the following section examines the linkages between adolescents' pursuit of more autonomy, their material desires and the ways in which they navigate the family context.

Images of the 'successful migrant': urban consumption and homecomings

Any migrant – man or woman, young or old – attempt to asserts him- or herself as a successful migrant through being well dressed and groomed when returning home or in photographs chronicling his or her life as a migrant. The materiality of migration is well known across West Africa, even if desired commodities and their value have changed in the course of time (Hahn 2004; Piot 1999: 170–171). This angle on migrants' self-representations reiterates their continued links with the rural community; however, it is important also to include material practices in the city. Before becoming migrants, children in the Bisa region admired those who returned to the village for their smart looks and their knowledge about other places, and they took note of how adults spoke of various migrants. Most of them were used to only getting one or two sets of new clothes per year, so they greatly admired clothes that were not worn thin and bleached by the sun. This inevitably influenced both their perception of what it would take to be deemed a successful migrant and their enactment of this social category.

Abounding with temptations, the city is a place where young migrants can easily spend their earnings on food, clothing, snacks, video clubs and game halls, in a way that is not possible in villages in the Bisa region, where the supply of leisure activities is generally restricted to market days, and those requiring electricity are few and far between.[6] I am not suggesting here that adolescents are attracted by the bright city lights or that they leave their rural home out of boredom, but rather that a new range of activities and entertainment opens to them once they are in the city. Fifteen-year-old Boureima, who left his aunt's house in Ouagadougou after a dispute over a pair of jeans, often spent his evenings exploring the bustling streets of his neighborhood. He lived with different employers, but instead of watching television at home with his host, he was out buying snacks and paying the entry of 50 CFA francs [8 cents] to watch videos in one of the clubs. Disapprovingly, one established migrant noted that the boy had once squandered his entire wage of 5000 CFA francs [8 euros] this way and that, additionally, the boy kept on moving from one employer to the next without asking the advice of his brother and uncles. Although Boureima eventually accepted the advice of his older brother concerning the need to save up, he chose to leave most of his wage with his employer instead of giving it to his brother for safekeeping. Unfortunately, his employer was unable to pay up when he wanted to leave, and thus Boureima lost his savings.[7]

The critiques of boys like Boureima make obvious that adolescent migrants are left little space for reworking their social position in the city. Other migrants dismissed what could, relative to the boys' limited income, be seen as sumptuous spending. As a contrast to the young Zairian diamond miners described by de Boeck (1998), whose momentous consumption of bottled beer, women and consumer goods had become a marker of success within the mining community, adolescent Bisa migrants' consumption of entertainment was seen by adults and peers alike to fall outside the local idioms of wealth and status. Two issues appear to be at stake. Those who were seeking to negotiate their age by asserting themselves as autonomous challenged the social hierarchy. Failing to act in ways that others recognized as appropriate for juniors, their enactment of relational social status was disregarded as 'not having understood'; that is, as being immature. While Zairian diamond miners may have been judged in similar ways, they were able to transgress such criticism because of the peculiar environment in which they lived, and because of the links drawn between swift accumulation, witchcraft and the need to make sacrifices (de Boeck 1998). Adolescent migrants in Ouagadougou and Abidjan live in the midst of a dense network of established migrants who gain social and material status from the presence of junior members of their kin group, whether they do so by exploiting their labor, by taking on parental roles or by invoking patronage relationships. This is why the critique of consumption practices frequently was intertwined with misgivings about not seeking the advice of, or attaching themselves to, seniors.

The other issue relates to individualistic consumption that satisfies a young migrant's cravings without his building social relationships through conviviality and gift giving. Twenty-three-year-old Souleyman was criticized by his friend for overspending on clothes. Well spoken and with some secondary education, Souleyman talked himself into well-paid jobs, but, according to his friend, was then sacked because he did not work hard enough or was suspected of being dishonest. 'Souleyman is like that. If he has no money, he might take some from his employer's cash drawer. He cannot save! If he buys something, one week later he's already sold it. We've got the same wage – 25,000 CFA francs [38 euros] per month – but Souleyman hasn't bought anything and he borrows money regularly. He doesn't drink, but spends lots on clothes. He is dressed like a "big man"[8] even before he has arrived!'[9] This critique foregrounds the display of wealth and how it is received by others. It contrasts with the way in which young women's display of consumed goods in northern Nigeria is associated with their integration into a social network (Platte 2008). While these young women's accumulation of wealth was premised on their adherence to well-established social pathways for adolescent girls, that is, accruing wealth in the marriage process and relying on senior relatives to maximize this wealth, the investment going into adolescent Bisa migrants' enactment of 'being successful' through the display of smart clothes is perceived as ephemeral and untimely. Given the size of their income, such consumption practices tend to be at the expense of accumulating wealth, and thus this behavior undercuts their social position in the rural social system. Incapable, if not unwilling, to be part of the dependencies and interdependencies within the rural household, these adolescent migrants do not follow the accepted social path of gradually contributing more and more to the household economy. They are thus criticized for showing disinterest in maintaining kinship relations.

Whenever I saw Souleyman, he was dressed in jeans or track suit bottoms, a sports jersey and a beanie. Although his clothes were never faded or worn thin, his dress style was a far cry from the labels of the big fashion houses worn by the *sapeurs* of Central Africa and the *coupeurs décaleurs* of Côte d'Ivoire, who compete for status and power through stylish dressing and conspicuous consumption in the urban nightlife (Hansen 2004b; McGovern 2010). In fact, Souleyman's dress style gestured at the globalized hip-hop culture; on the one hand an image of modernity among poor youth and a symbol of their marginalization (Weiss 2005: 116) and, on the other hand, a reflection of clothing markets blending second-hand clothing, mass-produced clothes from China and to a lesser extent surplus, mass-produced clothes from the North (Scheld 2007: 240). In a study of dress practices and globalization in Dakar, Suzanne Scheld pointed out that people distinguish between second-hand clothes from the global North and Chinese imports of counterfeit designer clothes. The latter are perceived as being of low quality, but are nevertheless very popular as their affordability allows consumers to present themselves in new clothes more often (Scheld 2007: 240). The quantity of imports from China also makes Chinese counterfeits widely accessible. In South Africa, for example, 80 out of 100 imported T-shirts come from China (Carmody and Owusu 2007: 510). For adolescent migrants from the Bisa region, the availability of Chinese-produced clothing implies that they can buy into the hip-hop style or, at least, combine one or two new items with second-hand clothes. In a small way, they try to shed their rural/newcomer/poor appearance by participating in urban life and, in Souleyman's case, by asserting a certain urban style through his clothing. As is obvious from the critique voiced by Souleyman's friend, and mirroring diverging attitudes among young rural migrants in Dakar, not all young migrants buy into this strategy for enacting success. Some rural migrants, argued Scheld, emulate the dress styles of urban youth to avoid being labeled as newcomers and backward. Others, however, criticize urban youth for showing off, while relying materially on older relatives and lacking moral values and a work ethic (Scheld 2007: 243).

The image of the well-dressed successful migrant is full of contradictions. While adolescent migrants are scorned for their spending to look smart in the city, they are expected to be well dressed when they return home. Adolescent boys' return outfit was usually a pair of new jeans, a Chinese-made sports jersey or a second-hand shirt, sneakers or at least sandals of a better quality than the usual flip-flops, and baseball caps. They adorned themselves with cheap eye-catching necklaces and, if they could afford to do so, with watches and MP3 players. Bakary, a 20-year-old shoeshiner, who had worked in Ouagadougou in the dry season for three years, explained that he was planning to use his savings of 100–600 CFA francs [15–90 cents] per day to buy jeans and other clothes, in order to be able to change his clothes. When he and two of his younger brothers (cousins) prepared for their return to their village and were buying new clothes, they started a mock bargain about a wristwatch to check out the price, but ended up, much to their surprise, with a watch each, laughing at the fortunate price of 750 CFA francs [1 euro], but also regretting having spent the money.[10] On my next visit to their village, their fathers cheerfully wore nice new wristwatches. In this context, being well dressed in conjunction with offering gifts, even if only symbolic, is perceived as an instant marker of accumulation and of the ability to control one's consumption in the city. However, adolescent return migrants have to strike a subtle balance. Adults look at their self-representations with a measure of pride when adolescents are proving their commitment to their seniors, but with a measure of concern when they have spent almost all their money on clothing to demonstrate their new status as migrants. In this case, parents are concerned about their children's priorities. This brings out a third contradiction. While parents and other adults may be critical of adolescents' allocation of their sparse resources, they overlook that adolescents do not necessarily orient their consumption practices at adults. Twenty-one-year-old Moussa, for example, reaped much admiration among his friends when he returned after three years in Abidjan clad in black jeans, T-shirt and a bright yellow bucket hat. He had even had an ear pierced, something not seen in the village before.[11] In addition to being impressed with clothing, adolescents admire new language skills, accounts of other places and the ability of returnees to invite their friends to snacks and drinks on market days. Young returnees thus gain social standing vis-à-vis their younger peers. Having proven that they are streetwise, they are the ones to whom their friends and younger brothers turn when they seek a companion with whom to travel. In this way, the investment in clothing also becomes an investment in a nascent social network.

The parents of two brothers – Ibrahim and Abdoulaye, aged 18 and 23 years, respectively – regularly sent requests for small presents to their sons in Ouagadougou. As I was the vehicle of some of these requests, Abdoulaye entrusted me with a wristwatch for their father and a pair of flip-flops for their mother on one of my journeys to the Bisa region. However, when they received a request for a contribution of 20,000 CFA francs [30 euros] for their grandmother's funeral in early 2006 – at a time when Ibrahim had just lost his job, and Abdoulaye was trying to set himself up as an itinerant tradesman – Ibrahim traveled back to the village to explain the situation to their father. Their difficulties were taken as adequate explanation and the demands for assistance decreased until their mother fell seriously ill in early 2008. After having worked as a contract laborer on a construction site without being paid, Abdoulaye was still unable to meet his father's request, but Ibrahim had moved to Abidjan and was able to send 50,000 CFA francs [76 euros] for medical expenses. Apparently disappointed, his father requested more. But the intervention of another young migrant, who had recently returned from Abidjan, made him reconsider. It was difficult for migrants, Ibrahim's friend explained, to find good employment, and their average wages had shrunk to half of what they were before the civil war. This convinced the father that Ibrahim's consumption patterns were still oriented toward the rural social system.[12]

The gap between the discourse of intergenerational reciprocity and young migrants' actual investments brings out how contingencies in the urban informal economy impacts the morality of migration. It is difficult to use regional labor migration as a means to gain social standing, for adolescents as for older migrants. What is particularly interesting, however, is that practices in Bisa families offer a contrast to the portrayal of rural families elsewhere. Scheld, for example, described rural families in Senegal as gluttonous and ignorant of the hardships young migrants experience in the cities (Scheld 2007: 238). Interviews with adolescent Bisa migrants and their families indicate that rural adults have understanding for the economic constraints among young migrants in Ouagadougou and Abidjan. While maintaining reciprocal ties is an important element of being acknowledged as successful, defaulting neither breaks family relations nor obliterates the possibility of being seen as a 'good person'.

Returning migrants of all ages, who have managed to save, bring back commodities such as mobile phones, ghetto blasters, bicycles, mopeds or cars, offering gifts of varying value and kind to relatives and friends, and possibly invest in farming equipment, cattle and plots of urban land. The increased availability of cheaply produced consumer goods following the opening of the African markets to imports from China has changed consumption patterns. Price reductions have made the goods affordable to an even wider segment of the population. In Ghana, for example, the price of a mountain bike imported from China dropped from US$67 to US$25 [from 58 to 21 euros[13]] over a two-year period in the early 2000s (Carmody and Owusu, 2007: 512). The bicycle, which was one of the most treasured items among adult male migrants to bring back in the 1960s (Hahn 2004), is still treasured among children today (de Lange,

2006). Despite speaking of the gift they ought to bring home, the first larger goal for the majority of adolescent migrants from the Bisa region was in fact to buy a bicycle. With the changing prices, this had become an attainable goal. A cheap Chinese bicycle imported from Ghana cost 25–30,000 CFA francs [38–46 euros] in 2007, while the better quality blue Peugeot bicycle that bestowed more status on its owner cost 45–50,000 CFA francs [69–76 euros]. The less successful individuals, or those who had stayed in the city for a shorter period of time, made do with a second-hand bicycle. Apart from giving the boys a new mobility – an important point for adolescents who otherwise have been used to walking 15–20 km to get to the nearest town – a bicycle earned them merit with their family and friends. Not only did it demonstrate their savoir faire, but it was also a commodity that could be lent out, creating social debts that the lender would take advantage of later. Thus having a bicycle was an asset for adolescents in consolidating their social standing.

With the rapid increase in mobile telephone communication, the purchase of a mobile phone ranged high on the list of desired purchases for adolescent migrants.[14] A mobile phone confers status on its owner because it is expensive and signals that the owner is in the lead of urban and modern practices. Similar to the bicycle, it has merit because others can receive or make phone calls although they might not be able to afford a phone. The price of a phone and of call time, however, barred most adolescent migrants in Ouagadougou purchasing one. In Abidjan, in contrast, having a mobile phone was common among young migrants. It was often cheaper to phone friends and relatives than to cross the city by public transport and risk being stopped by various security forces who demanded levies. Additionally, mobile phones made it easier and cheaper to keep in touch with the family in the village. A migrant cannot send a letter without remitting money, and this has become increasingly difficult with the economic and political crisis in Côte d'Ivoire. However, mobile phones also allow the rural family to call and explain all their problems that require financial assistance from the migrant. While adolescents are spared from some of the demands due to their low earnings, their self-representation as successful quickly draws them into the interdependencies of the household and only by remitting can they uphold the image of being successful.

Conclusion: adolescent migrants' material consumption

The emphasis on 'new' in discussions of the mobility-migration nexus is valuable for moving beyond the sedentarism entrenched in the social

sciences that continues to infuse the analysis of movement, and especially of adolescents' movement, with the idea of social rupture and the
sense of being uprooted (de Bruijn et al. 2001: 2; Malkki 1992: 31–33;
Sheller and Urry 2006: 208–209). However, the emphasis on the 'new'
sometimes stresses new technologies and recent trends in globalization
at the expense of historicizing mobility and the ways in which migration, in some places, has been a normal part of family life, and of childhood, for a long time (Hashim and Thorsen 2011: 11–13). Numerous
studies of adolescents' migration from poor communities have theo-
rized the linkage between economic motivations to migrate and
family decision-making processes to establish the complex ways that
adolescents exercise agency in such processes (Carpena-Méndez 2007;
Hashim and Thorsen 2011; Iversen 2002; Punch 2007). This chapter
set out to explore a different aspect of mobilities, namely, the relationship between work and consumption in adolescent migrant's lives, and
the role of migration, work and consumption in creating, maintaining
and breaking relationships. Adolescents move in order to participate
in a consumption-oriented, cash-based economy, which highlights the
intersection between adolescent development, globalization, migration,
work, consumption and self-representation.

In the Bisa region of Burkina Faso, adolescents' material consumption
is overwhelmingly premised on labor migration. Migrating to work is
not new, but the social mobility they can achieve is. The globalization
of supply chains and trade has made a much wider range of consumer
goods affordable to adolescents. Yet, globalization has also impacted
urban economies in a variety of ways. One impact that has seriously
negative consequences for the urban population is the structural adjustment programs and more recent neoliberal reforms that have increased
inequalities and affected the livelihoods of many poor (Hansen 2008:
101). Contractions in the urban economy impact the micro-enterprises
at which adolescent migrants work and often decrease their earnings
unexpectedly. In turn, this affects their consumption. However, with a
careful eye to their economy and by avoiding contingencies that might
devour their savings, adolescent migrants can purchase status-enhancing
commodities like bicycles, which in the past was the privilege of older
migrants. An additional outcome of globalization is the availability
of new commodities. The mobile phone has entered into adolescents'
desire and consumption in a way that perhaps parallels the older generation's interest in transistor radios. The symbolic value of these commodities is enormous, and underlines the importance of movement within
Bisa society. While the radio allows people to 'travel without leaving

home' – to gain knowledge and information from the world outside their community (Clifford 1992: 103) – bicycles and mobile phones accord more control to their owners. They can decide where and when to go and whom and when to call, whereas radio listeners must stick to the broadcasted programs. The most important symbolic attribute of bicycles and mobiles phones for adolescent migrants is, however, the potential for employing them to create social debts by letting others use them. These debts may extend across generations and circumvent hierarchical power relations. Global discourses, economics and policies impact on child migrant's lived experiences. While at one level these young people are victims of global neoliberal economies, they show that they can engage with globalization as consumers and buyers of global products. Work and consumption are part of growing up in the era of globalization. The ability to work and make independent purchases signals the transition from being dependent children to becoming young adults and successful migrants. Migration increases the opportunities to become consumers of global goods, and through consumerism, children and young migrants seek to gain higher status in their communities. Globalization then occurs on a continuum with the local, national and regional and global interactions.

It is impossible to separate consumption from social relationships in a context within which social relations are everything. Adolescents move within a dense network of kin and other relations, and they hold a subordinate position within this network. That such relationships are complex and two directional is well established (Andersson 2001; Ferguson 1999; Jamal 2001) but the commoditization of seniors' reciprocation of adolescents' work adds a new dimension to the moral underpinnings of rural-urban relationships. Adolescents have room to negotiate their relational age, but only in circumstances in which rural relatives are critical of the established migrant's spending priorities. Finally, the availability and affordability of new globalized clothes and dress styles brings out the contradictory ways in which adolescent migrants' enactment of the 'successful migrant' is received by adults and peers. Mirroring Mary Beth Mills's study of consumption among rural Thai girls in Bangkok (Mills 1997), this chapter shows that adolescents have aspirations to particular identities and lifestyles that are different from the poverty back home. They balance giving symbolic gifts to their parents and other significant relatives to be a 'good child' with their own ideas of how a successful migrant should dress and what he should do. It is important to remember that adolescents do not only see themselves in relation to adults. Just as important perhaps are the ideas and reflections shared by friends of a similar age about the repertoire of social positions that are worth pursuing. While, on the one hand, adolescent migrants are acutely aware of their marginalized position in the urban space, they imitate and reinterpret the public attitudes, styles and practices of the elites to make an impression on others. Unable to live these ideas in the city, they transpose them to the village and act them out there, only to find out that flashy looks and extravagance are discounted by their seniors and only impress their peers briefly.

Acknowledgments

The author would like to thank all people in Burkina Faso and Côte d'Ivoire who took the time to participate in this research and taught her much about family relations in situations of migration. She also thanks the three reviewers for their most constructive critiques and suggestions. Research funding provided by the Development Research Centre on Migration, Poverty and Globalisation (Brighton, UK) and the Nordic Africa Institute (Uppsala, Sweden) was greatly appreciated.

Notes

1. Images in the global media and reports of young children working on cocoa farms in West Africa in the early 2000s, for example, triggered a series of interventions to prevent the worst forms of children's labor, and led to the initiation of a certification process of cocoa to ensure it had been produced without the use of child labor (cf. Ould et al. 2004; Baah 2010; Toler and Schweisguth 2011).
2. All names used in this article are pseudonyms to ensure confidentiality.
3. My initial interview with Boureima took place on March 4, 2005, the last one on March 19, 2008. In between, I also followed him through conversations with him, his grandmother, his maternal uncle, his older brother and the established migrant who had put me in contact with the boy.
4. Interview on the periphery of Abidjan, January 21, 2008.
5. The CFA franc has a fixed exchange rate to the euro: €1 = 655.957 CFA francs. In 2005, the minimum wage for adults employed formally in Burkina Faso was 28,811 CFA francs (43.92 euros).
6. Throughout the region, markets operate on a three-day rotation between different villages, and only in the rural towns do markets operate on a daily basis.
7. Conversation with an established migrant in Ouagadougou on May 8, 2005, with whom I had many conversations between March 2005 and March 2008.
8. The notion of the 'big man' is well known across West Africa, and symbolizes someone of influence and wealth. For young migrants, this has less to do with political power and elitism than with being a well-to-do established migrant.

9. I engaged with Souleyman and his friend at frequent intervals between March 2005 and March 2008, but more often with his friend, who used to update me on Souleyman's whereabouts when I could not find him. The cited material derives from conversations with his friend on November 19, 2006, and March 2, 2008, and was verified by observing Souleyman in his different workplaces.
10. Observations and interviews with Bakary and a group of shoeshiners from his village between March 3, 2005, and March 11, 2008. The last interview with Bakary took place in February 2007, some 100 km from Abidjan.
11. Observations and interviews with Moussa on February 24, 2005 (village), and February 4, 2007 (Abidjan), and with his mother, 21 April 2005 (village). I have known Moussa's family since 1997, and supported the founding of the women's village association in 2002, of which his mother is the secretary.
12. I have known Abdoulaye and Ibrahim's family since 1997, and had very frequent conversations with the two brothers in Ouagadougou from the very beginning of the research in early 2005, with Ibrahim in Abidjan in early 2008 and with their parents in the village.
13. The exchange rate in mid-July 2003 was US$1 = € 0.86889 (www.oanda.com)
14. This is a development that has taken place over less than a decade. In a small village in the Bisa region, which consists of 73 households, nobody owned a mobile phone in 2002. In 2005, ten households had acquired a mobile phone, and in 2008, almost half the households had one. These phones belonged to young or middle-aged men, who had either bought a phone themselves or had been given one by a migrant. As the village had no electricity, they cycled to the nearest town at regular intervals to charge the phone.

References

Abebe, T. (2007) 'Changing Livelihoods, Changing Childhoods: Patterns of Children's Work in Rural Southern Ethiopia', *Children's Geographies*, 5, 77–93.

Agarwal, S., Attah, M., Apt, N., Grieco, M., Kwakye, E. A., and Turner, J. (1997) 'Bearing the Weight: The Kayayoo, Ghana's Working Girl Child', *International Social Work*, 40, 245–263.

Alber, E. (2004) 'Grandparents as Foster-parents: Transformations in Foster Relations between Grandparents and Grandchildren in Northern Benin', *Africa*, 74, 28–46.

Andersson, J. A. (2001) 'Reinterpreting the Rural-urban Connection: Migration Practices and Socio-Cultural Dispositions of Buhera Workers in Harare', *Journal of the International African Institute*, 71, 82–112.

Awumbila, M., and Ardayfio-Schandorf, E. (2008) 'Gendered Poverty, Migration and Livelihood Strategies of Female Porters in Accra, Ghana', *Norsk Geografisk Tidsskrift – Norwegian Journal of Geography*, 62, 171–179.

Baah, F. (2010) 'Use of Children and the Issue of Child Labour in Ghanaian Cocoa Farm Activities', *Journal of Agricultural Extension and Rural Development*, 2, 198–204.

Bass, L. E. (1996) 'Beyond Homework: Children's Incorporation into Market-Based Work in Urban Areas of Senegal', *Anthropology of Work Review*, 17, 19–24.

Bledsoe, C. H. (1980) *Women and Marriage in Kpelle Society* (Stanford: Stanford University Press).

Bledsoe, C. H. (1990) '"No Success Without Struggle": Social Mobility and Hardship for Foster Children in Sierra Leone', *Man* (n.s.), 25, 70–88.

Bourdillon, M. C. F. (2006) 'Children and Work: A Review of Current Literature and Debates', *Development and Change*, 37, 1201–1226.

Bourdillon, M. C. F. (forthcoming) 'Introduction: The Place of Work in African Children's Lives' in M. C. F. Bourdillon and G. M. Mulumbwa (eds) *The Place of Work in African Children's Lives* (Dakar: CODESRIA).

Carmody, P. R., and Owusu F. Y. (2007) 'Competing Hegemons? Chinese versus American Geo-Economic Strategies in Africa', *Political Geography*, 26, 504–524.

Carpena-Méndez, F. (2007) ' "Our Lives Are Like a Sock Inside-out": Children's Work and Youth Identity in Neoliberal Rural Mexico' in R. Panelli, S. Punch, and E. Robson (eds) *Global Perspectives on Rural Childhood and Youth: Young Rural Lives* (New York and London: Routledge).

Castle, S., and Diarra, A. (2003) *The International Migration of Young Malians: Tradition, Necessity or Rite of Passage?* (London: London School of Hygiene and Tropical Medicine).

Clifford, J. (1992) 'Travelling Cultures' in L. Grossberg, C. Nelson, and P. Treichler (eds) *Cultural Studies* (New York and London: Routledge).

Cordell, D. D., Gregory, J. W., and Piché, V. (1996) *Hoe and Wage: A Social History of a Circular Migration System in West Africa* (Boulder: Westview).

De Boeck, F. (1998) 'Domesticating Diamonds and Dollars: Identity, Expenditure and Sharing in Southwestern Zaire (1984 – 1997)', *Development and Change*, 29, 777–810.

De Bruijn, M., Van Dijk, R., and Foeken, D. (2001) 'Mobile Africa: An Introduction' in M. De Bruijn, R. Van Dijk, and D. Foeken (eds) *Mobile Africa: Changing Patterns of Mobility in Africa and Beyond* (Leiden: Brill).

De Lange, A. (2006) *"Going to Kompienga": A Study on Child Labor Migration and Trafficking in Burkina Faso's South-Eastern Cotton Sector* (Amsterdam: IREWOC).

Dobler, G. (2008) 'From Scotch Whisky to Chinese Sneakers: International Commodity Flows and New Trade Networks in Oshikango, Namibia', *Africa*, 78, 410–432.

Dougnon, I. (2002) 'Migration de Travail ou "Trafic d'Enfant"? Mise en Perspective Historique: le Cas du Pays Dogon', le 10me Assemblée Générale du CODESRIA, December 8–12, 2002 (Kampala: Ouganda).

Ferguson, J. (1999) *Expectations of Modernity. Myths and Meanings of Urban Life on the Zambian Copperbelt* (Berkeley: University of California Press).

Ferguson, J. (2006) *Global Shadows: Africa in the Neoliberal World Order* (Durham, NC, and London: Duke University Press).

Gell, A. (1986) 'Newcomers to the World of Goods: Consumption among the Muria Gonds' in A. Appadurai (ed) *The Social Life of Things: Commodities in Cultural Perspective* (Cambridge: Cambridge University Press).

Goody, E. N. (1982) *Parenthood and Social Reproduction: Fostering and Occupational Roles in West Africa* (Cambridge: Cambridge University Press).

Guichaoua, Y. (2006) 'Non-Protected Labour in one West African Capital: Characteristics of Jobs and Occupational Mobility in Abidjan, Côte d'Ivoire', *QEH Working Paper No. 132* (Oxford: Queen Elizabeth House, University of Oxford).

Hahn, H. P. (2004) 'Zirkuläre Arbeitsmigration in Westafrika und die Kultur der Migration', *Afrika Spectrum*, 39, 381–404.

Hahn, H. P. (2008) 'Consumption, Identity and Agency in Africa – Introduction' in H. P. Hahn (ed) *Consumption in Africa: Anthropological Approaches* (Münster: Lit Verlag).

Hansen, K. T. (2004a) 'Dressing Dangerously: Miniskirts, Gender Relations, and Sexuality in Zambia' in J. Allman (ed) *Fashioning Africa: Power and the Politics of Dress* (Bloomington: Indiana University Press).

Hansen, K. T. (2004b) 'The World in Dress: Anthropological Perspectives on Clothing, Fashion, and Culture', *Annual Review of Anthropology*, 33, 369–392.

Hansen, K. T. (2008) 'Localities and Sites of Youth Agency in Lusaka' in K. T. Hansen (ed) *Youth and the City in the Global South* (Bloomington and Indianapolis: Indiana University Press).

Hashim, I. M. (2007) 'Independent Child Migration and Education in Ghana', *Development and Change*, 38, 911–931.

Hashim, I. M. (2011) 'Learning and Livelihoods: Children's Education in North-Eastern Ghana', *Cahier de la Recherche sur l'Éducation et les Savoirs*, 107–126.

Hashim, I. M., and Thorsen, D. (2011) *Child Migrants in Africa* (London: Zed Books).

Hilson, G. (2008) ' "A Load Too Heavy": Critical Reflections on the Child Labor Problem in Africa's Small-Scale Mining Sector', *Children and Youth Services Review*, 30, 1233–1245.

Human Rights Watch (2007) *Bottom of the Ladder: Exploitation and Abuse of Girl Domestic Workers in Guinea* (New York: Human Rights Watch).

Imorou, A.-B. (2008) *Le Coton et la Mobilité: Les Implications d'une Culture de Rente sur les Trajectoires Sociales des Jeunes et Enfants au Nord-Bénin* (Dakar: Plan-Waro/Terre des Hommes/Lasdel-Bénin).

International Labor Office (2001) *Combating Trafficking in Children for Labour Exploitation in West and Central Africa: Synthesis Report* (Geneva: International Labor Office).

International Labor Office (2010) *Accelerating Action against Child Labour: Global Report under the Follow-Up to the ILO Declaration on Fundamental Principles and Rights to Work* (Geneva: International Labor Office).

Iversen, V. (2002) 'Autonomy in Child Labour Migrants', *World Development*, 30, 817–834.

Jacquemin, M. (2012) *'Petites Bonnes' d'Abidjan: Sociologie des Filles en Service Domestique* (Paris: L'Harmattan).

Jamal, V. (2001) 'Chasing the Elusive Rural-Urban Gap in Tanzania', *Journal of Contemporary African Studies*, 19, 25–38.

Katz, C. (2004) *Growing Up Global: Economic Restructuring and Children's Everyday Lives* (Minneapolis, MN: University of Minnesota Press).

Malkki, L. (1992) 'National Geographic: The Rooting of Peoples and the Territorialization of National Identity among Scholars and Refugees', *Cultural Anthropology*, 7, 24–44.

Massey, D. (1998) 'The Spatial Construction of Youth Cultures' in T. Skelton and G. Valentine (eds) *Cool Places: Geographies of Youth Cultures* (London and New York: Routledge).

McGovern, M. (2010) ' "This Is Play": Popular Culture and Politics in Côte d'Ivoire' in A. M. Makhule, B. A. Buggenhagen, and S. Jackson (eds) *Hard Work, Hard Times: Global Volatility and African Subjectivities* (Berkeley: University of California Press).

Mills, M. B. (1997) 'Contesting the Margins of Modernity: Women, Migration, and Consumption in Thailand', *American Ethnologist*, 24, 37–61.

Nieuwenhuys, O. (2007) 'Embedding the Global Womb: Global Child Labor and the New Policy Agenda', *Children's Geographies*, 5, 149–163.

Notermans, C. (2004) 'Sharing Home, Food and Bed: Paths of Grandmotherhood in East Cameroon', *Africa*, 74, 6–27.

Ould, D., Jordan, C., Reynolds, R., and Loftin, L. (2004) *The Cocoa Industry in West Africa: A History of Exploitation* (London: Anti-Slavery International).

Pacere, T. F. (2004) *Burkina Faso: Migration et Droits des Travailleurs (1897–2003)* (Paris: Karthala).

Piot, C. D. (1999) *Remotely Global: Village Modernity in West Africa* (Chicago and London: The University of Chicago Press).

Platte, E. (2008) 'Ostentation as Lifestyle? Conspicuous Consumption, Identity and Home Culture in Northern Nigeria' in H. P. Hahn (ed) *Consumption in Africa: Anthropological Approaches* (Münster: Lit Verlag).

Punch, S. (2007) 'Negotiating Migrant Identities: Young People in Bolivia and Argentina', *Children's Geographies*, 5, 95–112.

Razy, E., and Rodet, M. (2011) 'Les Migrations Africaines dans l'Enfance, des Parcours Individuels entre Institutions Locales et Institutions Globales', *Journal des Africanistes*, 81, 5–48.

Reynolds, P. (1991) *Dance Civet Cat: Child Labor in the Zambezi Valley* (London: Zed Books).

Roberts, P. A. (1988) 'Rural Women's Access to Labour in West Africa' in S. Stichter and J. L. Parpart (eds) *Patriarchy and Class* (Boulder: Westview Press).

Robson, P. (2010) *Ending Child Trafficking in West Africa: Lessons from the Ivorian Cocoa Sector* (London: Anti-Slavery International).

Scheld, S. (2007) 'Youth Cosmopolitanism: Clothing, the City and Globalization in Dakar, Senegal', *City and Society*, 19, 232–253.

Sheller, M., and Urry, J. (2006) 'The New Mobilities Paradigm', *Environment and Planning A*, 38, 207–226.

Thorsen, D. (2002) 'We Help Our Husbands! Negotiating the Household Budget in Rural Burkina Faso', *Development and Change*, 33, 129–146.

Thorsen, D. (2009) 'From Shackles to Links in the Chain: Theorising Adolescent Boys' Relocation in Burkina Faso', *Forum for Development Studies*, 36, 81–107.

Toler, D., and Schweisguth, M. (2011) *'While Chocolate Lovers Smile, Child Cocoa Workers Cry'. Abusive Child Labor in the Cocoa Industry: How Corporations and International Financial Institutions Are Causing It, and How Fair Trade Can Solve It* (San Francisco, CA: Global Exchange International).

United Nations' Development Programme (2007) *Human Development Report 2007/2008. Fighting Climate Change: Human Solidarity in a Divided World* (New York: United Nations' Development Programme).

Vischer, L. R. (1997) *Mütter Zwischen Herd und Markt: Das Verhältnis von Mutterschaft, sozialer Elternschaft und Frauenarbeit bei den Moose (Mossi) in Ouagadougou/Burkina Faso* (Basel: Universität und Museum den Kulturen).

Weiss, B. (2005) 'The Barber in Pain: Consciousness, Affiliation and Alterity in Urban East Africa' in A. Honwana and F. de Boeck (eds) *Makers and Breakers: Children and Youth in Postcolonial Africa* (London: James Currey).

Whitehead, A. (1984) 'Women and Men; Kinship and Property: Some General Issues' in R. Hirschon (ed) *Women and Property: Women as Property* (London: Croom Helm).

Whitehead, A. (1996) *Poverty in North East Ghana: A Report to ESCOR* (London: Economic and Social Committee on Research, Department for International Development [DfID]).

Whitehead, A., Hashim, I. M., and Iversen, V. (2007) 'Child Migration, Child Agency and Inter-Generational Relations in Africa and South Asia', *Working Paper T24* (Brighton: Development Research Centre on Migration, Globalisation and Poverty, University of Sussex).

Whitehead, A., and Kabeer, N. (2001) 'Living with Uncertainty: Gender, Livelihoods and Pro-Poor Growth in Rural Sub-Saharan Africa', *Working Paper No. 134* (Brighton: University of Sussex and International Development Studies).

5
New Youth Mobilities: Transnational Migrations, Racialization and Global Popular Culture

Diana Yeh

Introduction

This chapter draws on a project on so-called 'British Chinese'/'Oriental'[1] youth cultures to examine new forms of mobility among young people who have grown up as children of migrants. It traces changing mobility patterns, from the migration and settlement patterns of the parental generation to the physical and virtual mobilities of the next generation. Children of migrants move locally to participate in activities with ethnic and racial co-peers, take transnational trips and engage virtually as global youth. As the editors to this volume suggest, examining the short-term and the micro-movements of children and young people within major migration fluxes brings to light experiences that are presently invisible and undertheorized. By using the concept of 'mobility-in-migration', they capture new complex, changing forms of movement that occur in response to migration and global economic and social change. By discussing how the mobilities of children of migrants are shaped by family transnational migrations, this chapter illustrates how shifts from childhood to youth intersect with migration trajectories. However, by tracing the ways in which young people also craft their own forms of movement, it considers how their present mobilities, shaped by processes of racialization, relate specifically to a localized global youth culture shared with both migrant and nonmigrant co-racial youth and thus transcend pathways forged by familial and ethnonational ties. This chapter therefore argues that these young people cannot be understood solely as children of migrants and that their mobilities must also be examined within broader processes of racialization, the transnational migrations of other young people and the globalization of culture. A central theoretical aim of the chapter is to bring together the literatures on migration, mobility, racialization and global youth cultures. My analysis stands in line with recent studies of transnational migration that complicate the dichotomy between 'migrants' and 'nonmigrants' and between 'first' and 'second' or subsequent generations of migrants by exploring their shared social fields and overlaps in their experiences (Levitt and Glick-Schiller 2007; Levitt and Jaworsky 2007). Research within the mobility paradigm, however, has also expanded understandings of human movement beyond migration by examining the myriad ways in which a range of people, not just 'migrants', live 'mobile' lives (Urry 2007). Meanwhile, work on cultural globalization explores the impact of the global flows of people, culture, ideas and information on people's lives whether they themselves move or not. Despite this, children of migrants are still primarily studied as indicators of the degree of their families' 'assimilation' or 'integration' into 'receiving' countries, and thus associated with settlement (Olwig 2003; Gardner 2012). Scholars have begun to examine their virtual or corporeal movements, but usually within the context of transnational familial links to an ancestral homeland. Thus, the very construction of the categories 'children of migrants' or 'the second generation' can lead scholars to overlook their mobility tout court or focus only on those forms of movement associated with their migrant parents. So far, there has been little research on children of migrants as mobile young people in their own right, who create their own forms of mobility and shape their own paths of movement. Nor has there been sufficient attention paid to the centrality of processes of racialization in studies of youth migration and mobility.

This chapter therefore examines the different forms of mobility – virtual and physical – unfolding locally, transnationally and globally – in the lives of young people who have grown up as children of migrants and are racialized in specific ways. Subject to a 'model minority' discourse that revives racial discourses on the capacities of particular 'Oriental' bodies, young 'British Chinese' and others subsumed within this category[2] are largely invisible in the anxious and often racialized debates that construct youth as a threat and in more celebratory accounts of global youth cultures. Yet, in the last decade, as a response to continuing marginalization and racial discrimination in British society, they have begun to create new social and cultural spaces, including what they call – despite the highly contested nature of the term 'Oriental' – 'British

Chinese'/'Oriental' 'nights', 'clubs' or 'parties' (Yeh, 2014). In this chapter, I examine the different types of mobilities that participants of this nightlife practice, their intersection with the mobilities of migrant youth, and the centrality of both to the 'British Chinese'/ 'Oriental' night-scape. Although drawing on research among participants of officially 'adult' spaces, this chapter focuses on their transitions from childhood to youth and how these intersect with individual, transgenerational and new migration trajectories in 'superdiverse' (Vertovec 2007) contexts that are undergoing rapid change. It explores what it means to be young from a processual, multisited and contextual perspective. My analysis shows that these young people's present mobilities, shaped by processes of racialization, are informed by but also transcend childhood experiences of their families' migratory trajectories, as they forge new connections with people and places, and as their mobility both shapes and is shaped by changing local and global conditions. In locating the mobilities of these young people in the wider context of racialization, the transnational migrations of other young people and the globalization of culture, this chapter embeds migration research within broader processes of social transformation (Castles 2010).

Migration, globalization and youth

While studies of migration conventionally examine the long-term movements of people from one nation-state to another, often in the context of labor and settlement, in an increasingly globalized era marked by intensified movements of people, technologies and culture across borders, new approaches to migration and mobility have emerged. In recent decades, concepts of diaspora and transnationalism have offered a means of transcending earlier models of 'assimilation' by highlighting the way in which migrants forge identifications and social relations that transcend the nation-state. Much of this work, however, has focused on specific ethnic groups and their homeland connections (Anthias 1998). Recent studies, however, attempt to transcend the methodological nationalism and 'ethnic lens' of such research (Glick-Schiller et al. 2006; Olwig 2007). Transnational social spaces are now conceptualized as fluid social spaces that incorporate migrants and nonmigrants, not only in home and host countries but other sites around the world (Levitt and Jaworsky 2007). Scholars also examine nonethnic forms of migrant incorporation (Glick-Schiller et al. 2006), and both physical and virtual movements internal to the nation-state (King and Skeldon 2010; Parker and Song 2006).

Mobility research has also expanded understandings of human movement, by exploring its multiple forms and questioning rigid divisions between different categories of 'travelers', such as tourists, students and business people. While early research tended to associate physical and social mobility, couching movement as a positive, even liberating, cosmopolitan force, scholars now speak of 'regimes of mobility' to highlight the role of states and international administrations in determining people's ability to move and contributing to the 'glamorization' and 'demonization' of categories of mobile people (Glick-Schiller and Salazar 2013: 184). Until recently, research on cultural globalization has remained quite separate from questions concerning migration studies. Amid Samuel Huntington's vision of a 'clash of civilizations', debates have focused instead on the extent to which globalization is leading to the increasing standardization and uniformity of culture across the world. While some emphasize the power of multinational corporations in shaping consumer desires, others explore local appropriations of global products in forms of expression or as resistance. This study links questions of cultural globalization with migratory processes by examining the centrality of globalized forms of popular culture in the lives of children of migrants.

In doing so, it draws on insights from work in the diaspora paradigm, which emphasizes processes of racialization and locates youth as consumers and producers of global and transnational forms of popular culture (Sharma et al. 1996; Back 1996). Concepts of diaspora and hybridity, however, are highly contested (Anthias 2001), and in focusing on the 'hybridization' of 'diasporic' cultural identity and production among youth, discussions have often privileged ethnic-specific and panethnic 'marked' cultural forms (Brah 1996; Gilroy 1993; Hall 1988), rather than the 'virtually open-ended archives of differences' spread by global media (Appadurai 1996: 14). Scholars, for example, have argued that young Chinese in Britain have yet to develop a 'hybridized' culture (Parker 1995), but arguably overlook those that might not conform to reified conceptions of 'British Chineseness' (Yeh, 2014). This chapter extends this debate by demonstrating how global popular culture consumption and production, shaped by but also contesting processes of racialization, intersect with youth mobility, thus connecting work in the diaspora paradigm to questions of mobility, in ways that are rarely considered in migration studies (Castles 2010).

Youth mobility is itself marginal within migration research. Studies on migrant and immigrant youth tend to be bifurcated. The movements of migrant children are often examined within the context of their families' migrations and their place within the ethnic or transnational 'community'. More recently, there has been work on the autonomy of independent child migrants, focusing on development and poverty (e.g., Iversen 2002). By contrast, immigrant youth have conventionally been studied within an 'integration' paradigm, which focuses on the social and economic indicators of their 'assimilation', segmented or otherwise, into the 'receiving' society, and thus tend to be associated with settlement (Gardner 2012; Olwig 2003). Young Chinese in Britain are, for example, positioned as 'a model minority' due to their achievements in education and employment and subsequent social mobility (Archer and Francis 2007). Migrant transnationalism has generally been regarded as a first-generation phenomenon, although new research is emerging on second-generation transnational practices (Levitt and Waters 2002) and 'return mobilities' (King and Christou 2011). These, however, still usually focus on transnational movements and imaginaries that connect youth to a homeland in the context of family and ethnic ties, paying less attention to the wider social connections of young people that are significantly shaped but not necessarily delimited by racial identification. This chapter fills a gap in the research by examining the independent mobilities of children of migrants and their participation in transnational social spaces that transcend parental 'homeland' and ethnic ties and incorporate both migrant and nonmigrant youth across ethnic and sometimes racial divisions.

By bringing together these different bodies of research, this chapter examines the complex mobility of children of migrants in the context of the intersecting processes of racialization, the transnational migrations of people and the globalization of culture. The young people in this study were born to migrants, some migrated with their families, and most have taken familial transnational trips to the homeland. However, as they grow up and become aware of their position as racialized youth, they have also become independently mobile, virtually and physically and on multiple scales, and affected by the growing 'superdiversity' of Britain's cities (Vertovec 2007). I begin by discussing how their families' transnational and internal migration trajectories have shaped their childhood mobilities, and how global flows of people, cultures and technologies have fed into the construction of a 'mobile' 'British Chinese'/'Oriental' nightlife. I then discuss participants' attempts to 'go global' by connecting and traveling virtually and physically beyond the nation-state. Finally, I focus on the consequences of wider youth mobility on the lives of participants, by examining the impact of international students on participants' sense of mobility. International student mobility is an underdeveloped area of study (Dolby and Rizvi

2008; King and Ruiz-Gelices 2003), and existing research focuses mainly on those who move. This chapter contributes new debates by exploring how international students affect the lives of children of migrants.

In examining the mobilities of children of migrants as twenty-first-century young people, this chapter does not only describe the new forms of youth movement afforded by advanced globalization but also highlights 'the power and politics of discourses and practices of mobility in creating both movement and stasis' (Hannam et al. 2006: 2). These young people's lives show that celebratory discourses of globalization, which imagine a borderless world inhabited by jet-setting cosmopolitans, nourish aspirations that are easily thwarted in a society stratified by access to global mobility (Bauman 1998). While these young people are highly mobile, their lives – and indeed their very mobilities – remain structured by the political and economic forces of globalization, which exacerbate existing inequalities and exclusions.

'British Chinese'/'Oriental' nightlife and ethnography on- and offline

As other chapters in this book illustrate, in an increasingly globalized era, multisited ethnography (Marcus 1995) has become more common, as scholars 'follow' the movements of the people they study and conduct research in multiple localities or even on the move. To capture the mobility of today's generation of youth, researchers need to follow them as they engage in circular, serial, onward and virtual movements. As young people use web-based technology to mobilize and connect for both social and political purposes, virtual methodologies are an important emerging multisited and 'transtemporal' means of conducting research. This study draws on research conducted in London between 2010 and 2012 that combines ethnography in multiple online and offline environments. In migration research, scholars primarily explore the Internet as a space where virtual diasporas are constructed (Greschke 2012). However, like multisited research, virtual ethnography helps eschew such methodological nationalism and ethnocentrism. Rather than focusing on ethnic-specific websites, my fieldwork unfolded on promoters' and social networking sites, which reflected participants' concerns not only as ethnicized youth but more generally as young people.

Party promoters, disc jockeys (DJs) and musicians host their own websites and use social networking and other sites, such as Facebook, Twitter, YouTube and SoundCloud, to advertise their events and work by posting flyers, video footage and photographs of club nights and music samples. Clubbers also post their own photographs and 'chat' between themselves and promoters on these sites. 'British Chinese'/'Oriental' clubbing thus unfolds on- and offline. Alongside participant observation at events, where I met promoters, DJs, musicians and clubbers and observed their performances and interactions, I conducted online ethnography, which involved immersion in these sites. While I actively participated by joining as a member, I primarily employed observation without interacting with others; however, this was in line with the behaviors of the majority of members. Although I did not hide my role as a researcher, such observation still raises ethical issues of privacy, anonymity and the protection of subjects (Constable 2003). Ways of dealing with the ethics of virtual ethnography are highly contested, and as with all field research, must be developed in context. Although considering sites that do not require registration as in the public domain, where I have drawn on observation in sites requiring registration, I have not used direct quotations or described details that could identify individuals, but have used examples commonly found across the field.

In addition to participant observation on- and offline, I conducted in-depth interviews with nine men and one woman involved in 'British Chinese'/'Oriental' parties in several ways. Four were aged between 19 and 25, and six were in their 30s, but most had attended clubs since their teens and some since as young as 14. All except one still attend events as clubbers, but also work as website editors, DJs, club promoters or artists across England and Scotland. They were identified through the snowball method, but show that the scene is concentrated in London and organized mainly by university-educated young men. Nine had either ethnic Chinese and/or Vietnamese migrant parents born variously in China, Vietnam, Hong Kong or Malaysia. One is white English, and runs a club with 'a British-born Chinese' (hereafter 'BBC') whose parents are from Hong Kong, and a migrant from Malaysia. This reflects the fact that promoters work with others across the ethnic and racial divide, including, as discussed later, migrant youth. Eight were born in the UK, five in London, and the others in Glasgow, Portsmouth and Greater Manchester, although one grew up in Malaysia between the ages of one and seven. Two were born outside the UK, one in Holland and one in Trinidad and Tobago, but moved to the UK at the ages of seven and younger than one, respectively. Although seven participants were at the time of this research based in London, with the others in Newcastle, Nottingham and Bristol, most travel frequently to work or socialize in 'British Chinese'/'Oriental' parties in other cities. All were either attending or had attended university, although two had left without a degree. At the request of participants, real names are used in all cases except one, although some comments are anonymized to protect confidentiality. As participants and key informants of the nightscape, their views are not generalizable, either to others within 'British Chinese'/'Oriental' nightscapes or to 'British Chinese'/'Oriental' young people as whole. However, their narratives provide insights into complex mobilities of young people, whose lives unfold at the busy intersection of major migration fluxes and multiple cultural flows.

My interactions with participants confirmed the centrality of new technologies in their lives. After face-to-face field encounters and interviews, participants kept in touch through Facebook, emails and mobile phone texts and conversations. When participants were too busy to meet in person, or I was unable to travel, they suggested we use Skype or the telephone. Like multisited research, online ethnography and the use of such technologies can pose challenges to conventional ethnographic ideals of long-term immersion and bodily copresence in a demarcated field. However, Olwig (2007) argues that multisited ethnography provides rich data on nonlocal spheres of life that are increasingly important as people become more interconnected and mobile, and which are not easily captured by traditional fieldwork methods. Similarly, in studying 'British Chinese'/'Oriental' nightlife, which unfolds both on- and offline, I learned about different types of local and nonlocal interactions among participants, and analytical insights emerged from movement between sites. I was able not only to corroborate findings but to learn how participants renegotiate their identities in different contexts – to investigate the virtual and its relationship to the actual (Boellstorff 2012). As widely noted, the Internet is a space of identity play and performance. In this study, virtual ethnography allowed insight into the aspirations of young people as they sought to construct themselves as mobile subjects and into the role of technologies in facilitating such constructions. Observations and interviews, however, provided different perspectives on their mobility. The disjuncture between the two formed a central part of the analysis. The methodological approach of this chapter thus helps make visible how children of migrants are actually and aspirationally embedded in migratory circuits and mobile worlds, and reflects the 'global' nature of emerging forms of mobility among them.

Family migrations and childhood mobilities

Children of migrants grow up in 'social fields' informed by their parents' migration. Yet the traditional paradigm of migration – of migrants who move for work and settle long-term in 'host' societies – has often erased the complexity of family 'mobilities-in-migration'. For participants in this research, their parents' transnational and internal migration trajectories significantly shaped their experiences of growing up and childhood practices of mobility. Yet in their transitions to adulthood, as they begin to find themselves marginalized as racialized youth, they develop ways of practicing their own forms of mobility and forge new paths independently from their parents.

Studies on the 'Chinese in Britain' conventionally focus on the large-scale migrations of the 1950s and 1960s as a singular, one-way journey from Hong Kong into Britain. Several participants, however, spoke of more complex family trajectories. Kevin described his parents as 'immigrants from China'; his father arrived in London to study and work, but then moved to Malaysia, where he married, before returning to Britain. GK's parents were from Hong Kong, and went to Holland for work, where she was born, before they moved to the UK to work in a family member's takeaway. Johnny's father grew up in Malaysia, but went to Hong Kong for work, where he married before coming to the UK, and George was born in Trinidad and Tobago to a father from Hong Kong and a mother who is 'three-quarters Chinese'. Jon was born in London, but his family moved to Malaysia, where he lived until the age of seven, before returning to the UK. Participants thus grew up with understandings of the world in which distances are to be traversed for work, study and love.

These complex migration trajectories continued within the UK. Due to a concentration in the takeaway trade, which boomed in the 1970s, Britain's Chinese populations dispersed across the country to avoid coethnic competition, and are thus the most highly geographically dispersed of all ethnic groups. In the 1990s, 90 percent lived in wards in which only around 1 percent of the population were from the same ethnic group (Benton and Gomez 2008: 170). While not all participants came from catering families, they had similar stories of family relocations either across different parts of Britain or within different areas of Greater London. Steven was born in Glasgow, but his family moved to Norwich and then Bristol. Wayne was born in East London, but his family then moved to the northwest of the city, while Kevin 'moved around quite a lot from Hampstead to Colindale to Harrow'. Almost all spoke of being the only Chinese or 'Oriental' child at school, if not the wider locality, an experience engendering early feelings of ethnic and racial otherness, common among British Chinese youth (Parker and Song 2009).

As a result, further mobility was a feature of participants' childhoods. Steven spoke of 'traveling 15–20 miles' to meet Chinese friends. Even those whose parents had not relocated for work recalled travel as a requirement to be with other Chinese people. Jon recalled:

> There were no other Chinese people in Portsmouth, there were no Chinese around me…. So my cousins became the anchor. We lived by the sea, they lived in outer London, you know, Croydon, Feltham, but they used to come to see me.

Given the isolation of these migrant families from coethnic peers, and the prohibitive costs of traveling in terms of time and money, it is unsurprising that virtual mobility, in terms of the consumption of homeland media, was also a common feature in their lives. Parker (1995) has highlighted the importance of Hong Kong Chinese media among British Chinese families. Similarly, as Jon recalled, 'the thing that shaped me growing up was the fact that…once we started getting video recorders, they used to send over the Chinese soap operas in the '80s'. Yet, opportunities to access Chinese media in Britain, once limited to buying predominantly Hong Kong Chinese videos and music from Chinatown, expanded dramatically during the 1990s. For younger participants especially, their transitions into adulthood coincided with the new availability of Chinese satellite and cable television and the emergence of the Internet. Therefore, they consume 'Chinese' media, accessed both through their parents and independently. As Kevin, a DJ, said,

> Growing up, in the car my dad would have cassettes and he'd have a lot of Chinese songs, so…I do steal off my mum and dad's music collection, but then, more generally Chinese TV, Chinese movies. Especially with the Internet now, people just post Chinese songs, it's a lot easier to learn about new stuff.

Yet, with the rise of Asian cultural industries in the 1990s and of Chinese American hip-hop groups and rappers in the 2000s, unlike earlier generations of British Chinese, participants also began consuming – alongside global youth music popular at school – not only Cantopop from Hong Kong but also hip-hop, rap, techno and trance from China and Vietnam and by Chinese American artists. Their narratives, however, highlighted the significance of these artists not as Chinese but as *'Oriental'* role models, who challenged the racial stereotype of the invisible 'model minority' of 'nerds' and 'geeks' (Yeh, 2014). Participants thus also consumed nonhomeland Asian popular media, such as J-pop (Japanese pop) and, particularly, K-pop (Korean pop), and virtual ethnography also highlighted the popularity of nonhomeland Asian film stars, singers, models, dancers and other celebrities among them.[3] The rise of 'Oriental' superstars, who were famed for their good looks, for singing, dancing and rapping, enabled them to imagine themselves anew – as potential creators as well as consumers of global youth culture (Yeh, 2014). This illuminates the centrality of participants' experiences not only as children of migrants but, more specifically, as racialized youth. Virtual access to Asian stars encouraged participants to 'chase the dream' of working in the nightlife industries. Some started while still at school, with Kevin and Jay both making music in their early teens, and one participant promoting underage clubbing events around London at the age of 16. Yet, on leaving home and entering university, their activities expanded dramatically, as they came into contact, often for the first time, with coethnic and co-racial youth.

Complex family mobilities-in-migration shaped the physical and virtual mobilities of these children of migrants. Their transition to adulthood, however, coincides with racial subjectification, which they reinterpret through a consumption of Asian popular culture. Both familial and independent trajectories continue to shape their mobilities as young adults as they now seek their own work, leisure and love.

'British Chinese'/'Oriental' nightscapes: a mobile world?

Mobility, both virtual and physical, is a central feature of 'British Chinese'/'Oriental' nightscapes. Informed by their childhoods, participants continue to engage in internal mobilities and the consumption of global cultures in the formation of these social spaces. Yet, in doing so, they also respond to new changes brought by the restructuring of urban cities by global flows of people and capital, and the availability of online and mobile technologies. Their practices and aspirations suggest a generational transition from 'migrant' to 'mobile' identities.

Patterns of settlement of the migrant generation and processes of racial marginalization are the twin factors contributing to the formation of 'British Chinese'/'Oriental' nightscapes. The geographical dispersal of the Chinese across Britain has led to the emergence of different 'British Chinese'/'Oriental' parties in Newcastle, Edinburgh, Bristol, Manchester, Nottingham, Sheffield and other cities across Britain. Like the British Chinese websites discussed by Parker and Song (2009), these spaces provide rare opportunities for coethnic and co-racial interaction and dating and for the collective public consumption of Asian popular culture (Yeh, 2014). Events are sometimes organized around 'homeland' and nonhomeland popular culture, such as DiscoVietnam and K-pop parties, and often a range of Asian as well as global youth music is played. The South to North cultural flows in the 'British Chinese'/'Oriental' nightscape reflect how childhood consumption of Asian popular culture continues to shape the work of young people as promoters, DJs and musicians.

Further, while participants once traveled as children with their families to be with other 'Chinese', they now regularly travel as young adults, alone or with peers, but significantly, to be with not only other 'Chinese', but also 'Orientals'. In recent years, organizers have begun to respond to the rapid rise of international student mobility from Asia into the UK. In 2010–2011, China was the UK's largest sender, with 67,325 students in UK higher education institutions. Malaysia, Hong Kong and Thailand were also among the top ten senders (HESA 2010–2011). These demographic flows have significantly impacted the 'British Chinese'/'Oriental' nightscape. While it emerged from a desire to create opportunities for coethnic socializing, the large influx of students from these countries as well as from Japan, Korea, Singapore, the Philippines, Vietnam, Burma and Taiwan has enabled the expansion of the scene, transforming largely 'British Chinese' events into 'Oriental' parties.

The appeal of international students from Asia, as with local-born co-racials, emerges from a complex mix of racial and cultural identification. As James said, 'They like the same music, and behave in same way, that's why they like to socialize together'. While they may not speak the same language, being among Asian students provides 'British Chinese'/'Orientals' temporary relief from the 'tense and potentially vulnerable engagement' (Parker 2000) of interracial interaction. According to James, if 'the English come into an Oriental party, they'd ask: "Why are all the girls walking round holding hands and acting like school kids?" but the Thai, Malaysian Chinese, and Cantonese all have very similar behavior'.

Some promoters network among international students to create their own market. In Nottingham, Kevin created a club scene of around 2000 'Oriental people', including 'Burmese, Filipino, Taiwanese'. Most promoters, however, depend on the infrastructure of university societies to access the fluid international student market and on employing international students, who often socialize with co-nationals or other students from Asia (Spencer-Oatey and Xiong 2006). As one promoter explained, he employed an overseas student from Hong Kong as 'his network consists of Japanese and heavily South East Asian, Thai, Malay and Singapore guys, but he gets on very well with the Hong Kong guys and gets the Taiwanese as well'.

As well as responding to new demographic flows, promoters face challenges brought on by the increasing dominance of multinational corporations in the nightlife industries. The geographical dispersal of these parties, and their constant movement to different venues, not only reflects scattered migration patterns but also promoters' attempts to find affordable venues for a marginalized nightscape. This further requires the mobility of promoters, DJs, musicians and participants. While GK started a club night in Edinburgh, she later took it to Newcastle, and now collaborates with promoters in other cities. Now a DJ, Kevin regularly travels between London, Bristol, Manchester and Nottingham to play at events.

Given the constant change of venues and its fluid, scattered market, new media technologies play an essential role in providing a sense of stability to this mobile landscape, while contributing further to its reach. In addition to hosting websites and using Facebook and Twitter, participants also employ mobile phone technologies to broadcast their events. As GK exclaimed, 'I can't survive without What's App, I use it every single day!' The use of new technologies also has a significant impact on those too young to attend events – as Wayne, whose social horizons at his younger brother's age (16) were limited to a local karaoke, put it:

> To be honest, Facebook transformed, like, Facebook transformed, the whole world. When I was younger, I didn't know about ['British Chinese'/'Oriental' nightlife]. But now, my younger brother knows about everything that's going on cos of Facebook.

It is through these new technologies that promoters are able to attract a nationwide clientele of young people willing to travel across Britain to attend events. As Newcastle-based GK said,

> You can easily find out on Facebook if there's a Chinese party in London … you might see, oh, there's an event in London, I might go there, or there's an event in Sheffield, I might go there.

However, as these interview excerpts suggest, new technologies are not only used as tools by promoters, musicians and DJs for advertising purposes. As vehicles of globalization as well as its ideology, they are a valued means of performing mobility. As Elliot and Urry (2010) state, the 'freedom of movement … is the ideology and utopia of the twenty-first century'. Using various web-based applications, clubbers map the events they have attended, post photos of different nights and create timelines of their movements to prompt comments from others. As James said,

> In the old days, you'd just tell people you'd been there, but it's now becoming common nature where people'll've all been there, and all checked in on Facebook and taken a picture there, and loaded it up, and that's just become regular now.

New technologies are thus not only vital to the 'British Chinese'/'Oriental' nightscape but also facilitate the construction of mobile identities – through Twitter and Facebook, participants post minute-to-minute updates of their movements as they zigzag across urban cities to attend events. Among their posts are also stories of activities further afield – hen nights in Ibiza, romantic holidays in Europe and shopping trips to Hong Kong.

The 'British Chinese'/'Oriental' nightscape can thus be seen as a mobile world, defined by flows of people and cultures from the homeland and beyond, requiring the physical movements of participants as club nights move to different venues and cities, and partially unfolding in a virtual world. Mobility becomes a feature of the identities of those involved, but in ways that also transcend the nation-state.

Going 'global'

Among participants in this research, desires to be mobile are framed by discourses of globalization, which appear to afford different opportunities of 'going global'. Participants seek to develop 'British Chinese'/'Oriental' parties as a part of global youth culture by forging international collaborations, bringing in artists from elsewhere and promoting youth mobility. They also seek to engage in transnational mobility themselves. Yet, ultimately, they seem thwarted in their attempts to become part of a mobile elite circuiting a global nightscape.

'British Chinese'/'Oriental' or global nightscapes?

Participants' narratives demonstrated strong aspirations of developing international connections. For some promoters, the discourse of China's rise on the global stage presents new opportunities, specifically for Chinese youth, to go 'global', by forging transnational collaborations. Playkrown's vision statement, for example, states that

There are now increasing opportunities for China and Europe to collaborate … Chinese entertainment shall form an important bridge to reinforce the relationship between both parties.

Or, as one promoter, imagined telling Chinese companies,

'Look we could do a concert in London, you don't need to go to all these other promoters cos they don't speak your language and we're Chinese, so you should let us do it.' And to be fair they will do that cos … no matter what you do, the race thing is still a question, it's still there.

These comments reflect a common belief that diasporas act as a bridge between their countries of origin and places of settlement, and discourses specifically, that highlight the role of race/ethnicity in networking among the Chinese. Yet Benton and Gomez (2008) argue that there is little evidence of Chinese firms working with British Chinese, as they prefer to work with non-Chinese to access the UK market.

Participants in this research do collaborate transnationally, although not necessarily with coethnics in their parental 'homeland'. The K-pop team, run by two Malaysian 'BBCs', works with companies in Hong Kong and Korea, as well as the Korean government, in its attempts to export Korea's pop culture for economic and diplomatic benefits (Chua 2012). So far, K-pop has organized three junior events (for under 18-year-olds), subsidized by the Korean government for 200 people. One event was themed around the Korean flag. Other collaborations highlight how promoters seek to create a sense of 'British Chinese'/'Oriental' events as a part of global youth culture, by bringing in international artists and thereby contributing further to the mobility of youth. While DiscoVN, run by 'Vietnamese-cultured' James Dang, brings Vietnamese artists from the United States and Vietnam, most promoters work with artists who are unconnected to their parental 'homeland'. BBC Malaysian Kevin hosted Sam Lee of the rap group LazyMuthaFucka from Hong Kong. The K-pop team hosts artists from Korea, and Chi Nights hosts African Caribbean artists from the United States and the British Virgin Islands, showing connections across the racial divide.

Choices of artists reflect financial limitations and also, specifically, an online youth culture, in which children are increasingly constructed as consumers. A2 Entertainment held an 'all-age' talent show with Toronto-based Nu-Lite Entertainment, at which the judges included an online Korean Canadian artist and other 'Oriental' 'online singers' from Vancouver and Chicago. Promoters bring over 'YouTube super-stars' to provide British youth 'the opportunity to meet the stars they always see on YouTube for real'. For their 'London Foreign Exchange' concert, for example, Playkrown brought over Thai-born and Vietnam-born American YouTube rappers to perform alongside London-based Jay Differ. While the concert was an '18+' event, a 'meet-and-greet' was held for the underaged, 'so they know about us, and when they do turn 18, they're legal to come to our parties'.

Prizes at events include trips to Toronto, Hong Kong and Seoul, further promoting the transnational mobility of a few – but the desire for mobility among many – and in some cases, with contradictory results. In 2012, for example, the K-pop team helped advertise the Korean government's all-age 'Birth of an Amazing Star' talent show for broadcast on Korean television, which offered the winners trips to Korea. Despite the popularity of K-pop among 'British-Chinese'/'Orientals', however, the winners were 'five non-Orientals'. The significance of Korean stars as role models to young 'British Chinese'/'Orientals' in Britain was incompatible with the Korean government's desire to prove K-pop's 'cross-over appeal' – 'any Oriental person just wouldn't look right for what they wanted to achieve, which is to show that K-pop reaches non–Oriental-looking people'. What some scholars optimistically refer to as the creative local appropriations by youth of global popular cultural forms are easily stymied by the global political-economic intentions of nation-states.

In some cases the presence of global media companies in the UK can also enable promoters to export their cultural productions globally. GK's events are under negotiation to tour China, and 'it all started off with someone who went to our parties, who is from China, they ... said, "why don't you bring this to China?"' Meanwhile, the work of Kevin and other DJs was filmed by TVB for broadcast in Hong Kong. The Internet was also seen as a means of becoming 'global'. While K-Pop's iPhone App was downloaded in Japan and the Philippines, Kevin's fans are mainly in the US, while Jay Differ has followers in the US, Europe and Canada. GK emphasized the importance of her Internet podcast:

> If the podcast wasn't there, people from China or the US wouldn't know about the event we do in Newcastle, so there's a lot of DJs in America, in China, in Hong Kong that have actually heard of Go Ape events.

The young people in this study thus find different ways of developing 'British Chinese'/'Oriental' nights as a part of global youth culture, and in ways that can transcend the pathways of their families' migrations and are shaped by wider, especially but not exclusively Asian, youth culture. They engage with processes of globalization by becoming recipients and promoters of global youth cultures – and indeed of youth mobilities. Their position simultaneously as twenty-first-century young people, emerging artists or entrepreneurs and ethnicized and racialized children of migrants prompts them to engage with global youth culture and craft complex forms of hybridized cultures and identities. Marginalized within the racial landscape of Britain, they pursue opportunities and a sense of validation and belonging by building business links and connecting socially and imaginatively to other parts of the world. The interaction between their experiences of becoming an adult and of forging global links remains shaped by the broader structural constraints of globalization. Yet, as they begin to develop a sense of themselves as global citizens, they also develop new perspectives on familiar transnational journeys, as evidenced by their visits to the parental homeland and beyond.

From family trips to transnational partying

Like many children of migrants, the participants in this study often traveled with their parents as children to visit family in the 'homeland'. However, for most, their participation in 'British Chinese'/'Oriental' nightlife has altered the nature of travel from 'family trips' as children to 'business trips' or 'transnational partying' as adults. While these visits to Asia thus provide further evidence of 'return mobilities of the second generation', they also demonstrate the limitations of couching their visits in this way. Shaped by the young people's independent concerns, rather than those of their families, their travels are described as movements to new places or social spaces, which they did not experience as children, and which are a part of new translocal practices emerging from participation in the 'British Chinese'/'Oriental' nightscape.

Wayne, who visited Hong Kong every year with his family from the age of 14 to 18, now planned to go with his business partner:

> I never really got to enjoy the adult life, the clubbing scene, going to China by myself, whereas this year, it's different … if my market is the Hong Kong crowd, I'd love to see what their scene is like.

On her last trip to Hong Kong, GK visited her grandparents, but

> Over the whole duration of my two weeks there, I only spent two days with them because the rest of my days I spent catching up with

different people ... that was all because I'd done the whole Chinese events stuff.

The friendships she formed with international students who frequent her parties in Britain have expanded her horizons in her 'homeland': 'I go to Hong Kong or I go to China and I hit them up and they show me round and take me to clubs'. Rather than visiting family, she will now 'go shopping, go sing karaoke, go to bars and go to ... you *have* to go to Lan Kwai Fong and Tsim Sha Tsui'. Other participants also confirmed that, due to their nightlife work in Britain, they have become part of a transnational party network, as international students attend parties in the UK, return to their home countries and 'the word gets around'. As George, who visits Hong Kong twice a year, exclaimed,

> Apparently we're international! Every time we go to Hong Kong, it's like 'Hello Johnny, Hello George!' And I'm like 'I've never seen you before in my life, but how you doing?'

Connections in Asia can also have social benefits for life in the UK. Through their frequent visits to Hong Kong, Johnny and George played football in London with some Hong Kong stars and found that 'everyone was stopping them in Chinatown'. Rather than 'returns home', such trips to Hong Kong are constitutive of new translocal formations among the younger generations. More likely to frequent 'McDonalds' than 'typical Chinese restaurants', participants confirm Parker and Song's (2009) identification of Lan Kwai Fong as a popular 'hangout' for British Chinese youth. In George's words, it is 'a little London Hong Kong' made up of 'expats born or bred in Britain, the United States and Canada', who enjoy 'Hong Kong culture or Western culture in a Hong Kong environment'.

Scholars have highlighted how family narratives of 'return' are inherited and actualized by children (Reynolds 2008; King and Christou 2011). Two participants spoke of the parental influence on their thoughts of moving permanently to Asia. Yet such moves were not couched in terms of a 'return' to a 'homeland' for family purposes. GK, born to parents from Hong Kong, wanted to relocate not to her parents' 'homeland' but to China, which she saw less as an 'ancestral' homeland than as 'the future, the gold mine'. While Wayne also envisioned relocating to Hong Kong as a fulfillment of his family's orientation, 'cos that's how my dad sees it, he always says he's going to retire there', this 'return' was couched in terms of a 'lifestyle migration' (Benson and O'Reilly 2009):

Friends tell me it's like having a really long holiday…purchasing power is more, there's more variety of things to do there – going out, places are 24 hours, you don't need to be afraid that things aren't open, also like the leisure side, you go to massages, go to spas, everything's cheaper.

Yet other narratives show the stratified nature of mobility-in-migration. While some could not afford to travel, another explained that his family could not travel due to his younger brother's illness. Meanwhile, for Jay, who visits family in China and Vietnam 'every couple of years', such trips were not so much about the new adult pleasures of transnational partying as reminders of the need for everyday subsistence:

It was a big shock to see the struggle that they were going through just like for food, I mean, feeding the family and stuff…seeing how my cousins are living over there and how they're like 'Oh, you've always got nice clothes, or you're always like, you've got nice stuff'…they're not privileged enough to have the same.

Visits to the 'homeland' and other parts of Asia are thus experienced differentially by participants in this research. While some may continue to visit with their family, most also have experiences of traveling as independent adults. In these cases, their visits are not shaped primarily by family ties, but by wider transnational mobilities among both diasporic and migrant youth.

Fragile Mobilities

Participants partially achieve their aspirations to 'go global', as demonstrated by their transnational mobility, their international collaborations and the movement of their cultural products from the North to the South. Yet this sense of global mobility is fragile, dissolving in the presence of international students, who are so vital to these nightscapes.

While offering co-ethnic and racial identification, international students also constitute a necessary market, within an economy increasingly dominated by corporate ownership, which aims to attract highly mobile global capital (Chatterton 2010). As Wayne said,

We target a crowd which is more international, like for overseas students, cos they're the ones that can provide us with the bar spend that enables us to get a nicer club.

As this suggests, attendees of these clubs are ordered hierarchically according to spending power, but as important is their conversance with the 'habitus' of the elite. One high-end club promoter described his target market as students from 'global cities' – 'Kuala Lumpur, Singapore, Bangkok, Hong Kong, Seoul and Tokyo', who were not only 'the premium rich' but also 'fashion aware, know the good stuff, know their brands of vodkas'. Excluded from this were students from mainland China, who 'don't go to nightclubs and [are] so unaware of what to do'. The hierarchy between different international students, however, was not as pronounced in participants' discourses as that constructed between international students and local 'BBCs'/'Orientals'. In a highly stratified scene, the latter were aligned with 'locals' as the least lucrative: 'The BBCs and the locals, they tend to pre-drink and they don't really spend at the bar'.

In the 'exclusive geographies' of the nighttime economy (Chatterton 1999), local 'BBCs' are, like mainland Chinese students, also perceived to lack the social and cultural capital required to fit in at high-end clubs. According to one promoter,

> They're too hip-hoppy, with their street wear...you've got these 19–20 year olds from Hong Kong and Singapore, they know good stuff, and you'll get comments: 'Why would you come into a club wearing that?'

As this promoter acknowledged, exclusive clubs 'alienate' those from a 'technically working-class background', especially young men: 'They're never going to impress the ladies and they know that'. Local BBCs are also seen as a risk due to potential violent behavior. Thus, international students constitute a vital market for the 'British Chinese'/'Oriental' scene, but one that leads to the construction of 'British Chinese'/'Orientals' as economically, socially and even morally inferior (Yeh, 2014).

This is equally felt among the promoters themselves. Even mainland Chinese students, although excluded from the most elite clubs, were perceived by some as 'better off' than them, disrupting past hierarchies in which, as one participant admitted, 'the Hong Kong Chinese were a little bit higher up and the mainland Chinese were the dregs', due to UK citizenship rights. As another told me,

> When I was younger, I used to think...people from China, they just want the red passport...BBCs would say, 'Ah these girls that come here and they want to get in with these BBC guys, they just want a red passport'.

While this participant 'used to call them Fresh-off the Banana boat', increasing contact with mainland Chinese in the clubbing scene, 'who can be quite snobby', has thrown doubt on this formulation:

> Why would they want a red passport when they've got more money than you? You know, they probably got a better family background, they're not in the typical BBC chop-suey or restaurant. Why would they want a red passport?

Local British Chinese, who once felt privileged by UK citizenship rights, now feel themselves lacking in a global hierarchy. The 'red passport' fails to afford the mobility that is perceived to be enjoyed by the global elite, as 'they have money, right, they have a lot of money'. As James said,

> The rich kids, you go to Phuket or Hanoi or wherever at a certain time of year and they'll all be there. They all socialize on a global level. They're all cut from the same cloth.... It's about marketing, the upmarket world, the glamorous clubs, the big money – they mix together.

As he continued, 'The guys from KL [Kuala Lumpur], you can almost guarantee they've been clubbing in Singapore, they probably transited and been out in Bangkok, they've probably been to Hong Kong'. By contrast, local 'British Chinese'/'Orientals' 'club at home and that will be it'.

In addition to their perceived wealth and social cachet, the temporary stays of international students heighten feelings of a comparative lack of mobility among participants. This, coupled with the international mobility of other local youth, can have a devastating impact on the children of migrants, who lose both a market and friendships. As Kevin, who built up a party scene in the Midlands, said,

> now everyone's graduated and dispersed across the world ... a lot of my uni friends have gone abroad, either traveling or working ... a lot of international students have gone back home. Before I kinda knew everyone who came to my events, and by the fourth year, I didn't know anyone. I lost that personal connection, and it didn't feel as enjoyable or satisfying any more. I've moved back to London, where I've had to start again, from scratch. It's frustrating.

As this suggests, children of migrants may experience being left behind not only by their families but also by their peers. Youth mobility, then, has contradictory effects on them. While enabling the expansion of the 'British Chinese'/'Oriental' nightlife and of homeland horizons, in a neoliberal economy, the presence, and then absence, of international students also creates a sense of inferiority and of immobility. It highlights the thinness of participants' agency in fully participating in the global.

Conclusion

This chapter contributes to the emerging literatures on youth mobility by drawing attention to new forms of online and offline mobilities among children of migrants, a group usually associated with settlement. Locating their independent mobilities as racialized youth within family migrations that challenge 'old' notions of migration as arrival and settlement, and the contemporary global flows of people and cultures demonstrates their complex and dynamic nature within intersecting processes of racialization, migration and youth cultures. A focus on mobility within major migration fluxes draws attention to the relationship between the experiences of children of migrants and their families, between migrants and nonmigrants, and between dynamics of mobility and immobility. Young people use different types of mobilities for different purposes in response to changing social, economic and cultural circumstances over time and across different places. As children, their practices are shaped by their families' mobilities-in-migration, but in their transition to adulthood, they craft independent movements in response to racial subjectification that transcend familial and ethnic pathways. Through movement, they participate in translocal social fields that incorporate both migrants and nonmigrants, including both those who may and may not share their ethnic or racial positions. Their mobilities thus highlight a need for more complex understandings of the worlds in which they live, simultaneously, as children of migrants, racialized subjects and twenty-first-century young people.

These young people's lives capture a dynamic and situated agency as they respond to changing circumstances in the transition to adulthood through mobility. Within the particularities of their movements, there are varying degrees of 'thick' and 'thin' agency, which are experienced fluidly. Their use of global flows of people and cultures to craft new identities and cultures could be conceived as capturing 'thick' agency, the capacity to act within a broad range of options, not necessarily restricted by family relationships or structures of ethnicity and race. Yet in changing contexts, as subjectively experienced, that agency quickly thins. The way in which these young people draw on the global to feel at home in the local produces contradictory effects. Their narratives of mobility do not only reflect their actual practices but also the way in which technologies and discourses of 'the global' shape their aspirations, precisely, to become part of a mobile elite. Their active attempts to craft their identities as 'mobile' young people mask the conditions in which their mobility has been prompted by necessity and the way it is often thwarted.

There is tension between the aspirations and initiatives of these young people in taking advantage of the benefits of globalization, and the structural constraints that prevent them from being fully part of it. While engagement with the global promises a sense of belonging that cannot be found at a national level, they find themselves positioned on the margins of global processes. They are becoming 'mobile' as they actively respond to their position as racialized children of migrants by drawing on the opportunities afforded by travel, new migratory processes and global flows of culture and technology in the twenty-first century. Yet, their movements remain subject to neoliberal political and economic forces of globalization, in which different forms of mobility highlight – indeed, exacerbate – social stratification in highly unequal ways. The focus in this chapter on children of migrants who participate in specific social and cultural spaces does not allow for generalization of their experiences. Nonetheless, paying attention to new forms of mobility among youth embeds migration research within broader processes of social transformation and prompts an understanding of the lives of young people, even those who are not migrants, as simultaneously shaping and shaped by specific processes of racialization, intersecting transnational migrations and complex global cultural flows.

Notes

1. The terms 'British Chinese', 'Chinese' and 'Oriental' are often used interchangeably among participants, although sometimes with different emphases in meaning (for further discussion, see Yeh, 2014). My use of the term 'British Chinese'/'Oriental' reflects the unresolved, irreducible ways in which the terms are used. The use of 'Oriental' reflects a British context in which 'Asian', until the 2011 Census, referred to those from South Asia and their children. Here, despite its racial connotations, I follow participants' uses of the term, and use 'Asia' to refer to East and Southeast Asia.
2. Britain is home to ethnic Chinese from all over the world, but mainly Hong Kong, China, Malaysia, Vietnam, Singapore and Taiwan. Thus, the terms 'Chinese' as well as 'British Chinese' and 'British-born Chinese' are highly contested. In the 2001 Census, there was a separate category for 'Chinese' and a subcategory of 'Chinese: Other'. 'Chinese' thus effectively functioned as a racial categorization to include, for example, Filipinos, Japanese and Vietnamese.
3. The adoption of the term 'Asia' in some participants' narratives to refer to East and Southeast Asia (as opposed to British discourse in which 'Asia' usually refers to South Asia) reflects the growing significance of global discourses in their lives.

114   *Diana Yeh*

References

Anthias, F. (1998) 'Evaluating "Diaspora": Beyond Ethnicity?', *Sociology*, 32(3), 557–580.

Anthias, F. (2001) 'New Hybridities, Old Concepts: The Limits of Culture', *Ethnic and Racial Studies*, 24(4), 619–641.

Appadurai, A. (1996) *Modernity at Large: Cultural Dimensions of Globalization* (Minneapolis, MN: University of Minnesota Press).

Archer, L., and Francis, B. (2007) *Understanding Minority Ethnic Achievement: Race, Gender, Class and Success* (Abingdon: Routledge).

Back, L. (1996) *New Ethnicities and Urban Culture* (London: UCL Press).

Bauman, Z. (1998) *Globalisation: The Human Consequences* (Cambridge: Polity Press).

Benson, M., and O'Reilly, K. (eds) (2009) *Lifestyle Migration: Expectations, Aspirations and Experiences* (Burlington, VT: Ashgate).

Benton, G., and Gomez, E. T. (2008) *The Chinese in Britain, 1800–Present: Economy, Transnationalism, Identity* (Basingstoke and New York: Palgrave Macmillan).

Boellstorff, T. (2012) 'Rethinking Digital Anthropology' in H. A. Horst and D. Miller (eds) *Digital Anthropology* (London: Berg), 39–60.

Brah, A. (1996) *Cartographies of Diaspora: Contesting Identities* (London: Routledge).

Castles, S. (2010) 'Understanding Global Migration: A Social Transformation Perspective', *Journal of Ethnic and Migration Studies*, 36(10), 1565–1586.

Chatterton, P. (1999) 'Exclusive Geographies: University Students in the City', *Geoforum*, 30(2), 117–133.

Chatterton, P. (2010) 'The Student City: An Ongoing Story of Neoliberalism, Gentrification, and Commodification', *Environment and Planning A*, 42(3), 509–514.

Chua, B. H. (2012) *Structure, Audience, and Soft Power in East Asian Pop Culture, TransAsia: Screen Cultures* (Hong Kong: Hong Kong University Press).

Constable, N. (2003) *Romance on a Global Stage: Pen Pals, Virtual Ethnography and Mail-Order Marriages* (Berkeley, CA: University of California Press).

Dolby, N., and Rizvi, F. (eds) (2008) *Youth Moves: Transnational Mobility and Education* (New York: Routledge).

Elliot, A., and Urry, J. (2010) *Mobile Lives* (London: Routledge).

Gardner, K. (2012) 'Transnational Migration and the Study of Children: An Introduction', *Journal of Ethnic and Migration Studies*, 38(6), 889–912.

Gilroy, P. (1993) *The Black Atlantic* (London: Verso).

Glick-Schiller, N., Caglar, A., and Guldbrandsen, T. C. (2006) 'Beyond the Ethnic Lens: Locality, Globality, and Born-Again Incorporation', *American Ethnologist*, 33(4), 612–633.

Glick-Schiller, N., and Salazar, N. B. (2013) 'Regimes of Mobility Across the Globe', *Journal of Ethnic and Migration Studies*, 39(2), 183–200.

Greschke, H. M. (2012) *Is There a Home in Cyberspace? The Internet in Migrants' Everyday Life and the Emergence of Global Communities* (New York: Routledge).

Hall, S. (1988) 'New Ethnicities' in K. Mercer (ed) *Black Film, British Cinema* (London: ICA).

Hannam, K., Sheller, M., and Urry, J. (2006) 'Editorial: Mobilities, Immobilities and Moorings', *Mobilities*, 1(1), 1–22.

HESA (2010/11) 'Students in Higher Education Institutions', *Press Release 172*, <http://www.hesa.ac.uk/> Accessed June 1, 2012.

Iversen, V. (2002) 'Autonomy in Child Labor Migrants', *World Development*, 30(5), 817–834.

King, R., and Christou, A. (2011) 'Of Counter-Diaspora and Reverse Transnationalism: Return Mobilities to and from the Ancestral Homeland', *Mobilities*, 6(4), 451–466.

King, R., and Ruiz-Gelices, E. (2003) 'International Student Migration and the European "Year Abroad": Effects on European Identity and Subsequent Migration Behaviour', *International Journal of Population Geography*, 9(3), 229–252.

King, R., and Skeldon, R. (2010) ' "Mind the Gap!": Integrating Approaches to Internal and International Migration', *Journal of Ethnic and Migration Studies*, 36(10), 1619–1646.

Levitt, P., and Glick-Schiller, N. (2007) 'Conceptualizing Simultaneity: A Transnational Social Field Perspective on Society' in A. Portes and J. DeWind (eds) *Rethinking Migration: New Theoretical and Empirical Perspectives* (New York and Oxford: Berghahn Books)

Levitt, P., and Jaworsky, B. N. (2007) 'Transnational Migration Studies: Past Developments and Future Trends', *Annual Review of Sociology*, 33(1), 129–156.

Levitt, P., and Waters, M. C. (eds) (2002) *The Changing Face of Home: The Transnational Lives of the Second Generation* (New York: Russell Sage).

Marcus, G. E. (1995) 'Ethnography In/Of the World System: The Emergence of Multi-Sited Ethnography', *Annual Review of Anthropology*, 24, 95–117.

Olwig, K. (2003) 'Children's Places of Belonging in Immigrant Families of Caribbean Background' in K. Olwig and E. Gulløv (eds) *Children's Places: Cross-Cultural Perspectives* (Abingdon: Routledge), 217–235.

Olwig, K. (2007) *Caribbean Journeys: An Ethnography of Migration and Home in Three Family Networks* (Durham and London: Duke University Press).

Parker, D. (1995) *Through Different Eyes: The Cultural Identities of Young Chinese People in Britain* (Aldershot: Avebury).

Parker, D. (2000) 'The Chinese Takeaway and the Diasporic Habitus: Space, Time and Power Geometries' in B. Hesse (ed) *Un/settled Multiculturalisms: Diasporas, Entanglements, Transruptions* (London: Zed Books), 73–95.

Parker, D., and Song, M. (2006) 'Ethnicity, Social Capital and the Internet', *Ethnicities*, 6(2), 178–202.

Parker, D., and Song, M. (2009) 'New Ethnicities and the Internet: Belonging and the Negotiation of Difference in Multicultural Britain', *Cultural Studies*, 23(4), 583–604.

Reynolds, T. (2008) 'Ties That Bind: Families, Social Capital and Caribbean Second-Generation Return Migration', Sussex Centre for Migration Research, *Working Paper 46* (Brighton: University of Sussex).

Sharma, S., Hutnyk, J., and Sharma, A. (1996) *Disorienting Rhythms: The Politics of the New Asian Dance Music* (London: Zed Books).

Spencer-Oatey, H., and Xiong, Z. (2006). 'Chinese Students' Psychological and Sociocultural Adjustments to Britain: An Empirical Study', *Language, Culture and Curriculum*, 19(1), 37–53.

Urry, J. (2007) *Mobilities* (Cambridge: Polity Press).

Vertovec, S. (2007) 'Super-Diversity and Its Implications', *Ethnic and Racial Studies*, 30(6), 1024–1054.

Yeh, D. (2014) 'Contesting the "Model Minority": Racialization, Youth Culture and "British Chinese"/"Oriental" Nights', *Journal of Ethnic and Racial Studies*, 37(7), 1197–1210.

6

Forced Migration, and Material and Virtual Mobility among Rwandan Children and Young People

Giorgia Donà

Introduction

Research on global migration continues to be mainly about adult migration (Castles and Miller 2003), and the migration of children and young people is generally subsumed within that of adults or conceptualized as a separate, almost exceptional, phenomenon (Donà 2006). Yet, children and young people are increasingly part of global migration circuits (Hashim and Thorsen 2011; Salazar Parreñas 2005), and many of them simultaneously grow up and move, having to negotiate new ways of belonging (Ni Laoire et al. 2011) and develop new coping strategies and resilience (Ensor and Gozdziak 2010).

Among children and young people who migrate, there are those who do so voluntarily and those who are forced to move because of conflict and political unrest (Ahearn and Athey 1991; MacCallin 1996). According to the United Nations High Commission for Refugees, there are approximately fourteen million refugee children worldwide, including convention refugees, asylum seekers, and internally displaced, stateless and returnee children (Meda et al. 2012). Forced migrations represent the coerced dimension of evolving societies and 'how we deal with the discrete issue of the forcibly displaced will say much about our capacity to deal with this new reality' (Helton 2002: 7–8). The connection between large-scale forced migrations and individual small-scale mobilities is an underexamined dimension of these societal changes.

This paper brings together two bodies of literature that are usually kept separate: the forced migration literature that focuses on involuntary population movements and examines the impact of these displacements on individual and community lives, and mobilities research with its interest in everyday movements of people, objects, capital and information. Unlike the migration/mobility literature that mainly describes adult movements, this chapter examines the experiences of children and young people as they simultaneously grow up and move.

Forced migration and mobility

Migration, including forced migration, generally refers to large-scale movements of people from points of departure – usually understood as countries/places of origin – and points of arrival – conceptualized as receiving countries/settings. Migration is the 'collective action, arising out of social change and affecting the whole society in both sending and receiving societies' (Castles and Miller 2003: 21). It refers to long-term movements that individuals and groups undergo during and as a result of uprootedness, resettlement and integration. At macro-level, scholars are interested in the structural conditions (mainly political, legal and economic) that shape migration flows, and at micro-level, they research how these forces shape the decisions and actions of individuals, families and communities (Brettell and Hollifield 2013).

Globalization, defined as the proliferation of cross-border flows and transnational networks, has changed our understanding of migration, so far defined by the settler model, which explains how migrants integrate into economic and social relations, and the temporary model, which captures the experiences of migrants who move on a temporary basis to host countries and maintain relations with their countries of origin (Castles 2002). New technologies of communication and transport connected to globalization allow frequent and multidirectional flows of people, ideas and cultural practices, and it is important to understand their influence on new forms of mobility and incorporation (Castles 2002).

Mobility refers to 'the ability of people or machines to move information, the body, and/or goods between physical, mobile, or cyberplaces' (Buliung 2011: 1). The concept of mobility is broader, to encompass 'both the large-scale movements of people, objects, capital and information across the world, as well as the more local processes of daily transportation, movement through public spaces and the travel of material things within everyday life' (Hannam et al. 2006: 1). In their editorial introduction to the first issue of the journal *Mobilities*, Hannam et al.

(2006) set the agenda for mobility research, which, in addition to virtual and information technologies, spatial mobilities and materialities, includes migration, travel and tourism. The editors distinguish between static migration and mobility, which refers to the movement of people as a practice of everyday life.

Mobility research is interested in the use of local spaces like homes and public spaces (Barker et al. 2009), the street (Gough and Franch 2005), urban areas (Jensen 2009) and the outdoors (Benwell 2009), as well as the use of cars (Barker 2009). Researchers examine the unfolding of social relations, such as children's relations to adults (Kearns and Collins 2003), and the relation between human mobilities and immobilities, as in the unequal power relations that unevenly distribute motility (Pullan 2013). Mobility is studied mostly in peaceful societies and rooted places, rather than in those characterized by uprootedness and forced migration.

Very little research has addressed the connections between mobilities and forced migration (Gill et al. 2011). Yet human displacement can be more fully understood by examining either the ways in which a set of bodily, material, imagined and virtual mobilities and immobilities interact to produce population movements (Gill et al. 2011) or the ways in which population movements produce new forms of mobilities. Little existing research on mobility in the context of forced migration includes the analysis of forms of mobility during asylum (Zimmermann 2011), the ways in which the port of entry simultaneously conceals exclusion and shrinks spaces of asylum (Mountz 2011), the immobility of refugees in countries of first asylum (Mason 2011) and forced migrants' first return visits to places of origin (Muggeridge and Donà 2006).

In this chapter, I examine the connections that exist between mobilities and migration; I use the migration-mobility nexus to refer to the general link between the two concepts, while I adopt the term 'mobility-in-migration' that was presented in the introduction to examine in detail how multiple forms of mobility unfold within broader forced migrations. The chapter makes visible new dynamics of child mobility-in-migration as internally displaced, refugee and diasporic children and young people engage in multidirectional, multitemporal movements. As they grow up, they experience different forms of mobility, local and international, embodied and virtual, real and imaginative.

Rapid changes in information and communication technologies, a potent factor in the process of globalization, mean that young migrant people become mobile not only in material but also in virtual spaces. Recent years have seen an increase in the use of new forms of information and communication technologies for general populations (Arora 2012) and diasporic groups (Fortunati et al. 2012). The movement of information takes place between physical-, mobile- and cyberspaces (Buliung 2011: 1), giving rise to the e-diaspora, defined as a 'migrant collective that organizes itself and is active first and foremost on the web' (Diminescu 2012: 452).

In the context of forced migration, e-diasporas invent new forms of citizenship, community and political practices (Bernal 2006). For instance, diasporic members of Former Yugoslavia, and specifically the 'Yugonostalgic', use the Internet to stage and link together different 'Yugoslavias' and reinvent the nation from abroad (Mazzucchelli 2012). In online spaces, Palestinian organizations shift from being national communities to becoming transnational networks and solidarity movements that campaign for Palestinian rights and support the boycott movement (Anat 2012). In detention centers and refugee camps, forced migrants use technology to keep in touch with the outside world (Leung 2011), and accessing the Internet has beneficial effects on asylum seekers' well-being (Sturgess and Philips 2009). Karen refugees who originate from the border regions of Burma and Thailand and who have resettled in the United Kingdom use Internet-based technologies to 'keep in touch' (personal contacts) and 'spread the word' (political communication), thereby combining personal and political communications (Green and Lockley 2012). For young people, new information and communication technologies have become instrumental and symbolic tools that identify them as global citizens and members of global youth cultures. There is limited research on the role of new media among forced migrant children and young people. This chapter examines material and virtual mobilities of Rwandan children and young forced migrants.

From methodological nationalism to multisited transnationalism and netnographic e-transnationalism

The material presented in this chapter draws from research conducted with Rwandan children, young people, families and key informants in Rwanda, Uganda, Togo, the United Kingdom and Belgium between 1997 and 2013. In the field of migration studies to which this research belongs, three methodological frameworks can be identified: mono-sited research designs informed by methodological nationalism, multisited research in the context of transnational migration, and virtual-sited research among e-diasporas. While mono-sited research with specific groups and in bounded contexts continues to dominate in migration studies, there is an increase in multisited and multitemporal research, as this edited collection indicates, as well as a growing interest in netnography.

Research on forced migrants and refugees is still predominantly framed by methodological nationalism (Glick-Schiller 2010), in which the borders of the nation-state shape the boundaries of the research context either during resettlement in host societies, at refugee camps across borders or following return to the country of origin. The prevalence of mono-sited and mono-temporal studies framed by methodological nationalism means that researchers develop analytical categories of children defined by their migration contexts: children in conflict and those internally displaced who move inside countries of origin (Daiute 2010), refugee and asylum-seeking children who cross borders (Eide and Hjern 2013; Ní Raghallaigh and Gilligan 2010) and returnee children who go 'home' (Gladwell and Elwin 2012). In these categories, differences and specificity override similarities and connections, even though these children and young people are often the same individuals on the move.

My research with Rwandan children began as mono-sited research inside Rwanda in the late 1990s, and it was framed by methodological nationalism. Between 1997 and 2001, I was involved in three nation-wide studies on the protection and welfare of children living in difficult circumstances in postgenocide Rwanda. The studies examined family reunification for separated and unaccompanied children (Donà et al. 1998), street life involvement (Veale et al. 1998), and formal and informal foster care arrangements (Donà 2001). The children interviewed had experienced conflict, internal displacement and/or forced migration across the region. The studies deployed a similar methodology consisting of an initial review of policy documents and practice reports, followed by a period of empirical research consisting of interviews, focus group discussions and participatory research techniques with children; semistructured interviews and/or focus group discussions with family and community members; and interviews with government officials and service providers. The studies examined the experiences, voices and well-being of children in conflict, and of internally displaced, refugee and returnee children (Veale and Donà, 2002).

After leaving Rwanda, I continued to research the effects of violence on Rwandans abroad. In the United Kingdom I met Rwandans who had left the country in 1994 and moved to Europe. Marcus (1995) writes that rather than staying put, scholars need to 'follow' the movement of the people they study and conduct research in multiple locations or even on the move. Multisited research with migrant populations has increased since the burgeoning of transnationalism as a new field of study, when a methodological shift took place as a result of an increased awareness that migrants are not necessarily confined by national borders, but transcend them to engage in transnational practices. Methodologically, scholars of transnationalism have privileged multisited and comparative research methodologies to examine transnational practices among diasporic groups in different receiving societies and their relations to countries of origin.

In 2010, my involvement in multisited research that had begun in London expanded to Brussels, where colonial ties with Rwanda meant that many Rwandans had sought refuge there, and also to Togo and Uganda in Africa. This research was aimed at exploring the experiences of Rwandans abroad, including those of children and young people who had left with their families as refugees or who were born in the diaspora to families who had been affected by the conflict. It also represented a continuation of my long-term fieldwork in Rwanda, where for an additional six months in 2009, I conducted ethnographic research on the long-term effects of violence on 'bystanders' to violence, including children belonging to families of mixed ethnicity (Donà 2012) and young people who had been children at the time of the conflict (Donà 2011).

I have recently begun to examine the role of virtual spaces among Rwandans, including young people, in the diaspora as a result of 'following' participants' conversations, which included comments on how information technology and social media were changing the ways in which they connected to one another. Informed by digital globalization, there is a growing interest in the role of new media and information technology in social sciences research in general and in the context of migration. Ethnographic research online, also referred to as netnography (Kozinets 2010), is receiving increased attention as a methodological tool to study relations and practices of migrant and diasporic communities (Crush et al. 2012). The emergence of e-diasporas and diasporas in virtual sites (Dicks et al. 2005) results in the development of new research areas where technological innovations and migration intersect, as shown for instance in Horst's (2006) 'virtual dialogues' with the Somali community in the diaspora.

Although Rwandans in the country and the diaspora have embraced social media and information technology in the last few years, the study of the role of virtual spaces for forced migrant children and young people remains underresearched. For this chapter, netnography involved selecting sites that contained the terms 'Rwanda' and 'young people/ youth' in their title, and analyzing their content for themes related to 'mobility/migration'.

My involvement with the Rwandan community over time and across space has allowed me to capture transnational and transgenerational changes in context, and it is hoped that the examples presented in the following section give a sense of the passing of time and the developmental challenges associated with growing up in postgenocide Rwanda and in the diaspora. The chapter offers a methodological contribution by drawing together research that draws on multisited and/or multitemporal and virtual methodologies as I followed the research subjects over time and space. The methodology helps capture an emergent complexity within cross-border migrations where children and young people move for different purposes, across distances and over time within broader migration trajectories.

While different child/youth cohorts and their families were interviewed at different times and in different settings, all participants have been affected by the conflict, and their experiences are embedded in a forced migratory arc. Some of these children and young people have had firsthand experiences of conflict and displacement, while others are defined through their parents' forced migration: they all engage in mobilities of their own that link to conflict as the defining event.

Forced migration and mobility among Rwandan children and young people

Research on Rwandan children and young people has flourished since the end of the 1994 genocide in which Hutu extremists persecuted and exterminated ethnic minority Tutsi and moderate Hutus between April and July 1994. This research examined the conditions of child survivors of the genocide (Kaplan 2013), of traumatized children and adolescents (Gupta 1996; Schaal and Elbert 2006), and of young refugees in camps (De Smet 1998) and in the diaspora (Diamini and Anuza 2009). Most of this research is framed by methodological nationalism, with a focus on the genocide and its aftermath.

The emphasis on the Rwandan genocide has marginalized the dynamic in-and-out movements across the region during and after the genocide. The victory of the Rwandan Patriotic Front brought an end to genocidal violence in the country, but it propelled two intersecting waves of exit and return migration: almost one million Rwandan 'old caseload' refugees, including first- and second-generation children born in exile, voluntarily returned home from the diaspora, while almost two million Rwandans, including children, crossed the border to become 'new caseload' refugees at the end of the genocide. In 1998, almost one million 'new caseload refugees' returned to Rwanda following the closure of refugee camps in Eastern Congo (then Zaire). The tendency to frame the history of genocidal violence, refugee movements and repa-triations within the framework of national borders neglects the dynamic nature of minor movements and the connections that exist between local, national, regional and global movements.

As outlined in the introduction to this edited collection, the concept 'mobility-in-migration' is used to explain the way in which multiple forms of mobility take place within broader migratory movements. This chapter draws attention to how children and young people use different types of mobilities-in-migration, that is, mobilities within their migration trajectories, for different purposes in response to changing economic, social and cultural circumstances over time and across different places. The next section identifies forms of mobility that take place during and after conflict, and it shows that mobility is a common feature of chil-dren and young people's lives across migratory contexts that are gener-ally kept separate in the literature on internal displacement, regional refugee movements, diasporic migrations and repatriations. Multiple forms of mobility occur within the framework of forced migration, and these are ongoing and dynamic movements.

Mobilities in material space

Boasi lost his parents at the age of 10 in April 1994, and he was reunited with his maternal aunt in September of the same year.[1] He recalled that

> When people killed my parents, I took refuge in a sorghum field for two days. When I saw other people leaving Kigali, I went with them up to Gitarama Prefecture. There I met an old woman who took me to her house, and I stayed there for two weeks. Later on, she bought me to an orphan's center at Ruhango. The center was then moved to Gitarama. (October 1996)

Boasi's survival was made possible by rapid and dynamic movement to five different locations and to places near and far. His first hiding place was a field located in the vicinity. In mobility research, neighborhoods are usually explored as spaces of play (Barker et al. 2009), transitional spaces that signal the passage from home to school (Barker 2009), or social spaces in which control is held by street gangs (Gough and Franch 2005). During violent conflict, neighborhoods are simultaneously killing places and spaces of safety. From the onset of the Rwandan genocide, roadblocks were set up to intersect targets and prevent them from fleeing (Des Forges 1999). In a context of escalating violence that was exercised through the control of movement, mobility within neighborhoods and travel to places of origin became a survival strategy. Research on children's experiences during the genocide tends not to take into account the extent to which children's mobility occurred as violence escalated, and the ways in which movement was used as a survival strategy to hide and protect children. Damas Gisimba, the director of the Gisimba orphanage in which almost four hundred people took refuge, remembered that

> At the beginning of the genocide, as my neighbors knew me as a caring and compassionate person … it is for this reason that at first they thought that I could hide their children, and little by little that I could hide them too, and thus they joined me. (May 2009)

Neighborhoods where attackers, targets and bystanders cohabited were spaces of death and survival, and the transition from one to the other was dependent on a delicate balance between mobility and immobility. Physical buildings and spatial areas were transformed into spaces of safety because of the social features associated with them. In the neighborhood where the Gisimba orphanage was located, respect for and trust in Mr. Gisimba made it possible for those in need to use local mobility to the center as an initial survival strategy. In addition to survival in the form of protection, mobility within neighborhoods was also used as a survival strategy to ensure daily subsistence. The survival of the center's residents during the genocide required provisions. Only children who had been in the center for a long time and who were known in the neighborhood were sent out to collect water and food (African Rights 2003). Their mobility was possible because of established, preconflict neighborly relations, which could be exploited at a time of uncertainty and insecurity, transforming physical localities into spaces of protection thanks to the social characteristics of the people who inhabited them.

Movement to places of origin where individuals and families were known was similarly utilized as a survival strategy. Survival mobility was pursued with the understanding that the locality that one knew and where he/she was known would offer increased safety. Evariste, currently in exile in the United Kingdom with his wife and three children, recalled that, as the situation deteriorated: 'I sent the children back with my wife, while I stayed in Kigali to look after the property' (February 2009).

In a country of a thousand hills, attachment to places of origin meant that a return movement to known localities could be used as a coping strategy. Generalized insecurity and the widespread presence of roadblocks meant that the means of transport were actually transformed from material objects into spaces of protection. One such refugee, Innocent, was attending secondary school as a boarding student when he was told that it was not safe to stay at school anymore. He said, 'I went back in the car of the Bourgomaster of our commune. He was a friend of my father' (April 2009).

Children's experiences of using the car in peaceful settings (Barker 2009) and during conflict vary. During the genocide, the car acquired a symbolic status and became a safe space through its owner, who was usually someone in a position of power within the local area. Family connections and social relations were instrumental in ensuring the safety of children, and often this was achieved through mobility. The transformation of material objects that are mobile, like the car, into spaces of protection, which are usually construed as sedentary locations, shows how the relation between mobility and immobility is altered by conflict: mobile material objects are transformed into spaces of protection, and spaces of protection become mobile (like the center in which Boasi found refuge and which was later moved).

The complex relationship between mobility and immobility (Pullan 2013) is also visible in the case of refugees who cross borders in search of protection and find themselves 'stuck in transit'. Agnes, who lives in Togo with her children, said,

> It used to be easy to reach Europe from Lomé. When I arrived here, I tried all possible ways, but it did not work. Fake papers are useless now, one cannot use them as in the past. I have been caught two times, and I was put in prison with my children. (July 2009)

In spite of their forced immobility, Agnes and her children were mobile in two ways: mentally through their aspirations to reach the shores of Europe, and physically through their short-distance movements to the border. Mobility in this context is used not only for daily survival but also as a means to achieve one's aspirations of resettlement. Their efforts to leave Togo resulted in an additional type of coerced immobility in detention centers. As Agnes and her children attempted to reach the shores of Europe, Rwandans who migrated or were born in Europe engaged in other forms of mobility, as in short visits and 'return' trips.

Victoire and her husband moved to Belgium for educational purposes, and because of the conflict they decided not to return to Rwanda. Their daughter, Marie, was born in 1993 in Belgium, where she grew up. Despite not having lived there, Marie was very interested in learning about her parents' country of origin, and in 2008 she went to Rwanda for a short visit while her mother stayed behind. Victoire commented that

> She went back last summer with her stepmother, and she liked it. She is the one to ask questions when the uncles are around, while in the family nobody speaks if not in passing by like 'when I was in the forest'. (January 2010)

Young people born in the diaspora learn about the family's country of origin through visits by relatives who live in the diaspora, a type of short-term mobility, and through short 'return' trips they themselves take. For young people who are born in the diaspora, short-term mobility is a way to connect with the family's migration history and to belong. Mobility is not a survival strategy, but a means to address identity issues and strengthen social ties.

Taken in isolation, the examples of survival, return and aspirational mobilities presented above may appear irrelevant or marginal to our understanding of forced migrants' experiences, yet when examined together, short-term mobilities appear to be a consistent feature of children's and young people's experiences of conflict and forced migration. There is a nexus between mobilities as everyday experiences and migratory movements. Mobilities are embedded in broader forms of movement, and they act as constitutive elements that combine to form what we understand as large-scale forced migration. Thus, forced migration can also be conceptualized as the accumulation of diverse, fragmented and ongoing forms of daily mobility. The link between movements and mass displacements is currently overlooked, and the mobility-in-migration concept makes the connection and embeddedness explicit. In these varied contexts, mobility can be a survival strategy, a driving force to achieve one's aspirations, a means to explore identity issues and a way to strengthen social ties. The tension between mobility and immobility presented above exposes the constraints of movement, but it also shows the agency of young people during and after conflict.

Mobilities, developmental trajectories and family dynamics

Loss of family members and family separations are not uncommon during conflict and forced migration (Gupta 1996; Kaplan 2013; Schaal and Elbert 2006). Resulting changes in family structures and family dynamics have a bearing on the development trajectories of children and young people. Jonas, who was separated from his family in 1992 at the age of 13 and reunited with his older brother five years later, said,

I lived in Kibungo and we took refuge in Tanzania. I was sixth in the family, but three of them have died and I remain the third. I missed everything. Now, I am fed by my brother. My mother is very old, and I feel that I am missing many things in life. I am becoming an adult, and I want to have my own family and to be like the others. (October 1996)

Jonas was aware that the disruption of normal family relations had negatively impacted his life opportunities, marked him out as different from other young people, and left him disadvantaged. He also realized that the fact that war and forced migration took place during his transition from childhood into adulthood meant that his opportunities to take on adult roles, which included creating his own family, were impeded.

Many children and young people spoke of the ways in which conflict impacted them and their family lives, and in doing so, revealed something new and different: unlike the conventional understanding that conflict and forced migration result in changes in family structures and dynamics, they indicated how changes in family dynamics prompted them to engage in further mobilities. At the age of ten, Pierre fled Rwanda with his family and went to live in refugee camps in Tanzania. It was during repatriation that his mother died, and afterwards his father remarried. The belief that he was badly treated by his stepmother prompted him to leave the paternal house. He stayed with three other families, whom he later left to go and live on the street. At the time of the interview in November 2000, he was living with a foster family comprised of a widow and her six children, with whom he got along well.

It is often assumed that the 'family' is the best place for a child to grow up and that the natural family is the best form of care, with family reunification being the preferred solution to the predicament of unaccompanied and separated children (Veale and Donà 2002). Yet, one of the negative effects of conflict and forced migration is the breakup of existing families and the formation of new ones. Children cope with these changes in different ways, and ongoing mobility is one of their coping strategies. It includes, but it is not restricted to, family life, and Pierre's experience of life on the street is not unique. Interviews with 290 Rwandan street children showed that a high proportion of them were orphaned or had lost one parent, and that in spite of having guardians, they chose to lead an independent life on the street (Veale and Donà

2003). The street, usually associated with movement, acquires symbolic connotations of rootedness, and it becomes 'home'.

Agency exercised through mobility

Pierre's decision to move to the street and subsequently to go and live with a foster family offers an example of how agency is exercised through mobility within the arc of forced migration and repatriation. The examination of agency through a specific practice rather than in terms of personality characteristics or coping styles presents an innovative way to explore the ways in which children and young people manage challenging circumstances. Agency and mobility also intersect with life-course trajectories (Mills and Blossfeld 2005), as shown in the case of Innocent cited above. Between 1994 and 1998, Innocent moved multiple times, both inside and across borders. He said,

> Some time after the Rwandan Patriotic Army advanced to the south of the country, we escaped to Burundi. Once arrived there, I joined the Hutu rebellion. Three hundred of us left to join the rebels. Government soldiers fired at us as we made our way to the training camps, and only 40 arrived at destination. (May 2009)

His decision as an adolescent to join the rebel forces in Burundi and to risk his life as he traveled to reach the training camps – an example of mobility – shows his agency. Physical mobility to join the rebel groups was accompanied by social mobility from the status of civilian to that of trainee soldier and subsequent promotion to sergeant. Awareness of resentment toward Rwandans on the part of Burundian rebels prompted him to exercise his agency again through another type of mobility, namely his flight from the rebel group and return to Rwanda:

> I became informed that the Burundians wanted to kill all Rwandans at the end of the rebellion and that they were going to start with those rebels who had been at school. I came up with the excuse that I wanted to recruit more Rwandans to increase our contingent, and thus I managed to flee. (May 2009)

His return to Rwanda was accompanied by his difficult transition back into civilian life as a young man and it entailed further rural–urban mobility:

A benefactor brought me to Kigali, where I managed to resume my secondary education and to obtain my high school degree in law. I am not able to have a good job. I even tried to enter the national police, but so far I have not succeeded. My first marriage has failed, and so has the second. I survive with difficulty, I sometimes steal, and I do simple jobs to survive. My future is unclear. I do not know what lies ahead of me. (May 2009)

War and forced migration left a mark on Innocent's life prospects and impacted his current situation as a former child soldier and returnee in postgenocide Rwanda. His awareness of his situation and of his bleak prospects for the future is similar to that expressed by Jonas. Yet, their awareness of the impact of conflict and displacement on their lives shows that children and young people are capable of assessing their situation and of taking decisions in rapidly changing social environments.

Overall, these examples of mobility-in-migration show that children exercise agency through mobility and that mobility fulfills multiple purposes: it is used as a strategy to achieve social mobility, to improve life conditions and manage challenging events resulting from conflict and during forced migration. This section has highlighted the situated, bounded, relational agency as children and youth move in response to changing family needs, social circumstances and opportunities.

The next section offers another example of how young Rwandans exercise agency through the use of information technology and connect in material and virtual spaces. They are global citizens, who simultaneously maintain national identities, connect locally and participate in global youth cultures. While mobility in relation to material spaces and lived experiences was analyzed above, the next section examines an emerging trend that consists in promoting new forms of mobility through social media and in virtual space where children and young people are promoters, audiences and actors. Some of these young people have experienced the lived mobilities identified above when they were children, while others born abroad experience them in new ways that reflect Rwanda's transition from a country of genocide to a transnational nation. In this context, the mobility-migration nexus explains the ways in which these children and young people engage with material and virtual mobilities that intersect with their more permanent status of youth in the diaspora and are situated within the broad framework of diasporic migrations.

Promoting mobilities in virtual space

Inside the country and in the diaspora, Rwandans have embraced information technology and social media (Donà 2010; Rubagiza et al. 2011). Through Facebook, YouTube and other forms of new media, Rwandans promote, advertise and share information. Virtual sites created by and/ or targeted at young Rwandans in the diaspora include Rwandan Youth for Change (RY4C[2]), the Rwanda Youth Patriots/UK[3] and the Rwandan Youth Information Community Organisation (rYico[4]). These sites are a platform for social networking (e.g., the Rwanda Youth Patriots/UK), they promote awareness-raising and involvement in transnational politics (e.g., the Rwandan Youth for Change) and are used for fundraising purposes and to increase sociocultural understanding of Rwanda (e.g., the Rwandan Youth Information Community Organisation). In transnational social spaces, material and virtual mobilities come together and offer an example of the way in which migration and technological globalization intersect. Three main types of mobilities are identified and promoted in virtual space: mobility as political subject; sociopolitical mobilities in the diaspora; translocal ethnic mobilization. This section examines web-based social practices of Rwandan diasporic youth and how its members connect to homeland, organize political rallies and create transnational ties.

Firstly, mobility becomes the political topic of discussion when refugee movements are debated online to raise political awareness (Bernal 2006; Mazzucchelli 2012). The Rwandan Youth for Change Facebook page, for instance, reports that the Global Campaign for Rwandan Human Rights shows that an increasing number of young people are seeking asylum abroad in order to flee from oppression.[5] The controversial cessation clause, which forces refugees living abroad to return home on the grounds that the country is safe and that their refugee status should be revoked, is criticized, as is the coerced repatriation of refugees from Congo and the forced recruitment of young Rwandans for military training. These transnational sites create a virtual political platform through which opposition movements, composed of adult and young people, can criticize the government more freely than those residing inside the country.

Secondly, virtual spaces are used to promote sociopolitical mobilities in the diaspora. Under headings such as 'diaspora youth to convene in London'[6] or 'The Rwanda Diaspora Convention Europe', the first phase of which is a convention of Rwandan youth[7], young Rwandans are encouraged to meet and get involved. Short-term mobility helps sustain links with the country of origin and consolidate the formation of a distinct type of group identity (young-diasporic) through the articulation of a specific transgenerational identity as 'young Rwandans' living in the diaspora. They are different from other adult Rwandans living abroad and hold a specific diasporic identity as young Rwandans, distinct from those young Rwandans who still live inside the country.

Similarly, transnational nation-building is promoted by inviting young people in the diaspora to attend civic training called *ingando* (solidarity camps) or *itorero* (cultural schools) both in Rwanda and abroad. Since 2008, the Rwandan government has implemented *itorero* to promote national culture among young people in the diaspora, and, in August 2012, 281 youth from 19 countries went back to Rwanda and spent two weeks attending the fifth civic-training Itorero.[8] News of these sessions are reported online with comments such as 'after completing this civic training called Itorero, they now got a clear picture of their country and vowed to spread it to the rest of the world'.[9] Personal accounts posted online in a friendly and informal manner are used to share experiences, reach other young Rwandans and encourage them to have a sense of patriotism. For instance, upon completing her civic training, a young Rwandan girl posted the following blog:

> My perspective of Rwanda changed. ... The lectures (despite my poor performance due to language constraint) brought in me a certain surge of patriotism. I now look at myself as Munyarwanda girl – not as a country of my parents.

These short trips help young Rwandans learn about and connect with the 'home' country. Like other visits home (Muggeridge and Donà 2006), this mobility is distinct from permanent return, and helps create and maintain a sense of cultural and national identity among the transnational community, as shown by a comment posted by the same young Rwandan girl: 'I'm setting up a website to promote Ingando – targeting especially Rwandan young people growing up in the Diaspora'.

Thirdly, local mobility within receiving societies is promoted as a form of translocal ethnic mobilization. For instance, on the occasion of the celebration of the victory of the Rwandan Patriotic Front on July 4, the following invitation was posted:

> Highlights of the event for the 4th of July include: Intore Massamba in concert. Rwandan traditional dancers. RCA fundraising including a raffle for a return ticket London-Kigali courtesy of Ethiopian Airlines.

Documentary by Rwandan youth about their life in the UK. Films and documentaries about Rwanda. Showcasing different Rwandan products. More entertainment; more fun.[10]

While the event imitates the national ceremony that takes place in Rwanda, it never totally replicates it. It differs by its incorporation of aspects of life in the diaspora and its promotion of young Rwandans' initiatives, such as the documentary made by Rwandan youth about their life in the UK. The announcement also promotes short-term mobility through the possibility of winning a trip – a return trip – to Rwanda. The informal tone of the messages diffused in virtual space is congenial to the development of fluid social ties and entry into material and virtual spaces that can be occasional and open, as the following example shows:

> Guys dont forget there is a huge Rwandan youth event tmrw at '264 Romford Road, Forest Gate, E7 9HZ London' from 6:30pm. Entrance is £5 there will be music, food and drinks. Invite your fellow friends. thank u.[11]

In virtual spaces, young Rwandans abroad not only maintain ethnic ties but also participate in global youth cultures. Events promoted online include advertisements of African bands or sporting events. Such pleasure mobility is one of the features of global youth cultures, in which the national, transnational and global intersect through occasional mobility.

Also connected to global cultures are fundraising events that encourage development mobility. For instance, the post announcing that over 900 people attended AFROCONNECT III (rYico Keeping Memories Fundraiser[12]) or the Sponsor a Brick campaign (in partnership with the Department of Architecture at Brighton University[13]) bring together three sets of themes: national belonging and the commemoration of the genocide, youth cultures through the promotion of African music, and engagement with the development community through fundraising. The announcement also shows how the young Rwandan organizers transcend national boundaries of belonging by creating partnerships with local institutions and opening up the events to non-Rwandans.

In virtual space, local, national and transethnic identities coexist. Young Rwandans' agency is enacted through multiple forms of ad-hoc, occasional and short-term mobilities. In these contexts, mobilities fulfill different functions: pleasure, political and social. Globalization forces, traditional long-term migration and new mobilities intersect and contribute to the formation of *ye-diasporas* (young electronic): networks of young people who live in the diaspora and use virtual spaces as a platform to connect with other diasporic and nondiasporic individuals for a variety of purposes ranging from political to cultural, social to pleasure.

Conclusion

This chapter contributes to the understanding of an underexamined dimension of societal changes: the link between children and youth, large-scale migration and individual small-scale mobility. It draws attention to how children and young people use different types of mobilities-in-migration, that is, mobilities within their migration trajectories, for different purposes in response to changing economic, social and cultural circumstances over time and across different places.

It adopted an integrative approach to understand the lives of children and young people who underwent conflict and its consequences: two distinct bodies of literature were brought together, diverse migratory contexts were linked and different research methodologies combined. As such, the analysis offers a wide-ranging overview of the issues confronting children and young people as they grow up on the move, as well as provides an example of how researchers can methodologically reflect on their long-term engagements with the communities they study and present a more holistic understanding of the complexities of forced migrant processes.

Spatial and temporal connections were brought to the fore by methodologically engaging in multisited and multitemporal research as well as in netnography with the Rwandan community. The integration of 'old' and 'new' methodologies – ethnography and netnography – combined with the inclusion of a long-temporal span that documented the transition from mono-sited to multisited research with the same group, were instrumental in portraying a picture of the lives of Rwandan children and young people as they simultaneously navigated movement and grew up.

This chapter highlighted the centrality of mobility to the understanding of the lived experiences of Rwandan children and young people across space and time. The mobility-in-migration concept highlighted the ways in which multiple forms of mobility occur within broad forced and diasporic migrations. In spite of its invisibility in forced migration research (Gill et al. 2011), mobility was a recurrent feature of Rwandan children's and young people's experiences during conflict and subsequent movements; it was a common dimension of their experiences in disparate contexts; and it played a significant function in their lives. Children's and young people's movements are much more fluid and dynamic than is generally understood.

One of the chapter's objectives was to show the connections that exist across contexts that are usually separated in the literature on conflict and internal displacement (Daiute 2010), refugee and asylum seekers movements (Eide and Hjern 2013, Ní Raghallaigh and Gilligan 2010), repatriations (Gladwell and Elwin 2012), and diasporic migrations (Back and von Brömssen 2010). This integrative task was achieved by bringing together the literature on forced migration and on mobilities, and by using the mobility-migration nexus as the analytical tool to explain their intersection. In doing so, the chapter contributed to both fields.

Mobilities are an underresearched topic in forced migration (Gill et al. 2011), and this chapter brought to the fore their centrality and functionality. For instance, it showed that mobility and family life are connected in unexplored ways: not only conflict and forced migration alter family structures, but, more importantly, conflict-induced changes in family dynamics result in ongoing mobilities. It also showed that the agency of forced migrant children and young people can find expression through their engagement with mobility in material and virtual spaces. Survival, aspirational and pleasure mobility, as well as other topics, deserve further attention in the literature on forced migration.

Conversely, the examination of mobility in contexts that are not peaceful or locally rooted expanded conventional geographies of mobility research that tend to describe mobilities in Western peaceful societies, urban and rural areas (Barker et al. 2009; Gough and Franch 2005; Jensen 2009). By linking disparate contexts, the chapter shows that mobility fulfills multiple functions, and that they change in time and across contexts. Mobility is a survival strategy during conflict, a steppingstone to long-distance migration while one is stuck in limbo, a means to explore identity issues and a way to connect transnationally in the diaspora. Mobility is useful to fulfill physical, emotional, social, cultural and political needs.

Connected yet distinct from e-diasporas (Diminescu 2012: 452), a distinctive category of young-electronic (ye)-diasporas emerges. In virtual space, the representation of a distinct category of 'young diasporic Rwandans' takes place, through which they position themselves differently, both from other adult Rwandans living in the diaspora and from other young Rwandans residing in Rwanda. Rwandan ye-diasporas are the promoters, audiences and actors of mobility. They both promote, and are encouraged to engage in, sociopolitical mobilities and translocal ethnic mobilization through which transnational nation-building, which is independent from permanent return, takes place, and simultaneous participation in global youth cultures occurs.

To conclude, one of the ways in which globalization, defined as the proliferation of cross-border flows and transnational networks, has changed our understanding of migration, has been to show that mobility and migration intersect at multiple levels. Consequently, the settler and temporary models (Castles 2002) can best be replaced by the 'mobility-in-migration' model, which connects local and transnational journeys, individual and group movements, and the crossing of multiple peripheries and manifold centers of globalization.

Acknowledgments

Grateful thanks to the Leverhulme Trust for the Leverhulme Fellowship, which generously covered fieldwork expenses in Rwanda and Belgium and teaching leave (2008–2010). Many thanks also go to all participants and research assistants for sharing their time, experiences and insights over the years.

Notes

1. Respondents' names have all been changed in order to maintain anonymity and confidentiality.
2. <https://www.facebook.com/RwandanYouthforChange/info> Accessed August 7, 2013.
3. <http://www.facebook.com/pages/Rwanda-Youth-Patriots-UK/255482111327> Accessed August 7, 2013.
4. <http://ryico.org> Accessed August 7, 2013.
5. https://www.facebook.com/RwandanYouthforChange/info posted April 24, 2013, Accessed August 7, 2013.
6. <http://www.newtimes.co.rw/news/index.php?i=14648anda=41907> posted June 6, 2011, Accessed August 7, 2013.
7. <http://fr.igihe.com/politique/la-convention-de-la-diaspora-rwandaise-en-europe.html> posted June 28, 2011, with a note that it had been postponed; accessed August 7, 2013.
8. *Itorero* is a Rwandan civic education institution with the objective of teaching all Rwandese to retain their culture by promoting different values such as national unity, social solidarity, patriotism, integrity, bravery, tolerance, the dos and don'ts of society, etc.'. <http://www.rwandandiaspora.gov.rw/index.php?id=49> Accessed August 7, 2013.

136   *Giorgia Donà*

9. <http://www.rwandandiaspora.gov.rw/index.php?id=32andtx_ttnews[tt_ne ws]=56andchash=7046e5f2f3458459f0520c15d2a4a176> Accessed August 7, 2013.
10. Rwanda Youth Patriots/UK <http://www.facebook.com/pages/Rwanda-Youth-Patriots-UK/255482111327> Accessed August 7, 2013.
11. Rwanda Youth Patriots/UK <http://www.facebook.com/pages/Rwanda-Youth-Patriots-UK/255482111327> Posted on September 28, 2010; accessed August 7, 2013.
12. <http://www.rYico.org/> Posted April 28, 2013; accessed August 7, 2013.
13. <http://www.rYico.org/> Posted April 25, 2013; accessed August 7, 2013.

References

African Rights (2003) *The Gisimba Memorial Centre: No Place for Fear* (London: African Rights).
Ahearn, F. L., and Athey, G. L. (eds) (1991) *Refugee Children: Theory, Research and Services* (Baltimore: Johns Hopkins University Press).
Anat, B. (2012) 'The Palestinian Diaspora on the Web: Between De-territorialisation and Re-territorialisation', *Social Science Information*, 51(4), 459–474.
Arora, P. (2012) 'Typology of Web 2.0 Spheres: Understanding the Cultural Dimensions of Social Media Spaces', *Current Sociology*, online doi: 10.1177/0011392112440439.
Back, M., and von Brömssen, K. (2010) 'Interrogating Childhood and Diaspora through the Voices of Children in Sweden', *Childhood*, 17(1), 113–128.
Barker, J. (2009) 'Driven to Distraction? Children's Experiences of Car Travel', *Mobilities*, 4(1), 59–76.
Barker, J., Kraftl, P., Horton, J., and Tucker, F. (2009) 'The Road Less Travelled: New Directions in Children's Mobility', *Mobilities*, 4(1), 1–10.
Benwell, M. C. (2009) 'Challenging Minority World Privilege: Children's Outside Mobilities in Post-apartheid South Africa', *Mobilities*, 4(1), 77–101.
Bernal, V. (2006) 'Diaspora, Cyberspace and Political Imagination: The Eritrean Diaspora Online', *Global Networks*, 6(2), 161–179.
Brettell, C. B., and Hollifield, J. F. (eds) (2013) *Migration Theory: Talking across Disciplines* (New York: Routledge).
Buliung, R. N. (2011) 'Wired People in Wired Places: Stories about Machines and the Geography of Activity', *Annals of the Association of American Geographers*, 101(6), 1365–1381.
Castles, S. (2002) 'Migration and Community Formation under Conditions of Globalization', *International Migration Review*, 36(4), 1143–1168.
Castles, S., and Miller, M. J. (2003) *The Age of Migration* (New York: Guilford Press).
Crush J., Eberhardt, C., Caesar, M., Chikanda, A., Pendleton, W., and Hill, A. (2012) 'Diaspora on the Web: New Networks, New Methodologies' in C. Vargas Silva (ed) *Handbook of Research Methods in Migration* (Oxford: Oxford University), 345–365.
Daiute, C. (2010) *Human Development and Political Violence* (New York: Cambridge University Press).
De Smet, J. (1998) 'Child Marriages in Rwandan Refugee Camps', *Africa*, 68(2), 211–237.

Des Forges, A. (1999) *Leave None to Tell the Story: Genocide in Rwanda* (New York: Human Rights Watch).

Diamini, N. S., and Anuza, U. (2009) 'Trans-nationalism, Social Identities and African Youth in the Canadian Diaspora', *Social Identities*, 15(2), 227–242.

Dicks, B., Mason, B., Coffey, A., and Atkinson, P. (2005) *Qualitative Research and Hypermedia: Ethnography for the Digital Age* (London: Sage).

Diminescu, D. (2012) 'Introduction: Digital Methods for the Exploration, Analysis and Mapping of E-Diasporas', *Social Science Information*, 51, 451–458.

Donà, G. (2001) *The Rwandan Experience of Fostering Separated Children* (Stockholm: Radda Barnen).

Donà, G. (2006) 'Changing Migration Patterns and Responses in the Context of Child and Youth Forced Migration', *International Journal of Migration, Health and Social Care*, 2(2), 2–6.

Donà, G. (2010) 'Collective Suffering and Cyber-memorialisation in Post-genocide Rwanda', in M. Broderick and A. Traverso (eds) *Trauma, Media, Art: New Perspectives* (Newcastle on Tyne: Cambridge Scholars Press), 16–35.

Donà, G. (2011) 'Researching Children and Violence in Evolving Socio-political Contexts' in J. Pottier, L. Hammond, and C. Cramer (eds), *Caught in the Crossfire: Ethical and Methodological Challenges to Researching Violence in Africa* (Leiden, The Netherlands: Brill Publishers), 39–59.

Donà, G. (2012) 'Being Young and of Mixed Ethnicity', *Forced Migration Review*, 40, 16–17. <www.fmreview.org/young-and-out-of-place>. Accessed 14 April 2014.

Donà, G., Mukakizima, B., Muramutsa, F., and Kefyalew, F. (1998). *An Impact Study of Family Reunification* (Kigali, Rwanda: SCF UK and University College Cork).

Eide, K., and Hjern, A. (2013) 'Unaccompanied Refugee Children: Vulnerability and Agency', *Acta Paediatrica*, doi: 10.1111/apa.12258.

Ensor, M. O., and Gozdziak, E. M. (eds) (2010) *Children and Migration: At the Crossroads of Resiliency and Migration* (London: Palgrave).

Fortunati, L., Pertierra, R., and Vincent, J. (eds) (2012) *Migration, Diaspora and Information Technology in Global Societies* (London: Routledge).

Gill, N., Caletrio, J., and Mason, V. (2011) 'Introduction: Mobilities and Forced Migration', *Mobilities*, 6(3), 301–316.

Gladwell, C., and Elwin, H. (2012) 'Broken Futures: Young Afghan Asylum Seekers in the UK and on Return to Their Country of Origin', *New Issues in Refugee Research*, Research Paper 246 (Geneva: UNHCR).

Glick-Schiller, N. (2010) 'A Global Perspective on Transnational Migration: Theorizing Migration without Methodological Nationalism' in R. Bauböck and T. Faist (eds), *Diaspora and Transnationalism: Concepts, Theories and Methods* (Amsterdam: University of Amsterdam and IMISCOE).

Gough, K. V., and Franch, M. (2005) 'Spaces of the Street: Socio-spatial Mobility and Exclusion of Youth in Recife', *Children's Geographies*, 3(2), 149–166.

Green, G., and Lockley, E. G. (2012) 'Communications Practices of the Karen in Sheffield: Seeking to Navigate Their Three Zones of Displacement', *Asian Journal of Communication*, 22(6), 566–583.

Gupta, L. (1996) *Exposure to War-Related Violence among Rwandan Children and Adolescents: A Brief Report on the National Baseline Trauma Survey* (Kigali: UNICEF).

Hannam, K., Sheller, M., and Urry, J. (2006) 'Editorial: Mobilities, Immobilities and Moorings', *Mobilities*, 1(1), 1–22.

Hashim, I., and Thorsen, D. (2011) *Child Migration in Africa* (London: Zed Books).

Helton, A. C. (2002) *The Price of Indifference: Refugee and Humanitarian Action in the New Century* (Oxford: Oxford University Press).

Horst, C. (2006) 'In "Virtual Dialogue" with the Somali Community: The Value of Electronic Media for Research amongst Refugee Diasporas', *Refuge*, 23(1), 51–57.

Jensen, O. B. (2009) 'Flows of Meaning, Cultures of Movements: Urban Mobility as Meaningful Everyday Life Practice', *Mobilities*, 4(1), 139–158.

Kaplan, S. (2013) 'Child Survivors of the 1994 Rwandan Genocide and Trauma-Related Affect', *Journal of Social Issues*, 69(1), 92–110.

Kearns, R., and Collins, D. (2003) 'Crossing Roads, Crossing Boundaries: Autonomy, Authority and Risk in a Child Pedestrian Safety Initiative', *Space and Polity*, 7(2), 193–212.

Kozinets, R. V. (2010) *Netnography: Doing Ethnographic Research Online* (London: Sage).

Leung, L. (2011) 'Taking Refuge in Technology: Communications Practices in Refugee Camps and Immigration Detention', *New Issues in Refugee Research*, Research Paper No, 202 (Geneva: United Nations High Commissioner for Refugees).

MacCallin, M. (ed.) (1996) *The Psychological Well-Being of Refugee Children: Research, Practice and Policy Issues*, 2nd ed. (Geneva: International Catholic Child Bureau).

Marcus, G. E. (1995) 'Ethnography in/of the World System: The Emergence of Multi-Sited Ethnography', *Annual Review of Anthropology*, 24, 95–117.

Mason, V. (2011) 'The Im/mobilities of Iraqi Refugees in Jordan: Pan-Arabism, "Hospitality" and the Figure of the "Refugee" ', *Mobilities*, 6(3), 353–373.

Mazzucchelli, F. (2012) 'What Remains of Yugoslavia? From the Geopolitical Space of Yugoslavia to the Virtual Space of the Web Yugosphere', *Social Science Information*, 51, 631–648.

Meda, L., Sookrajh, R., and Maharaj, B. (2012) 'Refugee Children in South Africa: Access and Challenges to Achieving Universal Primary Education', *Africa Education Review*, 9(1), S152–S168 (UNHCR 2012).

Mills, M., and Blossfeld, H. (2005) 'Globalization, Uncertainty and the Early Life Course: A Theoretical Framework' in H. Blossfeld, E. Klijzing, M. Mills, and K. Kurz (eds) *Globalization, Uncertainty and Youth in Society* (London: Routledge), 1–24.

Mountz, A. (2011) 'Specters at the Port of Entry: Understanding State Mobilities through an Ontology of Exclusion', *Mobilities*, 6(3), 317–334.

Muggeridge, H., and Donà, G. (2006) 'Back Home? Refugees' Experiences of the First Visit Back to Their Country of Origin', *Journal of Refugee Studies*, 19(4), 415–432.

Ni Laoire, C., Carpena-Mendez, F., Tyrrell, N., and White, A. (2011) *Childhood and Migration in Europe: Portraits of Mobility, Identity and Belonging in Contemporary Ireland* (Farnham, Surry: Ashgate).

Ní Raghallaigh, M., and Gilligan, R. (2010) 'Active Survival in the Lives of Unaccompanied Minors: Coping Strategies, Resilience, and the Relevance of Religion', *Child and Family Social Work*, 15(2), 226–237.

Pullan, W. (2013) 'Conflicts' Tools: Borders, Boundaries and Mobility in Jerusalem's Spatial Structures', *Mobilities*, 8(1), 125–147.

Rubagiza, J., Were, E., and Sutherland, R. (2011) 'Introducing ICT into Schools in Rwanda: Educational Challenges and Opportunities', *International Journal of Educational Development*, 31(1), 37–43.

Salazar Parreñas, R. (2005) *Children of Global Migration: Transnational Families and Gendered Woes* (Stanford, CA: Stanford University Press).

Schaal, S., and Elbert, T. (2006) 'Ten Years after the Genocide: Trauma Confrontation and Post-traumatic Stress in Rwandan Adolescents', *Journal of Traumatic Stress*, 19(1), 95–105.

Sturgess, P., and Philips, C. (2009) 'Enhancing Internet Literacy as a Health Promotion Strategy for Refugees and Migrants', *Health Promotion Journal of Australian*, 20(3), 247.

Veale, A., and Donà, G. (2002) 'Psychosocial Interventions and Children's Rights: Beyond Clinical Interventions', *Peace and Conflict*, 8(1), 47–61.

Veale, A., and Donà, G. (2003) 'Street Children and Political Violence: A Socio-demographic Analysis of Street Children in Rwanda', *Child Abuse and Neglect*, 27(3), 253–269.

Veale, A., Donà, G., Muramutsa, F., Iyakaremye, I., Mukakizima. B., and Kalinganire, C. (1998) *Situation Analysis of Street Children in Rwanda* (Kigali: UNICEF, Italian Cooperation, Rwandan Government and UCC).

Zimmermann, S. E. (2011) 'Reconsidering the Problem of "Bogus" Refugees with "Socio-economic" Motivations for Seeking Asylum', *Mobilities*, 6(3), 335–352.

7
'I Wish, I Wish…': Reflections on Mobility, Immobility and the Global 'Imaginings' of Nigerian Transnational Children

Angela Veale and Camilla Andres

Introduction

Transnational migration, characterized by temporary or ongoing border-crossings, has been hailed as a means by which migrants can creatively sustain the economic life of their families while establishing connections and social networks in different nation-states (Vertovec 2007). Yet Al-Ali and Koser (2002) caution that transnational mobility is not equally accessible to all migrants; gender relations, household structures, legal status and access to entitlements can all act as barriers to migrant mobility. While the transnational migration literature emphasizes connected social networks across binational locations, it has insufficiently captured the 'stuckness' experienced by many African transnational migrants once they reach Europe and that of their children back home. The transition to motherhood can particularly constrain women migrants' mobility (Stock, 2012). The differently situated position of children with respect to transnational mobility is underresearched in the academic literature. While the children of the global elite can move with relative ease (Nette and Hayden 2007), the children of middle-class and poor families in the developing world, such as Africa, encounter significant barriers to transnational mobility. In particular, the left-behind children of European-based African migrant parents are part of an increasing population of children whose lives are defined not only by the opportunities but also the constraints of globalization.

The international migration of an African parent is often a collective family project in which the mobility of one individual is dependent on other family members remaining behind, including children and those who take on the obligation to care for them (Øien 2006). Decisions to leave children behind are complex. Parents may decide that young children should be raised in their land of origin, as they believe they will receive a better upbringing by being raised in their own culture (Bohr and Tse 2009; Whitehouse 2009). Migrant mothers worry about childcare and education (Dreby 2010). Some migrants migrate through irregular routes, making it costly or difficult to bring children (Dreby 2010). This is particularly the case when legal routes to migration are very restrictive, as is the case for African and other third country national (TCN) migrants seeking to enter Europe. This chapter contributes to the themes of this book by focusing attention on the lives of children who are arguably on the margins of globalization, that is, children in Nigerian transnational families who remain with caregivers in Nigeria when a parent migrates to Ireland. It focuses in particular on those children and migrant parents who experience their lives as immobile, such as because of a lack of economic means, legal obstacles to travel or to family reunification. It undertakes a child-centered analysis of dialectics of mobility-immobility as parents move and children remain behind, drawing attention to the consequences of irregular migration as children's family lives become structured by global migration regimes. It uses a psychological perspective to explore the 'global imaginings' of Nigerian-living transnational children in a world where their knowledge of the daily life of their parent and foreign-born siblings is mediated by media, technology, imagination and wishfulness.

It embeds children's lives in family networks with their local caregivers and transnational siblings and parents. It focuses on developmental trajectories, drawing attention to Nigerian transnational children who grow from childhood to young adulthood in migratory contexts in which they 'age out' from the possibility of family reunification with their parents and foreign-born siblings in Europe.

Finally, it is based on multisited, multitemporal ethnographic fieldwork in which the researcher moved back and forth between Ireland and Nigeria over a two-and-a-half-year period. This 'mobile methodology' means family members on both sides of the transnational divide in Ireland and Nigeria were brought into dialogue as the researcher moved between both worlds, creating a form of proxy communication through the mobility of the researcher for a parent whose movement was restricted for material or legal reasons.

Transnational children and global 'imaginings'

There is debate within the transnational migration research literature regarding the extent to which parent–child separation is a normative (Rae-Espinoza 2011) or stressful experience for left-behind children (Coe 2008; Heymann et al. 2009; Parreñas 2005; Suârez-Orozco et al. 2002). Transnational family research based on circular migration from within historical migratory communities with established child-fosterage practices shapes much of what is known about the impact of transnational family life for children. Åkkesson et al. (2012) found that transnational family members regarded separations as painful but normal, and they supported each other with thoughts that the migrant parent would be able to come back for a holiday after two years. Dreby (2010) argues that in Mexico, adult circular migration patterns are changing. Based on extensive fieldwork, she found that although Mexican families had traditionally endured short-term separations while a family member was abroad, separations were becoming long-term as a result of increased Mexico–US border surveillance, with negative psychological and educational consequences for children.

Presently, little is known about mobility within transnational family migration between Africa and Europe. Gonzáles-Ferrer et al. (2012) examined the length of child–parent separations among Senegalese migrants to Europe. They found that approximately 70 percent of Senegalese migrant parents and their left-behind children were living in different countries ten years after the initial separation. Return migration leading to reunification increased between two and five years after separation and thereafter decreased. However, family reunification in Europe was infrequent, although the probability of reunification increased after five years of separation and also if the migrant parent was a legal resident. This probably reflects the lengthy legal reunification application process. Compared to other migratory routes, such as from Latin American countries to the United States or Asia to the Middle East, migration from Africa to 'Fortress Europe' is challenging. Travel is expensive. For undocumented migrants, a European-wide system of border patrols and detention policies make traveling without legal permits risky. These factors may contribute to different transnational family patterns in Africa compared to those found in Latin America and Asia, possibly characterized by lengthier child–parent separations and less circular migration.

Time apart creates its own dynamics in transnational families. Carling (2008) describes how nonmigrants have difficulty understanding the daily lives of their migrant relatives as they cannot see for themselves the places in which they live and work. Dreby (2010) noted that lengthy parent–child separations result in 'time dislocations' whereby parents have a mental image of their children as they were years before, and they lose touch with their children's development. Both Dreby (2010) and Carling (2008) mention the centrality of the life of the imagination in transnational relating as parents, children and caregivers imagine the life of the other, and miscommunication, tension and hurt can enter relationships. Children grow up such that 'Ideas of the north pervade children's imaginations' (Dreby 2010: 19). Coe (2011) notes children had imaginings of 'abroad' that they described as urban, modern and with beautiful buildings in contrast to their own village life. Falicov (2005) asks what happens to the children of transnational migration and whether transnationalism creates 'real' connections or connections based on memory and imagination. In Mexican migrant communities, circular migration supports relatedness and intimacy (see Carpena-Méndez, this volume) as children experience their 'real' parent beyond the world of their imagination. This 'real-time' relationship results in shared experiences and social practices that support children's ability to engage in relating with their parent in the in-between time of their absence. Davis (2012) undertook an analysis of children's views of what they see as important in family practices. Children emphasized the face-to face, sensory aspects of relating, routine contact and shared everyday experiences as important to 'knowing' the other. Children used 'seeing' as a colloquial term to capture what they regarded as an integral part of close relationships; being able to 'look at their face', interpret 'facial effects', see 'what they look like', assess 'how they act' and their overall 'personality'. Children noted that routine contact and everyday shared experiences gave substance to coliving sibling relation-ships that nonresident relationships did not possess. Coe (2011) notes that in transnational families, children in particular felt the 'scattering' of the family and sadness if they were separated from siblings.

In transnational relating, then, it is clear that children engage in what we term 'global imaginings' whereby they imagine the other life of their migrant family members based on what they are told about it, the consumerist objects that come back from that other world, and the media. Within the developmental psychological literature, there is an argument as to whether the world of the imagination is a 'gap-filling' process whereby 'imagination is a process of resolving and connecting the fragmented, poorly coordinated experience of the world so as to bring about a stable image of the world' (Pelaprat and Cole 2011: 399) in the same way we view the frames of a comic book and 'fill the gap' between the fragmented images; or whether it is a creative, (not reproductive), enrichment or expansion of experience and understanding (Zittoun and Cerchia 2013). The former view would seem to require some ongoing experience of the world that is then reproduced in the world of the imagination, while the latter view goes beyond a more information-processing view of the world to draw on what is known but from there is created, expanded, to allow radically new perspectives. In the words of Zittoun and Cerchia (2013) 'imagination is not limited by the borders of the demand of socially shared or materially constrained reality, it allows an *as-if* mode – which can be fictional, playful, hypothetical, counterfactual, retrospective or prospective mode – to create, on a mental plane, alternative realities, recomposing the given or enriching it' (Zittoun and Cerchia 2013: 322). In real-world relating, joint participation in shared activities supports intersubjectivity and the ability of relating partners to engage in position-exchange. Position-exchange is the ability to take the perspective of another, to exchange social positions, to move out of one's own position in order to reflect on the situation of the other (Gillespie 2012). In the absence of direct experience of the physical or social position of the other, dialogue, narrative and other symbolic resources (photos, stories, images) allow one person to patch together an impression of the experience of the other (Gillespie 2012). This is a constructivist act in which one partner shifts from the here-and-now real world of '*as-is*' to an '*as-if*' position to imagine the world of the other (Josephs 1998; Zittoun 2007). This symbolic space is populated by content from the real relationship, but is also infused with content that may also inform this 'as-if' world. For transnational children in Africa, this includes information, images and expectations gained from television, movies and the consumption patterns of other returned international migrants. The question this chapter asks is how do Nigerian transnational children in Nigeria and Ireland negotiate relating in this complex global transnational space over extended periods of time, in contexts where there are significant constraints on child and/or migrant parent mobility?

Nigerian transnational families in Ireland

Nigerian migrants formed the largest population of African migrants to Ireland during its economic boom years 1996–2008, including significant numbers of women. The Nigerian population in Ireland is composed of proportionately more female migrants; their average age is 38 years old; and there are noticeably more children in the 10- to 13-year-old group when compared to other migrant groups (Central Statistics Office [CSO]

2012). Interestingly, 77 percent of households are categorized as mixed Irish-Nigerian households, with a child identified as the Irish person in a large number of cases (CSO 2012). A number of entry routes were utilized by Nigerian migrants to enter the country, including work permits and student visas. In addition, a common strategy in the period 1996–2008 was for Nigerians to enter the country through informal routes and claim asylum (Carling 2006; White et al. 2013). Many Nigerian migrants who entered the country through this route have since regularized their legal status through different mechanisms, although only 0.6 percent have been successful in gaining refugee status (Mberu and Pongou 2010). One way in which Nigerians have regularized their legal status is through an administrative procedure known as ICB/05, by which they had their residency application granted on the basis of having an Irish-born child. A 2004 referendum changed Irish citizenship laws so that children born after January 1, 2005 were no longer entitled to citizenship based on birth. Iroh (2010) argues that

> the very nature of the processes leading to such regularisation defined Nigerian migratory and transnational formations. That is to say, since the most common route to such legalization of residence was through becoming the parent of an Irish-born child, a regime akin to the interesting idea 'feminisation of survival' (Sassen 2002: 504) through a strategic deployment and practice of motherhood emerged. The 'feminisation of survival' situated the family – not only mothers and their Irish-born children but also their spouses and other children – at the centre of Nigerian strategies of survival. (quoted in White et al. 2013: 19)

When ICB/05 was granted, migrant parents had to sign a clause stating that they accepted they had no legitimate expectation to family reunification. In addition, from 2003–2011, it was the position of the Irish courts that 'a foreign national parent of an Irish-born child did not have an automatic entitlement to remain in the state with the child', and nearly 12,000 deportation orders were issued. Some deported parents, including Nigerians, chose to take their Irish-citizen child with them. In the Zambrano judgment (2011), the Court of Justice of the European Union (EU) ruled that Third Country National parents should be granted residence and the right to work in order to take care of their dependent EU-citizen children, in this case, their Irish-citizen children in Ireland. In Ireland, this has not extended to rights to family reunification, and applications for family reunification with spouses and dependent children may be made to the Minister for Justice and Equality and granted at his or her discretion.

An evolving strategy for family reunification is one in which many Nigerian migrants have reached eligibility for citizenship, obtained citizenship, and as naturalized citizens, have applied for long-stay visas for spouses and minor children. Such applications are also at the discretion of the Minister. For minor children who have become older than 18 years, applications for visas on their behalf are unlikely to be successful. Ireland does not have provisions that allow family reunification of adult children except, again, in exceptional cases. The Immigrant Council of Ireland notes that family reunification application procedures in Ireland take one of the longest times to process in Europe: 'Due to this system, a delay can imply that during the application process children lose their eligibility to reunite, as they have come of age in the meantime' (2013: 36). The Immigrant Council of Ireland states that

> Many individual respondents described the period that they had to wait for admittance of the family member as a period that their lives were on hold, void of sense, and paralyzing. It is difficult to make plans for the future (buying a house, starting an education) if one is not sure whether it will be possible to be together and build a life together. These effects are stronger as the procedure takes longer. Especially if the long procedure separated parents and children, this caused a lot of stress and anxiety. (2013: 102–103)

Transnational Nigerian parents in Ireland may not wish to seek family reunification with their children. However, if they do, they have to demonstrate stable, regular work and a relatively high monthly income requirement compared to other EU countries, and the legal framework means parent–child separations are likely to be over the long term. As can be seen, the migration regime in Ireland has influenced Nigerian transnational family formations so that many migrant parents in Ireland and their children in Nigeria remain separated over many years, with uncertainty as to how family life may be structured in the future.

Method

The material presented in this chapter is based on multisited, multitemporal ethnographic fieldwork with 18 Nigerian transnational families in both Ireland and Nigeria.[1] The 18 families were participants in a broader survey of 309 Nigerian migrant parents in Ireland, purposively sampled so that half of parents had children in Nigeria and therefore were living in transnational families, and of these, half had children in both Nigeria and Ireland. All survey respondents who were living in transnational families were invited to participate in the ethnographic study. A condition of participation was that the migrant parent consented for the researcher to visit their child and the child's caregiver in Nigeria. Furthermore, the child and caregiver also had to give their informed consent. A total of 18 families in the migrant parent survey met these conditions, and so all families who consented were included in the ethnographic study. Families therefore 'self-selected' to participate. We do not assume that their experiences are representative of transnational Nigerian families in Ireland, but the particularities of their lives offer situated case studies that draw attention to diverse and underresearched dynamics within some transnational families.

For the ethnographic study, participant observation, life histories and interviews were conducted with 18 migrant parents living in Ireland, with 23 children in Nigeria and with 18 of these children's Nigerian-based caregivers. Further, follow-up conversations by phone were carried out with research participants in Nigeria. In a number of families, interviews were also conducted with siblings (10) living in Ireland. Fieldwork involved movement back and forth between Ireland and Nigeria. The first contact with the field was made in Ireland in 2011 and was ended in July 2013. Fieldwork in Nigeria was conducted over two three-month periods – June–August 2011 and February–May 2012, and fieldwork continued in the intervening periods in Ireland until mid-2013. The researcher became a point of contact between migrant parents, children and their caregivers, a tool of 'connection' between the disparate geographic locations. For the purposes of this chapter, the analysis focuses on the theme of immobility that emerged as a central theme in the ethnographic work.

Survey results of the 309 migrant parents showed that, of the children in Ireland, 74 percent were born in Ireland, 17 percent migrated with their parent, 7 percent joined their parent in Ireland, and 2 percent came to Ireland and were later joined by their parent. Of the 309 migrant parent participants, over four-fifths had neither residency nor work permits on arrival in Ireland, and 81 percent claimed asylum. Nearly one-fifth (17 percent) were asylum seekers at the time of the survey. Of those no longer in the asylum system, many have gained work and residency permits as a result of their parentage of a child in Ireland under the ICB/2005 directive (see White et al. 2013). Also reflecting the profile of the Nigerian population in Ireland, a greater proportion of migrant parents surveyed were mothers. In mother-migrant cases, the father was the caregiver in 36 percent of cases. When fathers migrated, 69 percent of child caregivers were mothers. In total, half of families had a parent as main caregiver; nonparental caregivers were maternal relatives in most instances (31 percent), paternal relatives (8 percent) and other (7 percent).

Of the 18 families who participated in the ethnographic study, eight parents were registered as asylum seekers and were living in accommodation centers known as direct provision centers, seven of whom are migrant mothers. Of the others, six parents have leave to remain; two are undocumented; one is an EU citizen; and one parent chose not to disclose his legal status. Caregivers of their children in Nigeria were a grandparent (11), mother (1), father (2), aunt (1), uncle (1) and other relatives (2).

The migratory route: parent migration, child mobility

Migrant parents arrived in Ireland for many reasons, including socioeconomic reasons, fear for their lives or fear for the safety of their children. Carling (2006), detailing emigration from Nigeria to Europe, noted that structural obstacles, in particular tough European immigration legislation, have over time created a market for people and groups who use illegal means to facilitate migration. Perceptions of Europe as a place of opportunity and wealth lead people to take great risks for an opportunity to migrate (Carling 2006). Some research participants put their trust in people they did not know, and traveled to unknown destinations. The irregularity of the migration could be one reason why the process of migrating is shrouded in secrecy and silence in several families. A result of the secrecy is that the migration trajectory as told by the migrant parent and the child and his or her caregiver may not necessarily be the same story. The family members have diverging information about the migration, and children, in particular, tended to have little information about why their parent(s) left. In some cases information is purposively held back for one reason or the other. This is how it was experienced by Doris[2] – an elderly grandmother and the two granddaughters in her care: 'They left without informing us, and they just sent their address to us later. ... The children were staying with their grandmother on their father side. They were later brought here'.

This pattern emerges again in another family. Faridah, the migrant mother, explains why she did not inform her children and family about her migration until a few days before she left.

> When I got...when they got me the visa...the reason I didn't tell them [the family] from the beginning is that they don't need to

contribute anything, since someone will finance me, so I don't need to, you know, I just kept everything within me.

And just like the children, the researcher is told little about the migration trajectory, and is left with questions of 'who organized the travel and the visas, and why'? Faridah came to Ireland in 2001, and was granted leave to remain when she had a child born in Ireland. She also met her current husband in Ireland. At the time of the research, she had twin daughters born in 1997, living in Nigeria, and five younger children who were living with her and her new husband in Ireland. Faridah's life in Nigeria had been difficult from a very young age. The family struggled with poverty and violence. When Faridah migrated, she thought this would be the end of her difficulties. She was only able to arrange for her own migration, and it was decided right before she left that the children were to stay with her only living sister. Faridah recollects the day she told her sister and mother about her migration and the care of the children was negotiated:

> 'Look I don't want it to be a shock to you, it happens that I will be leaving within the next 2–3 days'. They said, 'Where are you going to? Abuja? You are always on the road'. This and that. I said that this is real. And my sister said: 'How do you do it? Where did you get it?' They were just imagining. Then I said: 'This is God's work, it's not by my power or by my mind'. But it was a shock to them. And they said, 'Are you going with your kids?' I said, 'No, they only got it [visa] for me only. As soon as I settle down, I come for my kids'. I was thinking something that would happen the next day, you know. But next day took years.

Not even her mother or her sister are let in on the details of Faridah's migration, and are only told about the migration a few days before she is leaving without her children. Faridah thought she would be able to reunite with her children in Ireland within a short period of time. Faridah has leave to remain in Ireland, and thus has the legal status dreamed about by the migrant parents in direct provision centers. This is the status that is imagined by both children in Nigeria and parents in Ireland as the legal status that will solve their problems of separation. But as the case of Faridah shows, poverty is also a very real restriction to achieving family reunification as she does not meet the income and job stability threshold. As family reunification fails to materialize, the care arrangement is renegotiated again and again over 11 years.

In the case of some families in our ethnographic study, the decision of a parent to migrate internationally was sudden. The migrant parent lacked information about the realities of life in Europe, in particular, about the difficulties of family reunification. As a result, caregiver arrangements were often put in place hastily and for the short term. Parental international migration sparked child mobility between households as caregiving arrangements had to be reorganized over time.

We see this in the case of Akono and Bejide, who migrated together three years ago, leaving behind three daughters in Nigeria. They have since had a new baby in Ireland. Until the parents migrated, the children lived with their parents near their parental grandparents. When they migrated, the oldest child was sent to live with her maternal aunt, and the other two children went to live with a pastor friend. He was unable to take care of them, and therefore they were sent to live with the paternal grandparents, before being moved to the home of their maternal grandparents.

Yet while looking at the caregiving arrangements over time, it should be kept in mind that the migration of one or two parents may not be the biggest change in the caregiving arrangement for a child. In another family, the two boys born in 1990 and 1992 agree that the biggest change in their caregiving situation was not in 2007 when their mother migrated, but back in 1999 when their parents separated. The two boys and their younger sister were sent to live with their paternal grandmother. In 2001, the parents divorced, and their two sons went to live with their father. Their younger sister went to their maternal aunt. Right before the fieldwork began in 2011, she was sent to live with her paternal uncle as she had become too unruly for her aunt. Parental divorce, compounded by parental migration, possibly introduced greater mobility into the children's lives than either event alone.

To contextualize these findings, the survey of 309 migrant parents showed that in mother-migrant households, following maternal migration, a third of children changed caregivers twice or more, and that in father-migrant households, 17 percent of children changed caregivers. Ethnographic findings suggest that divorce or family breakdown seems to result in greater mobility in children's lives postmigration. In a number of instances, the migration of a parent was one form of mobility in children's lives; children changed caregivers, sometimes siblings were separated, new families started, and multiple family members moved in different directions. The decision of a parent to migrate internationally is often poorly communicated and understood by children. They know their parent is in Europe, and many know that their parent is in Ireland, but 'Ireland' is a vague concept synonymous with 'abroad' or 'Europe'.

Stuck in mobility

Seven migrant parents in the ethnographic fieldwork were in the asylum process, and therefore were 'stuck' in mobility for multiple years. The environment at the direct provision centers visited by the researcher does not allow for a sense of safety or a feeling of 'home'. Parents are not allowed to have visitors to their rooms, and the common rooms are cold and have old, worn and unclean furniture. The center has an atmosphere of temporariness. It is a place designed for ushering people through. But as a residence for some families for multiple years, it is a depressing place that does not facilitate a good family life. This reality of life for the migrant parents and their children in Ireland is lost on the children back in Nigeria, and does not feature in the imaginings of their own potential life in Europe with their migrant parent, as portrayed in popular culture, on television and in commercials.

Titalayo lives in Nigeria with her two sisters, and is cared for by her maternal grandmother and aunt. Her father is a migrant with a new family in the UK, and has traveled between the UK and Nigeria for as long as she can remember. Her mother is an asylum seeker who has been living in a direct provision center in Ireland since 2005. Shortly after arriving in Ireland, she gave birth to twins, who at the time of the research were six years old. Titalayo, the second daughter, born in 1996, says,

> My life where I live is fun, but at the same time...how I wish my parents were also here. You feel they enjoy at that place and wish you were with them.... Ah the way (my mother) talks on the phone she too also misses us, and it makes her feel somehow sad that for so many years she cannot see her children, how they look.

Titalayo is satisfied with her life in Nigeria, but imagines the life of her mother 'at that place', imagines the life she is enjoying with the twins and 'you wish you were with them'. In reality, her mother is finding life 'harder and harder' in the direct provision center and feels she cannot return to Nigeria as she has nothing to bring back. This is a very painful situation for the migrant mother, a situation she cannot talk about without crying. For Titalayo, 'the tough part is when my mother doesn't send our provision money fast, and there is nothing with my grand-parents. It looks weird'. She compares her situation to other children, for example, 'when they come to school and say my mummy bought this for me'. She keeps in touch with her mother on the phone and on Facebook. She calls the other children to come and see her mum on

Facebook. One of the things that makes her sad is that 'they all know her on Facebook and greeted her on her birthday. Now we are in final year, I don't think they will get to meet her'. She has a sense of having a privileged life in Nigeria where she is well taken care of, eats good food, lives in good accommodation that is paid for by her parents in Europe and her maternal uncles. She feels loved and wanted by her grandmother and aunt. Yet she feels time moving on without any evidence that her mother is coming back or that she will go to stay with her mother in Ireland any time soon. In spite of a good life in Nigeria, she still clings to the hope of an imagined future in Europe. She wants to go to university 'Not in Nigeria, but abroad', where she imagines her future life with her mother: 'Everything is just like I wish, I wish. I wish there is a way that I can see my mum. And I know my wishes will come true one day'.

In these families, the children imagine the life of the migrant parent and siblings in Europe, and the life they could have together. But the way in which this is imagined is influenced by the age of the child, the care arrangement and the economic situation of the child in Nigeria, as well as the general perceptions of life in Europe.

Asa's mother, Alice, is also a migrant in Ireland and lives in a direct provision center. And like the mother of Titilayo and Ife, Alice came to Ireland in 2005 and had a child the same year. Asa was born in 2002, and was only three years old when her mother migrated. Asa struggled with feeling not only the loss of her parent but also the loss of being separated from the opportunities afforded by the West. Cultural globalization, the meaning and significance of the West, infuses relating and the juxtaposition of the hardship of life in Nigeria and ideas about this place that is far away complicates family life. And in the case of Asa and Alice, it is further complicated by the dire poverty of the family in Nigeria. Asa's grandmother and aunt (mother's mother and mother's sister) cannot afford regular meals for the nine children living with them and themselves. School fees are often paid late, and the children, grandmother and aunt all share one small room. The little room is crowded and damp, with both insects and mice visibly crawling around.

Alice migrated to seek asylum because she feared for the life of her unborn child. With the help of relatives and friends, she was able to come to Europe and claim asylum. At the time of the research, she and Obi were living in a direct provision center for seven years, awaiting the outcome of her asylum application. Now ten years old, Asa has no recollection of her mother. Both the migrant mother and the caregiver thought the child would be able to reunite with the mother before now. Alice and Obi are provided with food and accommodation and a small stipend as she does not have a right to work.

As the researcher moved between Ireland and Nigeria, it was clear that Asa and her maternal grandmother share a notion of Europe as a place where one goes to work, gets money and comes back to Nigeria as a wealthy woman, and that this has affected their expectations of the support the migrant mother should contribute. Asa and her grandmother gain their understanding of the global North from television, films and the gifts of clothes, toys, phones and electronics that they see other children of international migrants enjoy. This complete lack of knowledge about the realities of life in Ireland for those who enter the asylum system gave them no opportunity to foresee or to now imagine the difficulties the migrant faces.

This has made it difficult for the family to believe what the migrant mother is telling them. This has led to verbal confrontations between the caregiver and the migrant mother, which end with the mother crying and the caregiver then saying that she believes her. In Nigeria, Asa's grandmother explains, 'I thought that immediately when [daughter] left, she would get a job and would be sending money to me easily. It is not like that. She never knew it would be like that … I didn't expect that when she traveled abroad, we would continue suffering'.

Alice says that Asa expects her to send money and gifts:

> Yeah, and she wants everything. But she wants to be with me! If she's sad and I tell her 'don't worry I'm coming for you', she will shout and scream and tell her friends that 'my mum says she is coming to take me!!', you know. And inside of me I just … shh … I feel bad because I know I'm lying to her.

Asa has at times refused to talk to her mother because she does not know her. She has told her grandmother that she does not know this woman who calls, but never lets her see her. Yet Asa holds onto the idea of being reunited with her mother.

> *Camilla*: Where is your mother staying now?
> *Asa*: Europe
> *Camilla*: And how long has she stayed there?
> *Asa*: Since when I was small….
> *Camilla*: Since she left for that place, did she come back to see you again?
> *Asa*: No.
> *Camilla*: When you talk with your mum, what are the things you would talk about?

Asa: About the food I eat, school. I tell her that she should come and take me away.

Camilla: You tell her to come and take you. And what does she say?

Asa: She says that she will come and bring me there

It is difficult for Asa to know how the lives of those in the asylum system are constrained by laws that restrict the right to work. Within her lived experience, she expects a parent to be agentive, volitional and self-directed as in Nigeria. One cannot be 'stopped' from working should he or she wish to do so. It is difficult for Asa to understand the passivity of her mother, her inability to meet her material obligations and the immobility that keeps them separate. This makes her angry and sad at different times. The pressures of global consumption ('she wants everything') cause tensions that lead to a breakdown of trust in the parent–child–caregiver relationship. But Asa also believes 'she wants to be with me'. Asa imagines an idealized reunion in which her mother will bring her 'over there', so 'together-over-there' is a symbolic resource to deal with the pain of separation in the here and now, and 'as-is' is transformed into an idealized 'as-it-could-be'. Yet her mother, as long as she is in a direct provision center, is uncertain how long she will stay there, whether she will be granted leave to remain in Ireland or whether she and her twins will be deported back to Nigeria.

Methodologically, the consequences of the back-and-forth movement of the researcher between the family members in Ireland and Nigeria are that the researcher is able to tell the family in Nigeria that their daughter/mother really is in a center for people who seek asylum and that she is given food and shelter, but she is not allowed to work, and therefore cannot make money. As such, through her mobility, she enters into the realm of the 'real' in their relating. Asa and her grandmother said that they did not believe her until the researcher came and confirmed what the migrant mother told them. The migrant mother is relieved that they no longer think she is telling lies.

'They've only seen my artificial self'

Across transnational spaces, Nigerian children and their Irish-born siblings in our research were often aware of the existence of the other, but had little or no direct experience of each other. They have spoken on the phone, seen each other on Facebook, viewed photographs of the other, and in this way, incorporated each other into their emotional and imaginative lives. In general, children in Nigeria were older children, while their siblings in Ireland were still young. Titilayo has not met her twin brother and sister who were born in Ireland, nor the siblings (on her father's side) in the UK. When asked to imagine how the twins live in Ireland, she says,

> This year 2012 is going to be seven years. I think about, oh gosh, these children. They are born in Ireland, they have not even been to Nigeria, they've not even seen their grandma and grandpa before, and they have not even set their eyes on me before. They've only seen my artificial self (picture) and vice versa. ... The relationship is over the phone, so they don't even know if I am their sister. The relationship is not that close.... I am sad because I don't even know that much about them. I think it has to do with the government and only the government can make it change'.

Photographs and the mobile phone bring the siblings into relationship with each other, but it feels artificial rather than real. As noted by Davis (2012), Ife, Titilayo's youngest sister, laments that she has never had a face-to-face, sensory experience of relating. She attributes responsibility for this to 'the government', thus generating a distancing effect from holding her mother responsible. From her position in Nigeria, she reflects on their lives:

> The advantages there are: they will know more about Ireland, and some other places. They will have access to technology, and if they're old enough to get a job, they can make use of it. They will also know what their mum can do and not do. Those are the two advantages I know. The disadvantages are, they won't know their grandparents, sisters and brothers.

Unlike her, they will be able to travel, and they will have access to technology and the global work opportunities that that will afford them. 'Technology' symbolizes their potential future as global citizens. They also have real knowledge of their mother's situation rather than having an imaginary experience of her Irish life, as is her experience.

David is the eldest child of his parents, and he has three siblings in Ireland, two of whom moved to Ireland and one who was born in Ireland. Although his mother is in a direct provision center and is unable to send any money to support him and his grandmother, he says, 'I believe they are living a good life there', and by this he means, 'I mean they are able to do what they should be doing at their age'.

Across different interviews, it is clear that David has an image of life in Ireland and that it is a good life. This view is maintained in spite of the negatives that he hears from his parents, about the realities of life in a direct provision center, with little privacy, little money and a lot of worries. His 'knowledge' of Ireland is mediated by media and stories of Europe. Meanwhile, for siblings who have only known life in Ireland, Africa is a vague construct. David's younger brother, Timothy, is living with his parents in Ireland.

> *Timothy*: David is our brother.
> *Camilla*: Where does David live?
> *Timothy*: David, ehmm, Africa.
> *Camilla*: Where in Africa?
> *Timothy*: He's in Africa!! He lives there!
> *Camilla*: Africa is big. ...
> *Timothy*: Yeah!! But he lives there!
> *Camilla*: Which country?
> *Timothy*: South Africa. I don't know.

'David' is a concrete presence for Timothy, but his inability to imagine David in Africa conveys the challenge for young children of developing a relationship with their sibling who is far away. For children both in Ireland and in Nigeria, a wish to know and a sadness about being separated from siblings was very prevalent in interviews.

Developmental trajectories and political constraints

Interviews with grandparent caregivers and their grandchildren highlighted intergenerational differences in relation to mobility. The grandfather of Titilayo moved from the village to Lagos when he was 23 years old. He attended evening classes and became a mechanical engineer. His life expectation was 'whatever I want to do, I do'. He is happy with his life in Nigeria. He has a small pension, his grandchildren are living with him, and he is thankful for developments such as electricity that have made life more comfortable than when he was a child. His granddaughter, on the other hand, does not want to stay in Nigeria and has her sights set on going to university abroad. This has been her dream and intention since she was young. She feels this is important because of the course she wants to study:

> *Camilla*: And what course is that?
> *Titilayo*: Mass. com.
> *Camilla*: Is it 'mass communication' like reporting in TV?
> *Titilayo*: Yes.

A number of left-behind children, although not all, imagine their future to lie in Europe. Fatima, the daughter of Faridah, is attending a good school in Nigeria. Her migrant mother and her caregiver aunt prioritize education as important. Although her mother has leave to remain, she is unemployed in Ireland, and life is not easy for her. Fatima, however, says, 'I'm tired of this [Nigeria] country. Everything is not smooth....I think being with my mummy is the best'. 'Mother' and the place in which mother is living are fused together as an idealized and positive 'other' place where she could live in the future. Again, 'as-is' (this country) is found wanting compared to 'as-it-could-be' (Josephs 1998), which is an imagined, desirable (being with my mummy) but unlikely future.

Some participants showed their awareness of the structural constraints that concretely mediated this gap between real life now and an 'as-it-could-be' life in Europe. Two brothers in Nigeria were hopeful that their mother, who had acquired EU citizenship, would shortly be able to send for them and bring them to Ireland as she wants them to have 'a sound education'. However the eldest son, who was 20 years of age, was worried he would be ineligible once he turned 21 years old. He was very aware that he is getting older, moving toward young adulthood, and was likely to 'age out' of the chance to be formally reunified with their migrant parent.

Benjamin: Can I ask you something? I don't know if it's part of the interview.... Do you know if since now she [mother] has her Irish citizenship, she can get us a visa?

Camilla: I think so.... She may be able to get you a tourist visa for maybe 10 weeks because immediately you turn 18, they believe you are an adult.

Benjamin: So she can take my brother?

Camilla: Yes, but it also depends on how much you [mother] earn.

Benjamin: She told me if you're below 21, they still consider you a dependent, sort of.... They can give the visa, but make it difficult to get the papers? Does it take time?

Camilla: Yes. It takes lots of time.

Benjamin: Does it takes days or months? If it takes longer, by that time I will be above 21 because by June, I will be 21 and it will become even more difficult.... I went online to read about it and I saw that it takes time.

For participants such as Benjamin, their 'self' project is organized and constructed toward an imagined migrant future, including studying hard and researching about and waiting for the time of reunification with their migrant parent. This future 'as-it-could-be' organizes here-and-now development, a preadaptation for future mobility – but this goal is simultaneously becoming more out of reach.

Conclusion

The findings reported here relate to a particular context, that of children in Nigerian transnational families in Ireland who participated in a multisited, multitemporal ethnographic study. Due to structural factors of moving through the asylum process and lengthy processes of family reunification applications, migrant parents and their children were separated for lengthy time periods – and in the cases of those still in the asylum process, of an uncontrollable duration. For left-behind children, relating occurred in the technologically mediated world of phones and Facebook, in the material world of gifts and remittances, and in the symbolic world. Over time, it seemed that the symbolic world gained in importance in the absence of physical relating. A core analytic theme was relating in a virtual and imaginative space, and how the 'global' entered the mind and the emotional and relational world of the developing child in ways that had tangible consequences for development and social relationships. Children were engaged in making meaning of the content of their migrant parent's communications in the absence of direct experience of the context of their lives in Ireland. This is a fundamentally challenging developmental task. Children and their caregivers in Nigeria struggled to understand the migrant parents' perspective, as their exposure to media and television gave a perspective on life in Europe that made it difficult to understand the perspective of the migrant parent and to engage in position exchange (Gillespie 2012). The chapter drew attention to an underresearched form of mobility, that of imaginative mobility. This served a function both in 'filling a gap' (Pelaprat and Cole 2011) in transnational social relating and – following Zittoun and Cerchia (2013) – in creating an expansive sense of an imagined future, a globally mobile 'self'. We saw that the left-behind child felt not only the loss of the parent but also the loss of being separated from the opportunities afforded by the West. Migrant parents in turn struggled to meet the left-behind children's expectations that they have free access to the material goods of a global consumerist culture. Children experienced their economic and social position as being at the margins of globalization while wishing to be active participants.

The chapter embedded the migrant parent–children relationship in the context of other developmentally important relationships, such as children's relationships with caregivers and siblings. Siblings play an important role in children's development. A sibling is an individual who grows up and goes through similar stages just before or after a child, and sibling affection can be a source of support during stressful life events in a child's life (Dunn 2005). A child's peer relationships are often overlooked in childhood and migration literature, yet this chapter showed how keenly children felt their separation from brothers and sisters who were living elsewhere. Finally, this chapter was based on an innovative methodology that involved researching members of the same families who are living apart as a result of migration: the migrant parent, his or her child, the child's caregiver and siblings in Ireland and Nigeria. A possible reason migrant parents self-selected to be part of this study was the opportunity that the mobility of the researcher gave them to maintain a connection with their children in the face of their own current immobility. In this way, the chapter draws attention to dynamics of immobility within migration.

Notes

1. Financial support from NORFACE research program on Migration in Europe – Social, Economic, Cultural and Policy Dynamics is acknowledged.
2. Pseudonyms have been used for all research participants.

References

Åkkesson, L., Carling, J., and Drotbohm, H. (2012) 'Mobility, Moralities and Motherhood: Navigating the Contingencies of Cape Verdean Lives', *Journal of Ethnic and Migration Studies*, 38(2), 237–260.

Al-Ali, N., and Koser, K. (2002) *New Approaches to Migration? Transnational Communities and the Transformation of Home*, (London: Routledge).

Bohr, Y., and Tse, C. (2009) 'Satellite Babies in Transnational Families: A Study of Parents' Decisions to Separate from Their Infants', *Infant Mental Health Journal*, 30, 265–286.

Carling, J. (2006) *Migration, Human Smuggling and Trafficking from Nigeria to Europe.* [Online: International Organisation for Migration (IOM)]. <http://publications.iom.int/bookstore/free/MRS23.pdf> Accessed on April 13, 2014.

Carling, J. (2008) 'The Human Dynamics of Migrant Transnationalism', *Ethnic and Racial Studies*, 31(8), 1452–1477.

Central Statistics Office, Ireland (2012) *Migration and Diversity: A Profile of Diversity in Ireland.* (Dublin: CSO Office).

Coe, C. (2008) 'The Structuring of Feeling in Ghanaian Transnational Families', *City and Society*, 20(2), 222–250.

Coe, C. (2011) 'How Children Feel about Their Parents' Migration: A History of the Reciprocity of Care in Ghana' in C. Coe, R. Reynolds, D. Boehm, J. Hess, and H. Rae-Expinoza (eds) *Everyday Ruptures: Children, Youth, and Migration in Global Perspective* (Nashville, TN: Vanderbilt University Press), 97–115.

Davis, H. (2012) 'Affinities, Seeing and Feeling like Family: Exploring Why Children Value Face-To-Face Contact', *Childhood*, 19(1), 8–23.

Dreby, J. (2010) *Divided by Borders: Mexican Migrants and Their Children* (Berkeley: University of California Press).

Dunn, J. (2005) 'Commentary: Siblings in Their Families', *Journal of Family Psychology*, 19(4), 654–657.

Falicov, J. (2005) Working with Transnational Immigrants: Expanding Meanings of Family, Community and Culture'. *Family Process*, 44(4), 399–406.

Gillespie, A. (2012) 'Position Exchange: The Social Development of Agency', *New Ideas in Psychology*, 30, 32–46.

Gonzáles-Ferrer, A., Baizán, P., and Beauchemin, C. (2012) 'Child-Parent Separations among Senegalese Migrants to Europe: Migration Strategies or Cultural Arrangements', *The ANNALS of the American Academy of Political and Social Science*, 642(1), 106–133.

Heymann, J., Flores-Macias, F., Hayes, J., Kennedy, M., Lahaie, C., and Earle, A. (2009) 'The Impact of Migration on the Well-being of Transnational Families: New Data from Sending Communities in Mexico', *Community, Work, and Family*, 12(1), 91–103.

Immigrant Council of Ireland (2013) 'Family Reunification: A Barrier or Facilitator of Integration?', *Ireland Country Report*. Dublin: Immigrant Council of Ireland.

Iroh, A. (2010) 'Transition and Transformation: Nigerian Familial Formations in Ireland's Spaces of Regulation and Regimentation', *African and Black Diaspora*, 3(1), 69–89.

Josephs, I. (1998) 'Constructing One's Self in the City of the Silent: Dialogue, Symbols, and the Role of "As-If" in Self-Development', *Human Development*, 41, 180–195.

Mberu, B., and Pongou, R. (2010) *Nigeria: Multiple Forms of Mobility in Africa's Demographic Giant* <http://www.migrationpolicy.org/article/nigeria-multiple-forms-mobility-africas-demographic-giant> Accessed April 14, 2014.

Nette, J., and Hayden, M. (2007) 'Globally Mobile Children: The Sense of Belonging', *Educational Studies*, 33(4), 435–444.

Øien, C. (2006) 'Transnational Networks of Care: Angolan Children in Fosterage in Portugal', *Ethnic and Racial Studies*, 29(6), 1104–1117.

Parreñas, R. (2005) *Children of Global Migration: Transnational Families and Gendered Woes* (Stanford, CA: Stanford University Press).

Pelaprat, E., and Cole, M. (2011) ' "Minding the Gap": Imagination, Creativity and Human Cognition'. *Integrative Psychological and Behavioral Science*, 45(4), 397–418.

Rae-Espinoza, H. (2011) 'The Children of Émigrés in Ecuador: Narratives of Cultural Reproduction and Emotion in Transnational Social Fields' in C. Coe, R. Reynolds, D. Boehm, J. Hess, and H. Rae-Expinoza (eds) *Everyday Ruptures: Children, Youth and Migration in Global Perspective* (Nashville, TN: Vanderbilt University Press), 115–141.

Stock, I. (2012) 'Gender and the Dynamics of Mobility: Reflections on African Migrant Mothers and 'Transit Migration' in Morocco', *Ethnic and Racial Studies*, 35(9), 1577–1595.

Suârez-Orozco, C., Todorova, I., and Louie, J. (2002) 'Making Up for Lost Time: The Experience of Separation and Reunification among Immigrant Families', *Family Process*, 41(4), 625–643.

Vertovec, S. (2007) 'Circular Migration: The Way Forward in Global Policy?', *Working Papers No. 4* (Oxford: International Migration Institute, University of Oxford).

White, A., Dito, B., Veale, A., and Mazzucato, V. (2013) 'Transnational Migration and the Health and Emotional Well-Being of Nigerian Migrant Parents in Ireland and the Netherlands'. Conference on Transnational Families: Multi-Sited, Mixed-Method and Comparative Research Approaches, March 28–29, 2013, Maastricht: The Netherlands.

Whitehouse, B. (2009) 'Transnational Childrearing and the Preservation of Transnational Identity in Brazzaville, Congo', *Global Networks*, 9(1), 82–99.

Zittoun, T. (2007) 'The Role of Symbolic Resources in Human Lives' in J. Valsiner and A. Rosa (eds) *The Cambridge Handbook of Sociocultural Psychology* (Cambridge: Cambridge University Press), 343–361.

Zittoun, T. and Cerchia, F. (2013) 'Imagination as expansion of experience'. *Integrative Psychological and Behavioral Science*, 47(3), 305–324.

8
The Children Left Behind by International Migrants from Sri Lanka: Victims or Beneficiaries of Globalization?

Rajith W. D. Lakshman, Sunethra Perera and Reverend Pinnawala Sangasumana

Introduction

Development discourse often emphasizes the poverty reduction potential of international migration as a positive element of globalization in general and economic globalization in particular (Das 2009). The strongest evidence in support of this argument is the rapid/continuous increase in the flow of economic remittances bound to sending countries in the global south (De Haas 2005; World Bank 2005, 2011). Perhaps an even more appealing pro-poor property of these remittances is their resilience during global financial crises (see Sirkeci et al. 2012 for evidence during the 2008 crisis). The impact of migration, including that of the remittances, is felt the soonest and the strongest by the immediate members of transnational families left behind by the migrants. This impact, as all other globalization-related impacts, can either be a benign force (Dollar and Kraay 2002) or a malign one (Milanovic 2003). Migration and globalization are closely connected, yet the migration of people is often ignored in the literature on globalization. Children are also often excluded from our conceptualization of the world and research on globalization. This chapter, using data from Sri Lanka, looks at micro-level impacts of the international migration of parents on their children with a view to contributing to this debate from the angle of children. It offers an innovative contribution to the emerging literature on migration and globalization through an exploration of children's and families' engagement in migration that draws attention to multidirectional and multitemporal movements within individual, family and community migratory 'arcs'. It examines the lives of children, young people and families in different relationships to migration, including children and youth who are left behind, in response to changing global opportunities and constraints.

This chapter fits into the wider literature on migration, remittances and globalization that was dominated by economics until the introduction of the concept of social remittances by Levitt (1998). This change created the space to discuss alternative forms of remittances, such as social/cultural/political remittances, all of which affect globalization in ways that economic remittances do not (Levitt and Lamba-Nieves 2011). It follows that any analysis into how immigration affects the left-behind children, who are the focus of this paper, may also need to look beyond the economics. In fact, there is evidence that noneconomic remittances (Kandel and Kao 2001) are as important as economics ones (Durand et al. 1996) in determining the welfare of the children left behind. While the chapter attempts this with limited success, there still is an unmistakable economic bias in it. In fact, in what follows 'remittances' is used to mean 'economic remittances'.

The link between globalization, migration and development is strongly anchored on the relationship between remittance incomes and household consumption (De Haas 2005). There are at least three views on the remittance-consumption relationship: (1) remittances do not change household consumption patterns at the margin, (2) remittances affect household consumption behavior in a way that leads to a higher proportion of expenditure being spent on 'status-oriented' consumption goods (Chami et al. 2005), and (3) household members see remittances as a transitory income and spend most of it on investment goods (Adams and Cuecuecha 2010). While there is empirical evidence to support each of these views, the children left behind would probably benefit more if the third view were true, for household-level investments can enhance a broad range of impact areas relevant for children, including hunger, nutrition, health and education. Although all of these impact areas are critically important for ensuring child welfare, the present chapter exclusively focuses on the issue of the education of the children left behind. This is mainly a pragmatic decision influenced by the better quality of the available data on education in the target data sources.

There is an empirical literature that shows that remittances have provided support to better educate the children who are left behind (Asis 2006; Edwards and Ureta 2003; Kuhn 2006; Perera and Jampaklay 2011; Roongshivin 1985). This evidence is further strengthened and complemented by another strand in the literature that shows that remittances lead to the reduced labor force participation of the children left behind (Baland and Robinson 2000; Basu and Van 1998). However, the negative impacts of migration on the education of children are often associated with parental migration (Graham and Jordan 2011; Graham et al. 2012). The negative impacts of parental migration, which are frequently related to the malign face of globalization, involve psychosocial aspects that nontrivially impact the educational outcomes of these children.

In summary, the literature on migration and the education of the children left behind is characterized by two properties: (1) the quantitative work that links remittances with educational outcomes does not address psychosocial issues that arise from parental migration (e.g., D'Emilio et al. 2007; Edwards and Ureta 2003), and (2) the qualitative work that is based on psychosocial data that looks at the impact of parent migration often fails to quantify the said impacts (Castaneda and Buck 2011). These properties mark the contours of a specific gap in the literature that emphasizes that there are no studies that use large (national-level) quantitative data sets in conjunction with qualitative data to examine the impact of parental migration on children left behind. Save the Children (2006) and Perera (2009) use similar methods, but the former uses a micro sample and the latter uses census data, which does not lend itself to detailed socioeconomic analysis. Underlying this gap is a more serious issue in which any study that does not quantify its results, say, at the national level, runs the risk of escaping the attention of policymakers, and others that do not use qualitative data can only partially capture the comprehensive impact of parental migration. This chapter offers an innovative approach to understanding migration that intersects with individual and family life course trajectories. Its multitemporal and mixed-methods approach makes it possible to capture the ways in which children in different relationships to migration change and adapt to different circumstances over time. The lives of children and young people are embedded in migratory circuits that capture the 'global' dynamism of complex migration.

The present chapter contributes to filling the above gap in the literature by using national-level quantitative evidence alongside in-depth qualitative research to examine the effect of parental migration on the left-behind children.[1] By doing this we are able to, in limited ways, extend the discussion about remittances into the noneconomic realm. In particular, we identify a few instances in which social/cultural remittances may be at work. Another contribution of this chapter is that it contrasts the impact of mother-migration with that of father-migration, which has, so far, eluded the literature on children left behind. We emphasize this as a peculiar gender dimension of the impact of globalization on children left behind. A third contribution is the geographic focus of this chapter, which is a rare addition to the sparse literature on children left behind in Sri Lanka. Child and family migration is one of the changing manifestations of globalization. Differently from the traditional understanding of migration from South to North/West or from developing countries to developed ones, the chapter shows that there are varied migratory trajectories like East–East (from Sri Lanka to the Middle East). There is a sense of dynamic interaction between migration, growing up and broader contextual changes due to globalization. Increased connections exist among children and their siblings, parents, relatives, friends and communities living in near and distant places. More generally speaking, this paper for the first time uses data from a government household survey to generate migration statistics for the country. The Sri Lankan context is also an important addition to the present volume as it offers opportunities to discuss new mobilities in postwar conditions.

The remainder of this chapter is organized into six sections: literature on migration and children left behind in Sri Lanka; the quantitative and qualitative data sources used here; results from the quantitative analysis; results from the qualitative analysis; recent policy initiatives; and, finally, some concluding thoughts.

International migration from Sri Lanka and the children left behind

International migration is a prominent feature in the socioeconomic landscape of Sri Lanka. Two types of international migrants can be identified: (1) transitory labor migrants who mainly target Middle Eastern labor markets and (2) more permanent migrants. The Sri Lanka Bureau of Foreign Employment (SLBFE) estimates the first type be around 1.9 million individuals (SLBFE 2010).[2] A large number of these transitory/circular migrants are married and with children (Eelens et al. 1992; Save the Children 2006). The second type of international migrants, numbering at least 800,000 Sri Lankan citizens, is also referred to as a 'diaspora' (Collyer and Wimalasena 2007). The majority of the diaspora are ethnic Tamils who migrated to destinations in Western Europe, in Northern America or in Australia in several 'waves', including as refugees, following the outbreak of ethnic violence in the 1980s (Cheran

2003). As family reunion is possible for the 'permanent' migrants and/or they tend to migrate with their children or family, it is possible that the issue of leaving children behind would not apply to them.

As in most other Asian countries, the mass contract labor migration from Sri Lanka started in late 1970s. From then until now, the Middle Eastern countries continued to receive the highest proportion of labor migrants from Sri Lanka. The latest statistics suggest that a level as high as 84 percent is being absorbed by Middle Eastern countries such as Saudi Arabia, the United Arab Emirates (UAE), Kuwait, Qatar and Jordan (SLBFE 2010). A key feature of the Middle Eastern market, with massive implications for children, was that it mostly attracted low-skilled female migrants as housemaids. This was particularly the case during the 1990s (see Figure 8.1). In fact, Sri Lanka was often cited as proof of new (feminized) mobilities in the South Asian region (Piper 2008). However, as illustrated in Figure 8.1, this trend has since reversed, and the male and the female migrant proportions stand equal as at 2010. This trend reversal can be accounted for by the relative decline of the housemaid sector among migrants from Sri Lanka. For example, the sector declined from 66 percent in 1995 to 42 percent in 2010 (SLBFE 2010). It must, however, be noted that the above statistics are related to annual departure numbers only and that the absolute stock of migrants must still be overwhelmingly women.

The above historical trends/patterns could potentially change following what would arguably be the twenty-first century's most important single event for Sri Lanka: the end of 30 years of civil war in 2009. The Sinhala and Tamil nationalist movements contributed to the conflict that led to the pogrom of 1983, resulting in the deaths of many civilians of Tamil origin. After 1983, the ethnic violence escalated

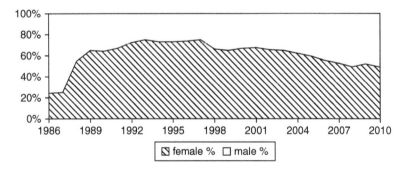

Figure 8.1   Departure for foreign employment by sex 1986–2010
Source: Based on data from SLBFE(2010).

into a civil war waged between the government of Sri Lanka (GoSL) and the Liberation Tigers of Tamil Eelam (LTTE). The violence in 1983 also caused a large number of Tamils to flee the country as refugees, bound mainly for India, Western Europe, Canada, Australia and New Zealand. Since the end of the war, however, the governments of some of these destinations have refused refugee status to recent arrivals from Sri Lanka. The end of the war has also opened up hitherto isolated areas of the country – namely areas in the Northern and Eastern provinces that were under LTTE control. These internal dynamics, which have international repercussions, are critical determinants of postwar new mobilities in Sri Lanka.

There is recent evidence that points toward significant out-migration from the Northern and Eastern provinces since 2009 (Jayathilake 2010; SLBFE 2010). There is also evidence that the profile of the migrant may also have changed after the war. For instance, the new (postwar) cohort of international labor migration from the Eastern Province is approximately 75 percent male (SLBFE 2010). This is in contrast to the pattern observed in other parts of Sri Lanka that has been dominated by females. The migrant numbers from the Northern/Eastern provinces should be interpreted carefully as these migrants, particularly the displaced ones, often use their addresses of temporary residence (e.g., in Colombo) when they register with the SLBFE. For this reason, the actual number of migrant workers from the Northern/Eastern Provinces may be substantially more than what SLBFE data suggests.

Methodology and data

This chapter uses a mixed method involving a quantitative analysis backed by an in-depth qualitative analysis to examine the welfare impact of parental migration on the children left behind. This analysis narrowly focuses on educational outcomes, albeit there are other aspects of child welfare that can be affected by parental migration, for example, physical health, psychological health, nutrition and happiness. The reason for this methodological decision lies primarily in our quantitative data source being richer in education-related data. The tabular, graphical and statistical tools used in describing and analyzing this data form the thrust of our quantitative work. The chapter quantifies the impact of parental migration by comparing the educational outcomes of children whose parents are abroad with the educational outcomes of the other children whose parents are either with them or are internal migrants. This quantitative analysis, on the one hand, provides important statistical evidence to understand the relationship between parental migration and the educational outcomes of the children. Moreover, the quantitative results form the basis for assessing the magnitude of the impact, which we believe adds value to the policy implications of this research. The qualitative analysis, on the other hand, is useful on its own and as a complement to the quantitative analysis. Qualitative information captured in case studies, for example, furnishes information that is nonquantifiable and hence is not captured in the quantitative analysis. In addition, case studies are useful to examine whether the observed quantitative relationships can be given a causal interpretation. This is particularly useful for this study because the cross-sectional quantitative analysis done here does not permit a rigorous examination of causal links. Case studies are a good way to overcome this issue, which is why we identified them as complementary to the qualitative data. We employ two sets of qualitative information: (1) qualitative data gathered from in-depth interviews with left-behind children and caregivers in 2008; (2) data from several qualitative in-depth interviews that were done with government and nongovernment officials involved in migration policy in Sri Lanka in 2012. The quantitative data source and the two qualitative data sources are introduced next.

Household Income and Expenditure Survey (HIES) 2009/10[3]

The HIES 2009/10 is the latest and the seventh in the HIES series conducted by the Department of Census and Statistics, Sri Lanka. This latest survey, for the first time in the HIES series, includes information from Jaffna and Vavuniya, two districts from the war-ravaged Northern Province. The HIES 2009/10 sampled 19,958 households and included some basic but useful information on household-level migration. It includes just two pieces of information on household members who had migrated: (1) the migrant's relationship to the head, and (2) whether the migrant is elsewhere in the country (internal migrants) or abroad (international migrants). We use this information to define a parent-migrant household as follows:

> **Definition 1:** A household in which *Wife/Husband* had migrated, leaving a *Son/Daughter* behind. [The emphasized are two relationships reported in the HIES.][4]

Admittedly Definition 1 is excessively strong, which would lead to an undercounting of parent-migration instances. For example, if a single mother migrates, leaving her children with her father, who is the grandfather of the children, the HIES cannot be used to identify theirs as a parent-migration household.[5] It follows that the population estimates presented below of households in which the parents are abroad should be considered as minimum estimates.

Table 8.1 provides the provincial distribution of cleaned/filtered data. The cleaning/filtering involved separating the households into two groups (1) those in which the head had no child(ren) or no spouse (i.e., the head is a widow/widower, divorced, or never married) or neither children nor a spouse and (2) those in which the head had child(ren) and a spouse. The first group was excluded from the analysis as it is not relevant for the present study. The second group of households is then separated using a four-pronged typology of households anchored around Definition 1. The four household types are households (1) with no migrants, (2) with only non-parent migrants (internal or international), (3) with an internal migrant parent, and (4) with an international migrant parent. Table 8.1 tabulates the estimated provincial distribution of each of these household types. The table reveals salient characteristics of the population: (1) approximately 2.5 million households have heads who do not have children or do not have a spouse or both; (2) about 0.11 million households have a parent who had migrated abroad leaving his/her children behind; (3) approximately 0.15 million households are with an internally migrated parent; and (4) the Eastern Province of the country has the highest proportion (4 percent) of international migrant-parent households, and Uva has the lowest (0.9 percent).

Perhaps the most significant, if not the most controversial, statistic reported in Table 8.1 is the overall number of international migrant-parent households. This is controversial because it is much lower than what is implied by other estimates, most notably those calculated by the SLBFE. The Bureau does not specifically estimate migrant-parent numbers, but supports the idea that a significant proportion of their estimated 1.9 million labor migrants are in fact parents. Our estimate, however, stands much lower. However, our estimate is supported by Perera's (2009) estimate that is based on the 2001 census. While the validation of existing estimates of migrant-parent numbers is not a key thesis of this chapter, these findings emphasize the need to reexamine the widely accepted estimates of international migration numbers in Sri Lanka.[6]

The HIES data can also be analyzed at the individual level; indeed, individual-level analysis is more appropriate when examining individual-level characteristics. The definition of children becomes crucial in this exercise:

Definition 2: A child is defined as an individual who is in the 0–19 age group AND is identified as a *Son/Daughter* of the *head*. [The emphasized are relationships reported in the HIES.]

Table 8.1 Estimated number of households in the population

Province	Head has no children or no spouse	Head is with children and spouse				
		Parent international	Parent internal	No migrant	Non-parent migrants	Total
Western	787,873	34,622	16,555	601,835	26,699	1,467,583
	53.7 percent	2.4 percent	1.1 percent	41.0 percent	1.8 percent	100 percent
Central	339,247	17,441	43,333	227,557	38,312	665,890
	50.9 percent	2.6 percent	6.5 percent	34.2 percent	5.8 percent	100 percent
Southern	319,135	8,235	19,634	250,325	26,724	624,054
	51.1 percent	1.3 percent	3.1 percent	40.1 percent	4.3 percent	100 percent
Northern	71,472	1,901	49	88,983	4,042	166,446
	42.9 percent	1.1 percent	0.0 percent	53.5 percent	2.4 percent	100 percent
Eastern	140,091	14,265	7,554	183,976	8,810	354,695
	39.5 percent	4.0 percent	2.1 percent	51.9 percent	2.5 percent	100 percent
North-western	324,905	14,272	18,120	266,258	11,815	635,370
	51.1 percent	2.2 percent	2.9 percent	41.9 percent	1.9 percent	100 percent
North-central	140,323	6,552	19,694	147,310	8,953	322,831
	43.5 percent	2.0 percent	6.1 percent	45.6 percent	2.8 percent	100 percent
Uva	150,209	2,958	21,265	145,360	20,362	340,154
	44.2 percent	0.9 percent	6.3 percent	42.7 percent	6.0 percent	100 percent
Sabara-gamuwa	249,071	6,154	12,710	216,280	15,962	500,177
	49.8 percent	1.2 percent	2.5 percent	43.2 percent	3.2 percent	100 percent
Total households	2,522,324	106,399	158,913	2,127,885	161,679	5,077,201
	49.7 percent	2.1 percent	3.1 percent	41.9 percent	3.2 percent	100 percent
Households with children (aged 5–19)	2,900,646	94,815	133,315	1,798,279	150,146	5,077,201
	49.7 percent	2.1 percent	3.1 percent	41.9 percent	3.2 percent	100 percent

Note: Population household numbers are estimated here on the basis of whether the household's head has a spouse and children. The households with children and spouses are then categorized according to their migration experience. The last row recalculates the numbers based on whether household has children aged 5–19.

Source: Authors' calculations based on HIES 2009/10.

For instance, the household sample in the HIES 2009/10 includes 85,403 individuals. Out of these, 35,254 are recorded as *son/daughter* of head of household. However, these sons/daughters include individuals who are older than 19 years. This study is not interested in the impact of parental migration upon these individuals. The HIES sample includes individuals who are in the 0–19 age group, but are not identified as *sons/daughters* of the head. These could be children who live with relatives or who are boarders. Clearly, the data is not sufficient to match them with their parents, which forces us to exclude them from this study. Definition 2 guarantees that only children who are unambiguously matched with their parents are included in the study.

Qualitative in-depth data 2008

The analysis extends further to examine the qualitative aspects of how parental overseas migration impacts children's school enrolment and educational outcomes. This analysis is based on the qualitative in-depth interviews conducted in 2008. The qualitative data was collected along with a household survey conducted in the Divisional Secretary (DS) division of Kalutara district in Sri Lanka.[7] We do not report a detailed analysis of the quantitative aspects of this data, which is discussed in detail by Perera (2009). The 54 key informants were selected from among children of migrants, children of nonmigrants, caregivers, return migrants, Grama Niladari (GN), which are the village-level administrative officers of the government, and schoolteachers for the qualitative in-depth study. The relevant ethical clearance was obtained prior to the conducting of these interviews.

Key informant interviews 2012

In order to justify and update the results of the qualitative and quantitative analyses done at the household level, we conducted semistructured interviews with key informants who have engaged directly or indirectly with different programs on children of migrant workers. Most of the key informants belonged to the executive rank in the relevant institutions. The interviewees included the manager of welfare of the SLBFE, the deputy general manager of social development of the SLBFE, the chief executive officer of the National Child Protection Authority (NCPA), the deputy commissioner of the Department of Probation and Child Care Services (PCCS), and the additional secretary to the Ministry of Child Development and Women affairs. In general, we focused on collecting information through the key informant interviews on different programs related to the children left behind with a view to seeing whether the gaps identified in this research are being addressed. This data that was collected in early 2012 was useful to confirm that our household-level results based on data collected in 2010 and in 2008 were in fact relevant/ valid at the time of writing.

Parent migration and the education of the left-behind Children: a quantitative analysis

This section quantifies the impact of parental migration on the education of the children left behind. This analysis looks at educational outcomes such as school dropout rates and household-level resource allocation for education. First, however, we look at the distribution of various types of migration households in our sample from the HIES.

Table 8.2 provides the estimated population number of children in selected age groups according to the migration typology defined earlier. Age groups 5 to 9, 10 to 16, and 17 to 19 were selected because they all run up to and culminate at an important state examination. Table 8.2 generates comparative profiles of children according to the typology of migrant households used here. The profiles reveal that (1) parents tend to migrate abroad less when they have children of age 0–5 (from among the four household types, the international migrant households have

Table 8.2   Population estimates of children (aged 0–19) by migration status of household

Child age	No migrants	Non-parent migrants	Parent internal	Parent international	Total
Age 0–5	1,495,142	172,978	99,504	55,610	1,823,233
	27 percent	29 percent	29 percent	24 percent	28 percent
Age 6–9	1,159,860	111,471	91,271	50,955	1,413,556
	21 percent	19 percent	26 percent	22 percent	21 percent
Age 10–16	2,015,484	209,890	114,759	88,100	2,428,233
	37 percent	35 percent	33 percent	39 percent	37 percent
Age 17–19	784,238	105,982	40,629	32,938	963,787
	14 percent	18 percent	12 percent	14 percent	15 percent
Tot Age 0–19	5,454,724	600,321	346,163	227,602	6,628,810
	100 percent	100 percent	100 percent	100 percent	100 percent
Other's	1,030,320	303,190	32,248	18,795	1,384,553
	19 percent	51 percent	9 percent	8 percent	21 percent
Head's	4,424,404	297,131	313,915	208,808	5,244,257
	81 percent	49 percent	91 percent	92 percent	79 percent

Note: The number of children in the population is estimated here on the basis of the household's migration type. The total number of children (aged 0–19) is then divided according to whether they are identified in the HIES as the head's children or not.

Source: Authors' calculations based on the HIES 2009/10.

the lowest proportion of children in this age bracket, 24 percent); (2) parents tend to leave behind older children and go abroad (39 percent is the highest among all migration types); (3) the above pattern in which migration is delayed until children become older and more independent is reversed in the case of the internal migration of parents; (4) the child age profile of households with no migrants is closest to that of households with non-parent migrants; and (5) the importance of Definition 2 is highlighted by the fact that only 92 percent of the children in households in which the parents have migrated are reported as the head's children.

Figure 8.2 presents the relationship between parental migration and the education of children by looking at the school dropout rates of their children. The dropouts are identified by the category 'attended in past'.[8] The pie diagrams in the top row illustrates that the school dropout rate among children whose parents have internationally migrated is 9.9 percent. This rate is marginally lower than the rate for households with no migrants (10.2 percent), but is higher than in households in which parents have internally migrated. This suggests that international, as opposed to internal, migration of parents is associated with higher dropout rates among children left behind. We analyze these results further according to gender in the bottom row in Figure 8.1. In summary, the six gendered pie charts confirm the following: (1) father-migration, whether internal or international, reduces dropout rates, whereas mother-migration increases it; (2) the above effect is even more accentuated when the mother migrates abroad; (3) there is no difference in the impact of father-migration according to whether the destination is internal or international; and (4) this impact is clearly migration related and not headship related (see that male and female headed nonmigrant households have identical pie diagrams). These are all extremely valuable findings when attempting to construct the parent-migration impact on children. However, the dropout rates of children do not say much about the impact of parental migration on the vast majority of Sri Lankan children (nearly 90 percent) who attend school. It is to this group to which we turn next.

The HIES provides additional information related to the education of children who attend school. We use this information to ascertain whether parental migration is associated with children's education. Of particular interest here is the time taken by children to travel to school. This variable is arguably a function of financial resources allocated by households to children's education. With better allocations for education, a household would be able to make decisions such as (1)

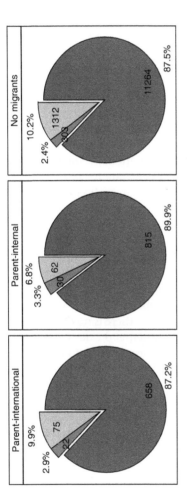
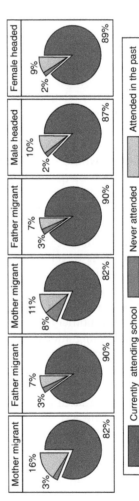

Figure 8.2 Household migration type and school attendance of the head's children in 5–19 age group

Notes: Children who are not attending school pending O/Level or A/Level results and those who have completed A/Level were excluded. Each of the pie diagrams in the top row is analyzed further in the pie diagrams in the bottom row according to gender of the parent-migrant or, in case of nonmigrants, the gender of the head. The percentage or the sum, or both, in each category are also reported. Non-parent migrant households are excluded here.

Source: Author calculations based on HIES 2009/10.

Table 8.3   Comparison of average time taken to travel to school

	Parent International	Parent Internal	No Migrants	Non-Parent Migrants
Parent International				
Parent International	4.6742 (5.4988)[a]			
No Migrants	1.7599 (2.8401)[a]	–2.9142 (–5.1243)[a]		
Non-parent Migrants	2.1960 (2.7264)[a]	–2.4781 (–2.4781)[a]	0.4360 (0.7536)	

Note: The table reports the difference between time taken to travel to school by children in different types of migrant households (left-hand side group minus the group on top) as well as the relevant t-statistic.
[a] significance at 1 percent level.
Source: Authors' calculations based on the HIES 2009/10.

purchasing/renting of houses nearer to schools that are in high demand, and (2) organizing quicker/safer modes of transportation (e.g., private instead of public transport). It is clear that these decisions are reflected in the time the children spend traveling to school.

Here we compare time spent traveling to school across the four types of children identified earlier. This comparison was done using the independent sample *t*-tests, the results of which are reported in Table 8.3. We used HIES data, first to calculate the average time taken by children according to the migration typology. The table reports the average time difference among the four types of children. More specifically, the table reports the average time taken by the vertical categories of children (named in the first column) minus the horizontal categories (named in the first row). The results of Table 8.3 may be summarized as (1) children in households with parents who are abroad spend the least time traveling to school (the estimated differences between their travel time and that of other groups are all statistically significant at the 1 percent level); (2) children with internal migrant parents spend the most time traveling to school; and (3) no statistically significant difference can be seen between travel times of nonmigrant households and non-parent migrant households. If we combine these results with the hypothesis that less time to school means more resources for education, then we have to conclude that the international migration of parents makes more financial resources available for their children's education. It is, however, not straightforward to reconcile this evidence of better financial resources at the disposal of migrant children with the earlier evidence that these children tend to drop out more, at least in the case of mother-migrant families.

There is a wide literature that links household expenditure on education to household remittances and, thereby, to the international migration of parents. Here we use a similar approach to infuse an interesting gender angle into the analysis. This work in based on household-level per-child expenditure on education, which is defined in the log-transformed form as the following:

$$Y_{edu} = \log\left(\frac{\text{Total expenditure on Education}}{\text{Number of Children in the HH}\,(5-19\,\text{age group})}\right)$$

Log transformation squeezes together the larger values in the data set and stretches out the smaller values. Without the log transformation, the distribution of per-child education expenditure would be extremely skewed. This is driven, on the one hand, by a large majority of Sri Lankans who rely on free public education (this includes free textbooks, meals and uniforms), with the result that their per-child education expenditure is very small. On the other hand, there is a much smaller group of households who can afford expensive private education. As a combined effect of these empirical realities, per-child education expenditure has a skewed distribution. Log transformation helps dissipate this skew and render the distribution more normal. This helps the comparison of density distributions of per-child education expenditure across the household types. Figure 8.3 plots three density functions: (1) for households whose mother has migrated abroad, (2) for households whose father has migrated abroad, and (3) as a control case for households with no migrants. The figure suggests that households with migrant mothers spend a lower proportion on education than those with migrant fathers.[9] The figure goes further to suggest that mother-migrant households allocated even less on children's education than households with no migrants. These results emphasize that the message that there are education-related benefits for children left behind is gender nuanced.

Qualitative evidence

The above quantitative results, while revealing some association between better educational outcomes for children with international

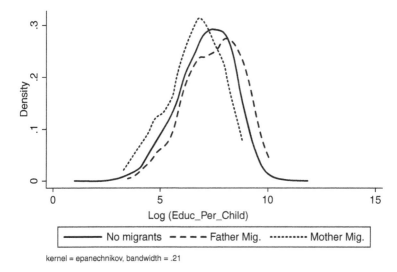

Figure 8.3 Kernel density plots of the logarithm of education expenditure per child (of age 5–19) by parent-migration type of households.

migrant parents, also revealed that father-migration is more compatible with those benefits. This section reexamines those results using a similar mix of scenarios, but through a qualitative lens. Here we look at narratives and other qualitative data on mother-migrant and father-migrant households in separate subsections.

Mother-migration and the children left behind

The qualitative data suggest that the majority of migrant mothers came from poor backgrounds and had resorted to migration as a survival strategy. In many cases, spouses of migrant women had low educational qualifications and were either unemployed or were in low-paying jobs. The majority of these women had chosen Middle Eastern destinations in which to work as housemaids. The mother's migration remittance becomes the main income of the family. The households become so dependent on these remittance incomes that the mothers keep renewing their contracts every two years. The main use of remittances, as identified by the interviewees, was for survival, for children's education, for buying a plot of land, and for building a house. Thus, mothers end up being absent from home for extensive periods of time. The majority of migrant mothers who are employed as housemaids in Middle Eastern countries had remitted their families an average of Rs.10,000–18,000 per month.

The proportion of remittance spent on children's school supplies and extra tuition classes varies depending on the children's age and the caregivers perception of the children's educational needs. Many children of migrant mothers attend tuition classes (additional tuition is common among children who attend public schools in Sri Lanka). Many migrant mothers remit money to the child's grandparents or other relatives instead of the child's father. This is to prevent the father from misusing the remittances, which is common. Some grandmothers manage the money while supporting the child's education and try to save some money as well:

> My daughter sends rupees 15,000 per month. About 10,000 is spent for food and other consumables and 2,500 for tuition fees and pocket money for the child. My granddaughter is sitting O/Level this year and grandson is in grade 7. I save 2,500 rupees each month. (Grandmother/Caregiver, age 62, F)

> My wife sends her salary to her mother. I am asked to get rupees 12,000 from her mother. It's enough for me and my son. I pay 1,600 for my son's tuition fees. The rest is spent on our monthly living expenses. (Father/Caregiver, age 38, M)

The mother's migration also has a positive impact on children's educational outcomes if the father plays a supportive role and manages child-care and the remittances:

> I passed my grade 5 scholarships examination this year. Now I live with my father. He does cooking and my laundry, and takes me to school and tuition classes. (Child of migrant mother, age 10, M)

Children of migrant mothers in our sample, especially the boys, tend to dropout after GCE O/L as they are keen to engage in a job to support their families and reduce the burden on their mothers. It may be possible to identify this as an effect of social/cultural remittances. Such social/cultural remittances with negative impacts on education have been reported before (Kandel and Kao 2001). All the children interviewed disliked the separation from their mothers, but they got used to it by constantly reminding themselves of the economic benefits of remittance.

International migration of fathers: the qualitative results
The fathers in the sample had migrated for higher wages and a higher standard of living than had the mothers. In contrast to the mothers,

all the migrant fathers had been employed before migration. With the recent initiatives by the GoSL, even the destination countries that the fathers choose are different from the mothers: South Korea, Malaysia, Italy and several other countries. Males are employed in higher-paid jobs, for example, as technicians, drivers and professionals. Many wives of migrant males had a higher level of education (senior secondary and above). The majority of wives are housewives, and they are expected to manage the household and perform childcare activities. Remittances were the only source of income for these families, as the wives were not employed. Poor families of migrant fathers also spent remittances on household survival, buying lands and building houses, and largely on educating children.

In-depth interviews with children, caregivers and schoolteachers reveal that the father's overseas migration has had a positive influence on children's school enrolment and educational outcomes. In fact, these children were much better off, educationally, than the children of nonmigrants, and of migrant mothers. This is, therefore, a sound confirmation of the quantitative evidence presented in the previous section. In fact, the case studies do more: they provide unambiguous evidence of a causal relationship between parental migration and children's education. For example, the case studies identify three reason why the international migration of fathers may lead to better education for the children left behind: (1) caregiving is done mainly by mothers; (2) a higher level of education of the primary caregiver (mother's education); (3) a higher amount of remittances received from migrant fathers, leading to high investment in the children's education; (4) a relatively higher quality of schools that the children attend; (5) the presence of extended family and a strong kinship support system; and (6) frequent communication of the father with the family and children left behind.

> Children of father-migrant families are better-off than children of mother-migrant families because children are emotionally closer to the mothers than to the fathers. (GN officer)

> Male-migrant families do not generate negative impacts on children's education as the mother is at home and she takes care of the children. Mothers are keen on children's education. They come to school frequently and attend regular parents' meetings. (Schoolteacher)

> We don't feel lonely. All our neighbors are relatives. If I/we need anything, they help; for example, taking the children to tuition classes. My husband calls every day. (Wife of male-migrant)

Remittances from migrant fathers are the primary, often only, income of these families. Children are able to appreciate the need for their fathers to work abroad, and they have adjusted to the situation by becoming closer to the mother and other relatives:

> I know he goes to make life better for us. That's the reason why we can continue our education – my elder sister is in medical college, and I am doing my A/Levels. We need more than 20,000 rupees for tuition fees and hostel fees per month. My mother is a housewife. So we heavily depend on our father's salary. My father calls twice a week. He asks about our studies. We share everything with him. I feel he is with us. Grandmother and grandfather stay with us. They also support us. (Child of father-migrant, age 17, F)

Summary of qualitative results

The key message from the qualitative data is that the socioeconomic backgrounds of father-migrant households are relatively higher than that of mother-migrant households. The reasons for migration and the final outcome from it, including the educational outcome for the children left behind, are determined by these differences. For example, differences between the school dropout rates, per-child expenditure on education and so forth are all related to this. Left-behind children of migrant parents could be argued to experience 'thinner' agency, that is, to act within very restrictive contexts with few viable alternatives. Yet, the description of their lives over space and time captures a dynamic and situated agency, which becomes activated and manifest at the point of interacting with their parents' moving-as-life-response to changing circumstances *within a life course trajectory*. Thus, research such as this should be extra cautious in interpreting quantitative results that ostensibly attribute the migration of mothers to the negative education outcomes among the left-behind children as passive recipients of remittances. The qualitative data makes it clear that the reasons are not that simple and highlight that more could be at work here: negative outcomes are in fact a reflection of the continued manifestation of poor socioeconomic standing of the mother-migrant families.

Recent policy initiatives targeting the children left behind

Even though there are government and nongovernment organizations working with women and children in Sri Lanka, none of them are exclusively responsible for the welfare of the children left behind. While this is indicative of the level of commitment and sensitivity to the issues faced by these children, it does create conditions that are more practical in nature. For example, even though the SLBFE under its mandate to project the 'families' of migrants has set up a program targeting the welfare of the children left behind in Sri Lanka, they are clearly not pressed hard enough to make the desired results happen.

The program conducted by the SLBFE has an education component that includes a scholarship program, training programs and a health component with limited intervention on health issues faced by the children. While this program has the potential to strengthen the positive impacts of the international migration of parents on their children's well-being, some officers at the SLBFE are skeptical about whether this has been achieved. They pointed out that there are crucial informational bottlenecks that prevent a fuller implementation of this program. For instance, the communication gaps among SLBFE, the caregivers and the migrated parents has prevented the benefits of this program from reaching as many as one-third of the eligible children. Although all officials acknowledge the devastating effect of a lack of information, even now there is no database on children left behind. We were told about information-gathering methods such as collecting information through schools and open advertisements, which have failed to register adequate information coverage. A better method would be to gather information at the time of the migrant parent's departure or at the time of his/her registering with SLFBE, but the information sheet used at these points does not include information about the children who are left behind.

The lack of information is a problem in other ways also. For instance, the key informants in this study kept emphasizing the difficulty in identifying the main caregiver of the children left behind. This is mainly because parents make informal arrangements with potential caregivers that are hard, if not impossible, to monitor. The violation of verbal agreements between migrated parents and caregivers creates conditions that negatively impact the children. Confirming these facts, the chief executive officer of NCPA highlighted the need for having legally enforceable agreements between migrated parents and caregivers that can help enhance child protection.

In order to establish a national policy on international labor migrants, a National Advisory Committee on Labour Migration (NACLM) is being formulated with the involvement of various governmental and nongovernmental stakeholders. A key objective of this committee is to provide effective protection and services to migrant workers and their families who are left behind. As such, the committee was seen in recent months pushing important policy decisions, particularly in relation to female international migrant workers. The GoSL has now imposed minimum standards for women migrant workers. As an example, the minimum age for women who seek foreign employment as housemaids was recently increased from 18 years to 21 years, and now there is even a maximum limit of 40 years. Further, women with children aged five or below are prohibited from overseas employment. Those seeking overseas employment are now required to have a minimum of level 3 qualification on the National Vocational Qualification (NVQ).

The present research, which provided quantitative evidence emphasizing that the migration of mothers is associated with low educational outcomes for their children, gives limited support to these policy decisions. However, as mentioned earlier, these quantitative results should be interpreted carefully. If, for example, mother-migration is a reflection of the premigration vulnerability of her family, then putting laws in place to prevent mothers from migrating will in fact put these children in even more dire conditions.

Conclusion

This paper looked at the welfare of children left behind by Sri Lankan migrants and interpreted it as an assessment of the impact of globalization on these children. It offers an innovative contribution to the emerging literature on migration and globalization through an exploration of children's and families' engagement in migration in response to changing global opportunities and constraints. The study's multitemporal and mixed-methods approach makes it possible to explore how migration intersects with individual and family life course trajectories, and to capture the ways in which children in different relationships to migration change and adapt to different circumstances over time. The lives of children, including those left behind, and their families are embedded in migratory circuits that capture the 'global' dynamism of complex migration.

Previous literature on Sri Lankan migrations had repeatedly highlighted the negative aspects of this experience. We too observed similar patterns when the children of all international migrants were pooled together. For instance, the welfare levels (measured here exclusively along educational parameters) of children of international migrants were inferior to those of internal migrants and nonmigrant parents. However, in contrast to the previous studies, our data was rich enough to separate the results according the gender of the migrant parent. It revealed that negative welfare outcomes were more common among mother-migrant households. By synthesizing these quantitative results with the qualitative results, we were able to expose a selection bias in mother-migrant households. In other words, households in which mothers decided to migrate had poorer socioeconomic backgrounds well before the migration took place. It is this ex-ante backwardness that is picked up in most analyses as negative migration impacts, and often erroneously identified as ex-post migration impacts.

It must be emphasized that this research must not be interpreted as evidence in support of preventing mothers from migration. To the contrary, we were able to observe that they in fact are the most in need of additional income such as remittances. Our results suggest that the experience of mother-migration can be made a beneficial experience by ensuring that they obtain better-paid jobs and leave their children in good hands. In this light, certain policy measures taken by GoSL make sense and are encouraging, but much remains to be done. In fact, quite a lot is being done to target the welfare of the children left behind. But our interviews with officers in charge of these programs gave the impression that these efforts were made in the dark, without knowing whom to target. Thus, the most important issue in relation to the welfare of children left behind boils down to making them more visible in the statistics.

Notes

1. Corresponding author: tel: +44 1273915611; email: R.Lakshman@ids.ac.uk.
2. In what follows, we show that these numbers are a gross overestimation of international contract labor migration.
3. We thank the Department of Census and Statistics, Sri Lanka, for providing access to this data.
4. The only other migration-related information in the survey is the information on remittance incomes.
5. No separate code is available in the HIES to identify the head's grandchildren, who are coded as *Other Relative*.
6. See Perera (2009) and footnote 5 of Perera and Jampaklay (2011) for more details on this.
7. Grama Niladari (GN) Divisions are the lowest level (at the village level) of regional administration in Sri Lanka. Each GN Division has a GN officer who is responsible for the village-level administration. Several GNs together make up a DS division, which is the next highest level of regional administration, followed by the district, which comprises several DS divisions.
8. Section 2 of the HIES includes children awaiting O/Level and A/Level results, as well as those who finished A/Levels in this category. But we filtered these out before doing this analysis.

9. Although this is evident through visual inspection, it can also be confirmed using the Kolmogorov–Smirnov test, which is superior to the classic t-test. The two sample K–S test statistic between the distributions of mother-migrants and father-migrants in Figure 8.3 is 0.2896 ($p < 0.01$). In other words, Figure 8.3 suggests that the density of father-migrant households stochastically dominates that of mother-migrant households.

References

Adams, R. H., and Cuecuecha, A. (2010) 'Remittances, Household Expenditure and Investment in Guatemala', *World Development*, 38(11), 1626–1641.

Asis, M. (2006) 'Living with Migration: Experiences of Left-behind Children in the Philippines', *Asian Population Studies*, 2(1), 45–67.

Baland, J. M., and Robinson, J. A. (2000) 'Is Child Labor Inefficient?', *Journal of Political Economy*, 108(4), 663–679.

Basu, K., and Van, P. H. (1998) 'The Economics of Child Labor', *American Economic Review*, 412–427.

Castaneda, E., and Buck, L. (2011) 'Remittances, Transnational Parenting, and the Children Left Behind: Economic and Psychological Implications', *The Latin Americanist,* 55, 85–110, <http://www.childmigration.net/Castaneda_Buck_2012> Accessed October 14, 2012.

Chami, R., Jahjah, S., and Fullenkamp, C. (2005) 'Are Immigrant Remittance Flows a Source of Capital for Development?', *IMF Staff Papers*, 52(1), 55–81.

Cheran, R. (2003) *Diaspora Circulation and Transnationalism as Agents for Change in the Post Conflict Zones of Sri Lanka*, Berghof Foundation, <http://www.berghof-peacesupport.org> Accessed October 20, 2012.

Collyer, M., and Wimalasena, P. (2007) 'Linking Migration Sub-systems in Sri Lanka', *Sri Lanka Journal of Population Studies*, 10, 25–47.

D'Emilio, A. L., Cordero, B., Bainvel, B., Skoog, C., Comini, D., Gough, J., Dias, M., Saab, R., and Kilbane, T. (2007) *The Impact of International Migration: Children Left Behind in Selected Countries of Latin America and the Caribbean* (New York: UNICEF) < http://www.unicef.org/socialpolicy/index_46050.html> Accessed April 17, 2014.

Das, D. K. (2009) *Two Faces of Globalization: Munificent and Malevolent* (Cheltenham and Camberley: Edward Elgar Publishing).

De Haas, H. (2005) 'International Migration, Remittances and Development: Myths and Facts', *Third World Quarterly*, 2(8), 1269–1284.

Dollar, D., and Kraay, A. (2002) 'Growth is Good for the Poor', *Journal of Economic Growth*, 7(3), 195–225.

Durand, J., Parrado, E., and Massey, D. S. (1996) 'Migradollars and Development: A Reconsideration of the Mexican Case', *International Migration Review*, 30(2), 423–444.

Edwards, A. C., and Ureta, M. (2003) 'International Migration, Remittances, and Schooling: Evidence from El Salvador', *Journal of Development Economics*, 72(2), 429–461.

Eelens, F., Schampers, T., and Speckmann, J. D. (1992) *Labour Migration to the Middle East: From Sri Lanka to the Gulf* (Cardiff: Kegan Paul International).

Graham, E., and Jordan, L. P. (2011) 'Migrant Parents and the Psychological Well-Being of Left-Behind Children in Southeast Asia', *Journal of Marriage and Family*, 73(4), 763–787.

Graham, E., Jordan, L. P., Yeoh, B., Lam, T., and Asis, M. (2012) 'Transnational Families and the Family Nexus: Perspectives of Indonesian and Filipino Children Left Behind by Migrant Parent(s)', *Environment and Planning A*, 44, 793–815.

Jayathilake, D. (2010) *From Pot to Fire: A Glimpse into the World of Those Trafficked in Sri Lanka* (Colombo, Sri Lanka: ILO).

Kandel, W., and Kao, G. (2001) 'The Impact of Temporary Labor Migration on Mexican Student Outcomes', *International Migration Review*, 35(3), 1205–1231.

Kuhn, R. (2006) 'The Effects of Fathers' and Siblings' Migration on Children's Pace of Schooling in Rural Bangladesh', *Asian Population Studies*, 2(1), 69–92.

Levitt, P. (1998) 'Social Remittances: Migration-Driven Local-Level Forms of Cultural Diffusion', *International Migration Review*, 32(4), 926–948.

Levitt, P., and Lamba-Nieves, D. (2011) 'Social Remittances Revisited', *Journal of Ethnic and Migration Studies*, 37(1), 1–22.

Milanovic, B. (2003) 'The Two Faces of Globalization: Against Globalization As We Know It', *World Development*, 31(4), 667–683.

Perera, S. (2009) *International Contract Labor Migration and Children Left Behind in Sri Lanka: The Impact on Children's Education*, PhD Thesis, Mahidol University.

Perera, S., and Jampaklay, A. (2011) 'International Migration and Children Left Behind: Impacts on Children's School Enrolment in Sri Lanka', *Sri Lanka Journal of Population Studies*, 12/13, 81–100.

Piper, N. (2008) 'Feminisation of Migration and the Social Dimensions of Development: The Asian Case', *Third World Quarterly*, 29(7), 1287–1303.

Roongshivin, P. (1985) 'Some Socio-economic Consequences of Thailand's Labor Migration to the Middle East' in United Nations Economic and Social Commission for Asia and the Pacific (UNESCAP) *International Migration in the Pacific, Sri Lanka and Thailand* (Bangkok, Thailand: United Nations).

Save the Children (2006) *Left Behind, Left Out: The Impact on Children and Families of Mother Migrating for Work Abroad* <http://www.crin.org> Accessed April 17, 2014.

Sirkeci, I., Cohen, J. H., and Ratha, D. (2012) *Migration and Remittances during the Global Financial Crisis and Beyond* (Washington: World Bank Publications).

SLBFE (2010) *Annual Statistical Report of Foreign Employment*. Sri Lanka Bureau of Foreign Employment <http://www.slbfe.lk/> Accessed October 14, 2012.

World Bank (2005) *Global Development Finance: Mobilizing Finance and Managing Vulnerability* <http://www.worldbank.org>.

World Bank (2011) *Migration and Remittances* <http://go.worldbank.org/0IK1E5K7U0> Accessed April 17, 2014.

9
Ways of Being a Child in a Dispersed Family: Multiparenthood and Migratory Debt between France and Mali (Soninke Homeland)

Élodie Razy

Introduction

Although literature on child migration has developed considerably over the last decade, it has tended to focus on intra-African migration and one-way south to north migration (Razy and Rodet 2012). The themes of north to south and circular childhood migration remain understudied, and its educational, social and cultural objectives are mostly ignored. Although children are at the heart of family practices (Basch et al. 1994; Rouse 2002), the nature and function of the children's mobility within migrant families to the family, and the community more broadly, in the process of transmission and reproduction as well as social and cultural change has been overlooked. A transnational perspective has developed (Baldassar and Merla 2014; Bryceson and Vuorela 2002; Levitt and Waters 2006; Mazzucato and Schans 2011; Olwig 2007; Parreñas 2005), but family and kinship dynamics have not been an important feature of the research, particularly in Africa (Grillo and Mazzucato 2008). Similarly, the ethnographical data and efforts at conceptual clarification have long been absent even though the notion of the 'transnational family' domi-nates[1]. Indeed, the criteria of membership and the morphology of the 'transnational family' are rarely specified (Le Gall 2005), and local family structures are often ignored. The family is defined as nuclear or extended, and is synonymous with 'blood ties' in a Euro-American-centered sense even though 'nonblood ties' can be included, as Bryceson and Vuorela (2002) state. The local definition of consanguinity and the kinship system (the rules of filiation, alliance, germanity or residence, attitude systems, the institution of fosterage and pseudo-kinship), and also practical kinship have only a peripheral place (Van Djik 2002).

Child migration in Africa generally takes place in migrant societies (De Bruijn et al. 2001; De Bruijn and Brinkman 2011), even though movements are accentuated by circumstances and fosterage (Alber 2003; Goody 1982; Lallemand 1993). Structural reasons for independent child migration are related to work (Castle and Diarra 2003; Grier 2004; Hashim and Thorsen 2011; Lord 2011), survival (Einarsdóttir 2006), education and training.[2] These reasons are inseparable from each other, and are sometimes associated with issues of alliance or pledges related to education and domestic work (Castle and Diarra 2003; Lallemand 1988, 1993; Razy 2007c). Emancipation and social mobility are the keywords of scholarship on child migration that is classified as 'independent'[3], but the notion of independence is often unquestioned. The processes of decision-making about migration are complex: children generally migrate with their parents or other kin (or follow them). Where this is not the case, departure is frequently approved or known by one of the parents or a member of the family circle. Most migrant children are not young persons who wish to assert their independence by breaking away from their family, as can be the case for older youth, who are mostly incorrectly referred to as 'children' within the academic literature, yet who may not be considered as children in local terms (Rich 2010; Thorsen 2007; Timera 2001; Ungruhe 2010). This confusion between children, adolescents and young people makes the youngest of them invisible, while allowing to be referred to as part of a whole, an extended category (0–18 years or even older) endowed with agency, yet vulnerable and inevitably deserving protection. Such a process can be seen as a lack of knowledge about various local divisions of life span around the world, and reflects the influence of the psychology of development within a universalized, static political framework (considering the child as a minor regardless of whether he/she is 6, 11 or 16 years of age). The distinction between children and young people, which is culturally and socially relevant in many contexts, is rarely subjected to in-depth analysis. Finally, removing contradictions from debates about the vulnerable and victimized child, the issue of the child's agency and his/her voice (Ensor and Gozdziak 2010; Lancy 2012; Razy and Rodet 2012; Szulc et al. 2012) requires us to consider the child as a thinking and sentient subject who acts – sometimes by not doing anything visible, but simply waiting – by taking account of the contradictory structural, social and cultural constraints that weigh down upon him/her. Contextualizing the child's voice – sometimes without the spoken word – by moving away from a universalist vision of childhood can mark the beginning of an ethical reflection on the conditions and risks associated with given words (Guillermet 2010) such as agency, its possible degrees, nature and expression.[4]

In this chapter, I focus on the movement of children between Europe (France) and Africa (the Soninke homeland, Mali), a phenomenon that has been neglected in the academic literature. The Soninke are the descendants of the inhabitants of Wagadu's kingdom (or Ghana), which declined in the eleventh century. The issue of Soninke migrations cannot be addressed without considering the original dispersion myth as an illustration of the structural and cyclical nature of the migratory phenomenon, which tends to speak of the 'dispersed family' (Dieterlen and Sylla 1992; Manchuelle 1997; Meillassoux et al. 1967; Pollet and Winter 1971). This chapter poses the question What does the movement of children mean for the children and families concerned, in the context of the long history of migration within the Soninke people and their relations with France, its former colonial power?

My fieldwork between Mail and France over an 11-year period from 1996 to 2007[5] is centered on the time I spent examining family and children's practices and having discussions about practices and, especially, spontaneous discussion. Theoretically, exemplarity takes precedence over representativeness by an in-depth and full-length study of individual cases (Fainzang 1994). In order to address all the dimensions of the phenomenon in context, it is also essential to call upon general anthropology and more specialized subfields (the anthropology of childhood and of migration) and to reach beyond the opposition between social and cultural anthropology (Godelier 2007). Through an in-depth longitudinal study of specific case studies, I try to explain how recurrences across different individuals reveal what people share beyond physical, cultural and social spaces. My approach is in line with multisited ethnography (Marcus 1995, 1998). The term 'locality' is, however, preferred to 'site' for local territorial involvement claimed by the participants (area, village, town, region, country). The term 'network' implies the structuring of various localities, individuals or groups.

By exploring a range of situations as demonstrated by extracts from cases of child migration, I will show that analyzing movement is relevant not only in order to have a better grasp of the role this plays in the construction of children's migration, identities and destinies but also for what it reveals about northern and southern societies. It shows how child mobility functions for children and for the social reproduction of the group. After analyzing the dominant perception of this migration in literature and highlighting any shortcomings, I will look at two types of circular movement by children in greater detail, as well as its gendered character and purpose. This chapter reveals short- and longer-term child mobility, 'to-ing and fro-ing', or what the editors refer to as mobility-in-migration, which extends concepts of transnational families as bilocated (here and there) in order to capture children's small, short-term movements and longer movements, their comings and goings so that children's lives are lived, to some extent, in 'in-between' spaces. In this respect, the chapter contributes new insights into how children in the dynamic, responsive nature of historic migration trajectories respond to changing global migration regimes. I will then show how the anthropology of kinship and the notions of multiparenthood and 'migratory debt' enable us to better understand child migration. This proposal focuses on the embeddedness of child mobility within child, family and historic migratory arcs as personal and collective objectives are pursued through migration. Finally, I will examine the historical background of these factors.

Soninke waves of migration between France and Mali and Mali and France: where are the children?

In this so-called 'caste-ridden' society with its long-standing Muslim tradition, there is historical and demographic evidence of the migratory phenomenon that has molded society during the precolonial, colonial and postcolonial periods (Manchuelle 1997). Malian men's enlistment in the military navy at the beginning of the twentieth century and later in the merchant navy paved the way for emigration to France at the end of the 1950s. This movement intensified in the 1960s due to the high demand for labor in Europe. Migrants were single men who sent money back home, both to pay for the day-to-day upkeep of their families and to develop religious, health and education infrastructures (Barou 1978; Daum 1998; Quiminal 1991; Timera 1996).

This system was destabilized by new French immigration laws. In 1974, following the 'closing of borders', migrants continued to enter France illegally. The law on family reunification was promulgated; its aim was to allow immigrants to live as a family, subject to certain restrictive conditions with regard to resources and housing. Most men working in France preferred or had to leave their wives and children at home and those who were legally in France could visit them regularly, thus perpetuating this migratory model over time. In practice, migration took more varied forms. Women arrived (legally or illegally), ordered in most cases to leave their firstborn children with their husband's patrilineage. They arrived in France one after another or took turns migrating, entering monogamous or polygamous households. The husband could decide to bring just one of his wives or to send one of them back at a given time (Quiminal 2002; Razy 2006). Children were born and grew up in France, and some of them were to be at the heart of 'new forms' of circular migration – from the mid-1980s to the present day. Others, born in Mali, would legally or illegally arrive in France between the ages of 15 and 20, according to the conditions of family reunification and current nationality law.

Immigration and nationality laws introduced by successive governments in France produced disparities (Fassin et al. 1997) that were reflected within families in which siblings did not have the same legal status. In 1973 (before the 'closing of borders'), the French government reformed the sole right in order to automatically grant French nationality to children born in France (regardless of whether one or both of their parents were French citizens). From the mid-1980s, immigration became an important issue in the political arena, while the extreme right-wing party's vote (Front National) increased. Subsequent legislation took place in an ambivalent context in which the status of children born to foreign parents became a crucial and sensitive matter.[6] The *Pasqua-Méhaignerie Law* of July 22, 1993, obliged children born in France to foreign parents to officially ask for nationality between the ages of 16 and 21 years. A further reform, the *Guigou Law* (September 2, 1998), balanced blood and sole right: a child acquired French nationality on his/her 18th birthday if he/she had lived temporarily or regularly in France for up to five years between the ages of 11 and 18 years. If his/her parents agreed, a child could ask for French nationality when he/she was 13 years old. On reaching 16 years of age, a parent's permission was no longer needed.

On the whole, European immigration policies have become hard line and led to a diversification of migratory strategies in the villages of the Senegal River Valley. Barou (2001: 316) describes a 'modern vision of the *noria*',[7] citing the example of a man who 'scheduled' the birth of a child in France in order to then send him to the village, where he invested in his schooling so that he could later replace him in France. The father combined family upbringing in the village with his schooling and the acquisition of French nationality.[8] This example shows how the child can become a resource that can be fitted into the political context.

With an emphasis on 'second generations' and their integration into France, sociological literature has neglected the migration by the children and young descendants of African migrants.[9] French-speaking academics have done little to pursue the possibilities opened up by transnational studies, which have from their part failed to take into account the practical aspects of family dynamics and the children's role.[10] This has been true of migrations by children of Soninke origin. These children have only appeared in the literature in recent years, just as women remained invisible for a long time, due, in particular, to their limited presence in the public sphere (Kuczynski and Razy 2009; Razy and Baby-Collin 2011) and to researchers' lack of interest in women's and children's lives in-between between nation-states and social and cultural spaces, especially in the case of Africa (Grillo and Mazzucato 2008).[11] Migration is discussed briefly in terms of 'returns', focusing on the comings and goings and the family dynamics involved in the rotation of spouses (Bodin and Quiminal 1991; Poiret 1996: 448; Quiminal 1995), sometimes due to illness (Rezkallah and Epelboin 1997) and also highlighting the conflicts between generations and lineal relatives. Authors mention the threat of the return of women and/or children and/or adolescents[12], which is described as a 'sanction' or 'punishment' (Pradelles de Latour 2001; Quiminal 2002); the strategies for marrying off daughters (Nicollet 1992; Quiminal and Bodin 1993; Quiminal et al. 1997; Timera 1999); and the imagined return of parents to their homeland (Poiret 1996).[13]

This overview raises questions about the way in which women's and children's circular movements are taken into consideration and also shows the ambiguity of the concepts used, which in turn is evidence of the political dimension of this research and of the difficulty in Europe, particularly in France, of thinking politically about multiple identity, multiparenthood (Razy 2010) and changing living arrangements.

In this first section, I drew attention to the gaps in current understanding and how terms such as 'returns' and 'punishment', references to origin, and more theoretical concepts such as 'transnational family' and 'independent child migration' fail to capture a circular movement of children, which I will now examine as a particular type of migration that affects children, regardless of the length of time, the frequency or the stage of life at which it occurs. This is thus a shift away from an instantaneous compound logic regarding migration based on a sedentary vision (here or over there/now) toward a certain in-betweenness and repetition – or potential for it which can turn it into a circular movement. Indeed, without necessarily occurring or being repeated, this circular movement is usually present in the minds of those involved (children or adults), as it is part of the journey's and migration's imaginary based on men's experience. In addition, the choice of this concept also serves here to signify the placing of the child's mobility into the institutional framework that represents the so-called "traditional" circulation of children.

To do so, I want to explore a range of situations illustrated by extracts from children's accounts in order to gain an understanding of the details and objectives of child movement. This will make it possible to establish a provisional typology, useful for addressing the political, symbolic and imaginary question about the status and identity of the children.

Understanding the morphology of the movement of children

Holiday periods

A first type of movement of children involves one or several trips from France to the country of their parents' origin, Mali, during the school summer holidays, with or without a parent, and a return to France for the start of school in September.

Moussa S. is the third of five children of Kadyatou S., none of whom has ever been to Mali.[14] His mother, who has lived in France for 18 years without ever visiting her family in Mali, has always been emotionally very close to Moussa. He was 14 years old when he agreed to visit Mali with his mother. In his mother's village, everyone spoke Soninke, so it was not easy for him to communicate. He slept and ate with his mother. Sometimes he became a little bored: 'I wanted to go home, I was fed up, I missed Dad'. With his 'brothers' (his agnatic uncle's sons[15]) he played football, went to other villages on foot or on horseback, and once went into the fields: 'I tried to pull the plough, but it was too hard for me so I asked to hold the animal. They said as a joke that I had no strength and couldn't play football. It's tougher than at home, more brutal'. As a joke they called him *'lembure'* (bad child) and 'French' and said: 'Children from France are incapable, they don't know how to do farm work'.

Moussa found that he had grown through this 'beautiful experience'. He had matured and gained some perspective. He spoke about how lucky he was to be in France, and compared his life there to the difficulties and inequalities that exist in Mali. At the end of the trip his 'French' identity was reaffirmed both in his personal reflection and in the views of others in the village and the country: 'I feel French but a small part of me is Malian. When I came back I felt different. I felt more like I was in Mali than in France and then I felt French again'.

Moussa's account shows that the journey serves, in part, as a rite of passage (improving language, learning new skills, playing in a new way, experiencing new feelings and belongings) that changes his status both in France and in Mali from his own, his mother's and his family's perspective.

Even though his intention is to revisit Mali, he did not go back there since I met him. He is unlike other children whom I met who visit their families there every year or two. In the last case, the circular movement is actualized whereas in Moussa's case, it remains potential.

Long-term stays

A second type of movement from France to Mali does not involve a return at the start of the school year, but, as is often assumed in the literature (cited earlier), it is not systematically synonymous with 'punishment'. The stay generally exceeds three months, has a formative dimension and is a key part of the child's upbringing. In some cases it is a sort of rite of initiation. Resistance by children is rare and virtually impossible in Mali. The sentiments expressed by the children whom I met (especially those under ten years of age) revealed a sense of injustice and sadness. Their only way of expressing agency was to ask adult outsiders for help in order to return to France (see case studies below: Bintou and Manda B.; Mamadou C.).

Children born in France can be taken to the village irrespective of their gender, between the ages of two and three years – the usual weaning age in the village – to be raised there in their own patrilineage or that of their mother. Here, the departure takes place before socialization outside of the family begins, that is, before the child starts nursery school. At that age, the child is not familiar with the French language nor with the social and cultural codes that can be experienced at school (body techniques, table manners, relationships, play and games).

The T. family: The six children of the first wife of Mr. T., who were born in France, were brought to the village at two or three years of age, in the order of their births. The boys went to school there, but the girl did not. In 1996, at the age of 16, the eldest, a girl named Jeneba, arrived in France as the second wife of a Soninke man with whom she already had a two-year-old daughter. She did not speak French. In 1998, her husband died, and she was drawn into conflict with her cowife, with whom she lived in France. Her father took her into his home again in France. A year later, she married a young Soninke man, took classes in French and gave birth to a second child. Three of her five brothers arrived in 2000 at the ages of 17, 18 and 19, and the remaining two arrived in 2002 at the ages of 17 and 18. All of them have French citizenship as a result of being born in France to a French father who had been born in a former French colony.[16]

A key difference in the mobility of children, which is attributable to gender, appears in the two stages described below when the girls are aged between seven and nine years, and for boys, when they are between 10 and 13 years. The varying lengths of contact time at school that is accepted by certain families within the host society depend on male and female roles, to which individuals must learn to conform, particularly through their upbringing.

It is mainly girls who leave France for Mali between the ages of seven and nine. In this instance, they learn how to become a wife and mother. In France, they have gained some basic skills at school (reading, writing and arithmetic), and are at an age when they are regularly asked to carry out domestic chores or look after the younger children. Here the 'traditional upbringing' of the girl, which has already been partially completed within the family in France (cooking, housework, childcare), is perfected in a process of assimilation in the village in Mali where the child learns on a day-to-day basis through repetition and imitation. Investment in the schooling of little girls and young girls varies greatly. It ranges from the total absence of any schooling to schooling of varying lengths of time at the *medersa* (or 'Koranic school') or the 'French school'.

Aminata K., aged nine, traveled from France to Mali for the summer holidays and did not go home with her mother in September. The little girl did not know what was planned for her. She said that she was now ashamed to speak French and that she did not like the food in the village: 'The only thing I like eating is milk and coffee', she said, showing partial identification with the community. She believed people were kind to her, but she felt sad. On arrival, she already knew how to cook, do housework and look after children, but she had learned how to 'go to collect water and grind millet' in the village, as she told me.[17]

Girls can then get married and move to another village, town or African country, or return to France (legally or illegally) at different stages of their lives. In this way they are embedded in a circular movement.

After the divorce of their parents (requested by the mother), Bintou and Manda B. (seven and nine years of age), who were born in France, where they used to live, were brought to the village during holiday periods (in Mali) in 1995 and did not come back to France. They went to school in the village. In 2001, the eldest, who was then 15 years of age, was admitted to High School, but got married during the summer after being beaten (because she had refused this marriage). The two sisters asked for help during the visit of a French representative of a twinning association to the village who planed their trip back. Contact was then made with the mother of the girls (who had remained in

France), and who had not seen them since 1995. In June 2002, they were brought back to France at the ages of 14 years and 16 years respectively, where they were reunited with their mother. The eldest daughter gave birth there, and then started her education again as her younger sister had done.[18]

For boys, this journey from France to the village or town (Bamako) generally takes place later, between the ages of 10 and 13. They include both 'problem boys' (boys with behavioral problems, delinquency and drop-outs) and boys with no problems who, like Mamadou C., have excellent academic grades.

Mamadou C. was 12 in 1997 when he arrived from France to the village to spend a year in the family of his agnatic uncle as his brothers had done before him. I got to know him while doing fieldwork on early childhood. He led a solitary existence, made toys with recycled materials, did not join in with the children of his own age, and did not really play. Mamadou repeated his wish to go back to school in France when he talked to me. He did not go to school in the village. Mamadou finally returned to France after a year spent in the village and went back to school. His younger brothers and sisters will also have this experience, but will not stay as long. At the age of 16, motivated by the desire to get to know their parents' village of origin and to get to know their family, they will stay in the village for two months with their father over the school holidays. In this family, long stays and holidays were experienced in different ways by different siblings.[19]

The D. family. In 1999, at the age of 12, Demba (the eldest sibling) was sent to Mali to 'see the family, to learn how people before him lived their lives and to learn how to be self-sufficient' at the request of his agnatic uncle who was resident in Mali. Against his mother's wishes, he did not return to France at the end of the holidays. After two weeks spent in Bamako with his agnatic aunt (his father's sister), Demba spent a month and a half in the village, where he learned the trade of blacksmith with his agnatic uncle. After going to school in Bamako, he was then joined by his brother in 2000. They both returned (aged 17 and 15, respectively) to their parents' house in France in 2004.[20]

Schooling obtained in France can be supplemented at the *medersa* in the village or town, thus providing a dual education. Between the ages of 10 and 12, boys use to leave the family home to sleep in little collective houses with other boys of their own age, returning only in the daytime for meal. This can be referred to as the 'departure from home of the mother'. Permanently leaving the mother's side, gaining independence and starting work are all challenges that are faced during this time. They still have considerable learning ahead of them, as marriage, which comes later for boys, seems to be less of a concern for parents (Timera 1996).

On the other hand, girls who arrive in the village from France around the age of 13 are on the verge of marriage. The 'educational' aspect of the stay for the youngest girl cited above is limited: the marriage itself will be the equivalent of 'training', but this may be preceded by excision. Although not systematically performed, it is a strong sign of reappropriation by the group through the marking of the body to make the individual conform to the female model of wife and mother.[21] Carrying out this gesture at an advanced age on these girls coming from France restores the rite's initiatory value that it once had but that it has lost because it nowadays takes place within the first weeks of life in the village (Razy 2007a). The procedure involves young girls born in France who are often deemed not to be 'real Soninke' or to be lacking in Soninke identity. As a rite of initiation, excision assumes here a strong social and symbolic dimension: it is an essential prerequisite for marriage.

By the time they 'return' to France, which they left behind at different ages, the children have taken several crucial steps. The boys who return to France still single between the ages of 15 and 19 are deemed to have 'put on trousers'[22]; they have 'become men' and have to work and invest in their school work or training. Girls who have married may have already had children and often arrive after the age of 18. Boys are meant to 'return' one day, but this is not systematic for girls.

The two types of movement of children between France and Mali that were observed are embedded in different ways in an imaginary of circular migration.[23] The general objective of these visits, as stated by the parents, was to 'learn about culture' and 'get to know the family'. In both cases, the children's opinions were rarely solicited, and the movement was chosen for the children by adults. The two situations analyzed raise a number of questions about the identity of the individuals – an identity assigned by the parents, the family, the state; an identity claimed by the child him/herself; an obviously shifting and complex identity which is constructed between distinct spaces – and how a circular movement affects children's lives. The second, the long-term stay, expresses the lineage-based ideology that underlies a specific migratory process: child circular movement plays a crucial role in the multilocal family and, moreover, in the social and cultural organization beyond time and space (alliance, gender-based roles, education etc.). How and why is such a migration possible if not necessary? In the next section, I will try to address these points.

The directions of children's movements
(France/Mali and Mali/France)

Kinship and multiparenthood

While it is increasingly acknowledged in the literature that some children move around, what can be said of the spaces and individuals between which this movement takes place? It takes place between (multilocal) or beyond (translocal)[24] various locations, some of which are considered to be transnational.[25] Rather than speaking in terms of 'transnational social fields' (Basch et al. 1994), 'transnational social spaces' (Faist 1998; Levitt and Glick-Schiller 2004; Pries 1999), or 'imagined communities' (Vuorela 2002), it is more heuristic to produce a precise breakdown of the different levels of meanings employed in the discourse and practices. To do so, I propose to stop using 'transnational' as if it included all possible features of the family. 'Transnational' can then be considered as describing one feature of the family among others. Therefore, I suggest adding to the concept of 'social space'[26] with the concepts of physical – in some cases transnational – cultural, symbolic, cosmological or imaginary spaces (including legal and national definitions).

The movement of people between different parts of the world that, even though they are not unified, share common reference points (as in West Africa, for example) does not raise the same questions as the movement between worlds that are very distinct from each other in terms of kinship, matrimonial alliance, family formation, religion, childhood models and, more broadly, social organization. In Soninke society, in which the kinship system is patrilineal with a light matrilineal influence and in which the residence is patrivirilocal, the power is held by the elder, and the institution of fosterage is very developed. The child is the child of the lineage (Rabain 1994). In contrast, the biological parents are the only people responsible for the child under French law.

Without claiming to provide definitive answers, we should ask the question about how to define the family to which the children belong in order to better understand the spaces mentioned above. The children's family is undoubtedly a dispersed extended family in the image of the aforementioned myth of origin.

What can be said about the individuals involved in these spaces? Firstly, the parenthood approach distinguishes the biological parents from the social parents (Lallemand 1976), both of whom can assume parental functions (Godelier 2004; Goody 1982).[27] Secondly, multiparenthood is part of the institution of kinship (multikinship), which is defined in terms of practices and ideology (terminology, relations, pseudo-kinship, social organization, norms and attitudes) at the junction of several societies in which migratory configurations are concerned. Men and women have left a 'traditional' lineage-based patrilineal society and arrived into a 'modern' cognatic society in which the ideology of the nuclear family is dominant. Movements and fosterage are based on various factors during the life cycle of the children, between different parents or partners (Barou 1991, 2001; Goody 1982; Razy 2006, 2007a).

This dispersed multiparenthood-based configuration involves several kin – related or not – to the child's partners (members of the kin group, friends, neighbors, doctors and nurses, Koranic schoolmasters, teachers, associations' members, pupils, representatives of legal institutions, such as a judge or a state prosecutor, etc.) who are present or absent physically, but who take part in the child's life and make decisions daily or occasionally (see cases below). They later exercise one or several parental functions between the different spaces that, from a distance and at a particular time or period, can inspire conflict or agreement between France and Mali (see Razy 2007b, 2007c for further detail). The biological father and mother are not the only decision-makers: agnatic uncles and paternal and maternal grandparents, as well as other relatives or nonrelatives can play a key role between the two countries. In the D. family, the biological mother and father of Demba were in disagreement, but the agnatic uncle of the child living in Mali, by agreement with the biological father, obtained permission for his classificatory sons to join him there for stays in the village and the capital. The agnatic aunt was the central figure in Bamako, where the two brothers were schooled in French. Also, the time spent in Mali corresponded to the period understood to be between the 'departure from home of the mother', equivalent to a childhood sortie for the boys (around 10–12 years), and the 'wearing the trousers' period (around 15–17 years).[28] Bintou and Manda B. were also the subject of disagreements between parents and family.

It is usually within patrilineage that the instructions are formulated and that decisions concerning the stay, excision or the marriage of some children are taken. These decisions are made by the eldest agnatic uncle, often in opposition to the biological mother and sometimes in agreement with the agnatic aunts, or with the paternal or maternal grandmother and in some cases with the uterine aunts (the sister of the child's mother).

While the concept of multiparenthood allows us to gain a better understanding of the contours of the dispersed family and the place of children within it, it does not fully explain the reasons behind children's movement.

The migratory debt: who are the children?

What I call the 'migratory debt'[29] (Razy 2007c) is that of migrants whose absence, although income generating, nevertheless has repercussions for all areas of family and village life, and is a key concept in the analysis of children's movement that is addressed in this chapter.

The 'repayment' of this migratory debt, apart from covering economic and material aspects (sending money, funding village projects, purchasing consumer goods, building houses, giving gifts) also has a social dimension (movement of women, children and young people, matrimonial alliances between the latter). When family reunification laws were first passed in France, we witnessed the departure of a number of women and the birth of their offspring outside the village. The consequences were initially a form of deprivation of the workforce (domestic work and work in the fields) and of the child-rearing function of the woman within her husband's patrilineage and, to a certain extent, within her own patrilineage. Similarly, the birth of children who belonged to this same patrilineage deprived it of its primacy, particularly in terms of upbringing. The migratory debt that was incurred when the women left was provisionally 'repaid' by the children who were born prior to their mothers' departures and left in the village.

Payment of the debt not only kept the individuals concerned within the kinship network, but it also contributed to the reactivation or maintenance of links within the dispersed family. The general and intergenerational economy of the network is therefore continued. Conversely, payment of the debt can be perceived as an agent of dislocation. This is the case when the fist-born has been left in the village following the mother's departure and cannot, for legal and/or social reasons, rejoin his/her siblings in France. For example, Taata A., a young woman whom I met in Paris in 2007, told me about her elder brother born and left in the village when her mother came to France. Tata's family in France adopted the ideology of the Western nuclear family and was no longer concerned itself with payment of the migratory debt but could not succeed in helping the young boy to come to France. Tata told me the extent to which her older brother, her parents and all the family living in France was suffering from his situation in the village.[30]

The act of taking in children, mostly girls born overseas, followed by their subsequent marriage, can represent the final repayment of this migratory debt.[31] A mother can request her son to send her one of his daughters who was born and grew up in France so that the daughter can help her during her old age in the village before that daughter gets married. This was the case of Aminata K. She was left in the village when she went there during the holidays at the request of her father's mother, who wanted help with her daily chores (cooking, housework, cleaning etc.). There was also the case of Awa G., whose agnatic uncles unsuccessfully opposed her refusal to marry and to go to Mali on holiday. In the Soninke homeland and in the Soninke community in France, people who do not live in the village play as big a part in alliance as those who do. Indeed, in the village, unions are entered into that may place Soninke relatives in France in a position of debt, as their absence does not relieve them from their obligations. Some repay, others do not, thus asserting themselves more in a process of individualization (Marie 1997), which can be closely linked to the 'migrant's status itself (Rabain 2000).

The balance of power that is established between the different players will determine whether the holiday trip takes place or not, whether it is maintained or whether it transforms into a longer stay, involving marriage for the girls and/or excision and 'return' or 'nonreturn' to France. Some parents submit to the authority of the elders, which sometimes takes the form of pressure from the family or village applied from a distance and within the community in France: the women have gone, the children must come back. Other parents agree from the outset to send their children to stay in the village. Mothers may support the plans, be kept out of them or be opposed to them. It would seem that choices relating to children often convey a certain reaffirmation of parental and lineage-based primacy and authority both in France and in the village, as well as a lack of understanding or rejection of the intrusion of the French state in 'private affairs' (Razy 2007b).

To clarify the political, symbolic and imaginary dimension of the migratory debt, it would be useful to deal with the status and identity of the children for whom the type of movement (holidays/long stays) and its objective (learning a trade, domestic or Koranic training, excision, marriage etc.) are indicators. First of all, we must question one of the terms used to describe their movement: 'return'. Do people belong to the country to which they are said to return? Is this place just a physical space or can it also be seen as an 'internal space'? Verbs such as: 'to go home', 'to come back', 'to return' do describe movements, but equally, they identify children and young people in a specific way: 'Soninke', 'Malian', 'French'. Can an individual 'return' to the country of his/her parents, where he/she has never been, when he/she makes a journey at the age of 12? Can an individual 'come back' to France at the age of 16 if he/she has only spent the first two years of his/her life there (Razy 2006)?

The response depends on the individual who is questioned: Are we talking about nationality, identity or a feeling of belonging? Is the person giving his opinion as a French or Malian legislator, the father who lives in France, the family in the village, the child or a young person? An examination of the current situation shows the ambiguity of the status and identity of the children concerned, as exemplified by the practice of excision of young girls in France and in the country of origin. By this act, those who carry out the excisions, the parents and their entourage, signify the fact that the child belongs to the Soninke community and his/ her eventual reappropriation by the latter. Another social environment, formed by volunteers, representatives of educational, medical or legal institutions, can also be called into play, revealing to the child another part of his/her identity.[32]

The first case is that of Assa F., aged eight years, who was threatened with excision during a holiday trip to the village even though her mother had been convicted in France for exercising this practice on her older daughters. This would seem to prove that neither sanction nor monitoring systematically protects the children from these practices. The father, who was very elderly, lived in France. He was first summoned by the school's doctor, and he telephoned the nurse in charge of the community health center in the village to order that his daughter should not be excised. A procedure (involving a thorough examination of the child by the medical authorities before and after the journey, a reminder of the law and prison sentences that can be incurred, the summoning of the father by a judge, and intervention by medical personnel in the village) was carried out on behalf of the different individuals concerned in France and in Mali.

In another case, Fatou J., a young girl of ten years who was not excised, confided to the volunteers who monitored her schooling in France. She was to be sent to the village during the summer without any planned return date (excision was suspected). After various fruitless attempts to discuss the matter with the family, the state prosecutor approved the opening of a file on the case. Measures were announced for a determined period after the father was summoned, and were then lifted by the judge some months later. Here again, a mobilization took place. The girl was not taken to the village, but the rupture between the association's volunteers and social services and the family resulted in the children's total isolation and various aggressive demonstrations by the father and Fatou's elder brothers against the persons involved. The identity implicitly claimed by Fatou when she refused excision did not coincide with her parents' desire for her to become a complete Soninke young girl. Even though the young girl spoke out, the long-term consequences of her act did not work to her advantage. She did not go to Mali, but could not attend the association's activities anymore and was isolated.[33]

I could cite numerous examples of court cases related to excision when criminal sanctions were declared.[34] During the court cases the French state reaffirmed that the parents did not have exclusive rights over their children and pointed out that all the 'children of the nation' (Bonnet et al. 2012) must be treated equally. Here, it was the status of the child and his/her identity that were at the heart of the debate: this child was torn between two countries, between two reference spaces, between different models of childhood. Sometimes, the attachment of the child to the nation-state was manifest or even publicly reclarified, while at other times he/she became the child of the other nation-state (Mali), the child of his/her parents, of his/her lineage or of his/her community who sometimes asks for help without receiving an answer.[35]

For Mamadou C. and Taata A., who are the parents of Moussa S., their children are 'French' because they were born and grew up in France. This does not however mean that those children have permanently left behind the social and cultural constraints of their parents' society, but that they are implicitly or explicitly allowed to make their own choice if they respect cultural and social values (religion, social organization, family). Taata A.'s parents allowed their children (boys and girls) to choose their partner within their cast (*hoore*, noble). Taata told me that one of her sisters married a young Soninke man without knowing exactly where he comes from. Later, the parents explained to their children that the young people were kindred (marrying within the family is particularly valued in the Soninke society). For others (the parents of Assa F. or Fatou J., for example), children must remain fully Soninke (religion, family, excision, alliance, gendered future and lineage power) despite their French nationality. Here, nationality has a practical rather than a social and cultural meaning. In the village, opinion is divided about these 'different children'. Sometimes they remain irreparably 'foreign' – *muukiyugo* (foreign boy), *muukiyaxare* (foreign girl), *muukilemme* (foreign child).[36] Identities that are given and experienced are endlessly renegotiated and conflict with each other over many years.

For the children themselves, the question of identity is raised more frequently in pragmatic and ordinary terms than in an abstract belonging feeling – even though they can mention their parents' social and cultural values as being their own – until it becomes prominent according to gender and age (identity is closely related to marriage). Identity is developed through daily activities and has its roots in an area, a school and specific social relations, but also in the sphere of intimacy, within the family, which is simultaneously a link and a place of expression of origin (visitors, food, clothes, videos). Movements for holiday stays or longer trips between two physical, social, cultural and imaginary reference points form the connection or 'disconnection' of their identity that is part of a multilocal setting.

A new phenomenon?

In conclusion, we must ask ourselves if this phenomenon is a truly new one. The contemporary migrating African child is often associated with the idea of independence on the one hand and with trafficking and exploitation on the other (Donà and Veale 2011; Ensor and Gozdziak 2010; Lancy 2008).[37] It must be noted that the majority of West African child migrations belong to social and historically rooted in families networks (Rodet 2009). The long history of migrations in Africa has provided a model of the spaces within which children migrate beyond borders (De Bruijn and Brinkman 2011; Hashim and Thorsen 2011). These have therefore been at the heart of translocality and multilocality issues (Razy 2010; Rodet 2009) for a long time.[38]

It is indeed the emergence of a new outlook, looking beyond unidirectional migration (toward the West), which is now center stage for reasons that are essentially political and which makes it possible to view this migration as a north-south/south-north movement. This migration is not new, but it is becoming visible, like that of adults, because it is becoming meaningful. We are therefore witnessing its extension, intensification, diversification and 'inversion'. Migration by school children, and later by third-level students, from Africa to Europe (with comings and goings) has been historically the case for the colonial and postcolonial elite (Bourgouin 2011; Vuorela 2002). It is currently becoming 'democratic' due to cheaper air travel and forces of globalization, while North-South child movement is developing in accordance with the intra-African model of sending the child to the family (to the village or to Bamako), in the context of new extra-African family migrations.

It is the diversification of migratory destinations that has given rise to new worlds of meaning that can be legally contradictory (for example, when does a girl become a woman and what is the age at which she can get married?) and to a movement of reciprocal ethnicization of the populations involved, which has already been observed by Whitehouse (2009) within Africa. In Brazzaville, for example, Malian migrants consider Congolese values and their own as 'inimical' and send their children to their village in Mali when they are a few years old in order to protect them.

With regard to child migration, the notion of movement comes back to a system put in place by the adults for the children: the children who stay in Mali for a long time (before leaving later) do not see themselves as the participants and the link within their dispersed family, but find that they are subjected to a situation that they find unjust. The children when on holiday grow more readily into the role they see themselves as having once they become adult (Moussa S.). More generally, there is a certain void that articulates the connections between the two places: in France there are few 'recognized' witnesses of changes in status. A young bride can leave the village and becomes a mother of 6 or 7 children abroad. The same people who live in France do not witness the deaths (their parents' death for example) that occur in the village and modify everyone's status in the family. Only trips abroad make it possible to express, by means of a process of 'space–time condensation', the two phenomena that are usually connected and disconnected by departures: the child is the vector of this updating of relations that is necessary for a certain cohesion of the dispersed family. The contradictions that occur were pointed out by Rouse (2002: 162–163): 'Moreover, the way in which at least some people are preparing their children to operate within a dichotomized setting spanning national borders, suggests that current contradictions will not be solved through a simple process of generational succession'. Conversely, Bourgouin (2011) suggests the emergence of a cosmopolitan individualist identity, (temporarily) free from family constraints. I have shown that children are connected within kinship and history migratory networks and that their own individual migration trajectory is very dynamic and creative but always historically and intergenerationally embedded. It is too early to make a decision on the issue, but it can be said that gender as well as locations involved in migration movements both in Mali and in Europe (rural/urban) are core issues related to the future of the dispersed family.

Conclusion

Although child movement between France and Mali represents a legitimate subject of study as it is structurally part of the Soninke society and its migratory history, as in many other societies, it is a topic that has long been ignored by researchers. It has been clearly demonstrated that this movement differs according to age and gender and takes two main forms: the (short) holiday stay and the long stay in Mali. The main concepts explored, those of multiparenthood and migratory debt, have opened up several potential fields of study related to the construction of spaces and identities between France and Mali and the constraints of the lineage-based logic. While certain aspects of this form of child migration can seem new, the structural record of this phenomenon as demonstrated by history and anthropology must not be ignored.

In this chapter, I chose to focus on child migration by putting children at the core of my research. By doing so, I showed how their circular movement is closely intertwined with the patrilineal-based kinship and alliance system in which fosterage takes part (multiparenthood) on the one hand and embedded in a debt system on the other hand. I called the 'migratory debt', a kind of community debt caused by the departure of women, as workforce and caretakers, and the absence of their children born abroad, as members of the patrilineage in the village. My analysis, based on multisited, multitemporal ethnographic fieldwork both in France and in Mali, asked whether this phenomenon is new or grounded in the past and identified its meaning and function within the social and cultural organization of the dispersed family. The use of the notion 'circular movement' allowed me to emphasize and thus critically analyze two close child migration forms and related concepts ('transnational family' and 'return') that are often used in the literature as well as by governments as static categories: migrants' children in France who go to their parents' country of origin for holiday and children who are sent there after being born and have lived in France for few years. The chapter captures an invisible and undertheorized dynamic, that of a 'to-ing and fro-ing', a mobility-in-migration that places the movements of children as central to understanding the new dynamics of an evolving historical migratory trajectory. The political dimension of this circular movement appears on a micro-level with a kind of (patrilineal) lineaged-, community- and gender-based cultural politics of childhood (Scheper-Hughes and Sargent 1999) and, on a macro-level with a nation-state and Western-based cultural politics of (migrant) childhood: both are dealing with the issue of identity, but in different ways. Moreover, the question What is a child? needs to be explored in a lifelong multisited and contextual perspective, to better understand the way of being a child (a boy or a girl) in a dispersed family.

In addressing child migration between Europe and Africa, it is essential to take into account the range of representations of childhood, of childhood statuses, gender and individual and generational life cycles and to think about the intra- and extra-African flows as being part of the same issue.

As an occasion for a 'postcolonial encounter' that has been rarely studied, child migration offers an open window on contemporary patterns of social production and reproduction as well as cultural and political resistance to them within our societies.[39]

Notes

1. On the blurred definitions of the 'transnational family', see Van djik (2002) and Razy and Baby-Collin (2011).
2. Here I am thinking of schooling (Lange 2003), generally in French, but this can involve religious instruction (medersa), without forgetting the learning of domestic chores and cultural skills (Razy 2007b; Whitehouse 2009; Gasparetti 2011).
3. Without the parents (Hashim and Thorsen, 2011).
4. Cf. Razy and Rodet (2012).
5. 1996–1997 and 2004 (Mali) and 1996–2007 (France).
6. A child born in France before January 1, 1994, whose mother or father was born in a former French colony is French.
7. 'From the name of an Arabic system of watering by to-ing and fro-ing with small baskets in succession' (Semin 2009: 102).
8. Children and parents themselves – mostly nonliterate – do not know their rights and the successive reforms of the law; therefore, they cannot easily take advantage of it.
9. There are a few exceptions (Barou 2011). This phenomenon has already been mentioned by Manchuelle (1997).
10. This obvious lack of interest in childhood migration was widespread until recently, particularly in the case of Africa (Evers et al. 2011; Hashim and Thorsen 2011).
11. It is in most cases in the nonprofit sector and/or state journals (following the commissioning of surveys) that data is produced by researchers, and less often in academic reviews (see Kuczynski and Razy 2009)
12. This joint 'women/children' approach contributes to the invisibility of children, which is itself merged into a blurring of the categories child/young person/adolescent.
13. Concerning the phenomenon in the US, see Whitehouse (2009) and Razy and Baby-Collin (2011).
14. A visit to Bamako in 2003 and to a village in the Soninke region (comments recorded in Paris between 2003 and 2007).
15. In the Soninke patrilineal kinship system, a man's children are also his brother's children. Children are thus considered as siblings. The eldest brother usually makes decisions for his and his brother's children.
16. Information was recorded in France during the period in which the family was monitored (1996–2002).
17. Information was recorded in 1997 in the village in the Soninke region.
18. Information recorded in Paris in 2003.
19. Information was recorded in 1996 in the village in the Soninke region.
20. Information was recorded in Paris in 2004.
21. With regard to circumcision, this is generally carried out in France where it is not prohibited, unlike excision.
22. This is a rite of passage that takes place at around the age of 15 (Razy 2007a).
23. I note that many children have never been to Mali during their childhood and that there are differences between siblings.
24. De Bruijn and Brinkman speak of 'a translocal community' (2011).

25. The exclusive reference to nation-states that is implied by the adjective 'national' (whether referring to it or moving beyond it) is certainly not relevant in all contexts (Hannerz 1996).
26. In the sense of the meaning employed by Condominas (1980).
27. Regarding the use of the concept and ideological and political issues related to its recognition, cf. Razy (2010).
28. See Razy (2007a)
29. A form of 'community debt' (Marie 1997) and 'debt to ancestors' (Bonnet 2009).
30. Information recorded in Paris in 2007.
31. Quiminal et al. (1997) addresses the issues of marriage for children born in France in terms of observing practices and norms and of the status of parents.
32. Participation in a literacy and homework-help association 1988–2007.
33. Information recorded in Paris in 2005.
34. Cf. Lefeuvre-Déotte (1997).
35. This is the case of children or young people who have tried to 'return' to France after being sent to Mali and who, once they have left the French national territory, no longer exist in the eyes of the French state, unless their request is communicated to the parents (cf. Mamadou C.) or the authorities (cf. Bintou and Manda B.) who remain in France.
36. Whitehouse (2009: 90–91) uses the term tabushi: 'The definition…comes from West African informants of many different ethnicities who use the term to refer to West African children born and especially raised abroad. This definition carries the pejorative implication that the tabushi is culturally inauthentic and lacks the mores and habits that anyone "born and bred in their ancestral West African homeland acquires early in life"'.
37. A specific example of this would be the 'denatured' version of the 'traditional' institution of fosterage.
38. On the notion of translocality in Africa, cf. notably Marfaing and Wippel (2004).
39. Asad (1973) speaks of the 'colonial encounter'.

References

Alber, E. (2003) 'Denying Biological Parenthood: Fosterage in Northern Benin', *Ethnos*, 68(4), 487–506.

Asad, T. (ed.) (1973) *Anthropology and the Colonial Encounter* (London: Ithaca).

Baldassar, L. and Merla, L. (eds) (2014) *Transnational Families, Migration and the Circulation of Care: Understanding Mobility and Absence in Family Life* (Research in Transnationalism), (London and New York: Routledge).

Barou, J. (1978) *Travailleurs Africains en France: Rôle des cultures d'origine* (Grenoble: Presses Universitaires de Grenoble).

Barou, J. (1991) 'Familles Africaines en France: De la Parenté Mutilée à la Parenté Reconstituée' in M. Ségalen (ed) *Jeux de Familles* (Paris: Presses du CNRS), 157–171.

Barou, J. (2001) 'La Famille à Distance: Nouvelles Stratégies Familiales chez les Immigrés d'Afrique Sahélienne', *Hommes et Migrations*, 1232, 6–25.

Barou, J. (ed) (2011) *De l'Afrique à la France: D'une Génération à l'Autre* (Paris: Armand Colin).

Basch, L., Glick-Schiller, N., and Szanton-Blanc, C. (eds) (1994) *Nations Unbound: Transnational Projects, Postcolonial Predicaments, and Deterritorialized Nation-States* (Amsterdam: Gordon and Breach).

Bodin, C., and Quiminal, C. (1991) 'Le Long Voyage des Femmes du Fleuve Sénégal', *Hommes et Migrations*, 1141, 23–26.

Bonnet, D. (2009) *Repenser l'Hérédité* (Paris: Archives Contemporaines).

Bonnet, D., Rollet, C., and Suremain (de), C.-É. (eds) (2012) *Modèles d'Enfances: Successions, Transformations, Croisements* (Paris: Archives Contemporaines).

Bourgouin, F. (2011) 'Des Individualistes Globaux: Ruptures et Discontinuités dans les Familles d'Élites Africaines Transnationales' in É. Razy and V. Baby-Collin (eds) *Autrepart* (La Famille Transnationale dans Tous Ses États), 57, 299–314.

Bryceson, D., and Vuorela, U. (eds) (2002) 'Transnational Families in the Twenty-first Century' in D. Bryceson and U. Vuorela (eds) *The Transnational Family: New European Frontiers and Global Networks* (Oxford: Berg Publishers), 3–30.

Castle, S., and Diarra, A. (2003) *The International Migration of Young Malians: Tradition, Necessity or Rite of Passage* (London: London School of Hygiene and Tropical Medicine), document paper.

Condominas, G. (1980) *L'Espace Social: À propos de l'Asie du Sud-Est* (Paris: Flammarion).

Daum, C. (1998) *Les Associations de Maliens en France: Migrations, Développement et Citoyenneté* (Paris: Karthala).

De Bruijn, M., and Brinkman, I. (2011) 'Communicating in Africa: Following Mobile Communities in Angola and Cameroon' in É. Razy and V. Baby-Collin (eds) *Autrepart* (La Famille Transnationale dans Tous Ses États), 57, 41–58.

De Bruijn, M., Van Dijk, R., and Foeken, D. (2001) 'Mobile Africa: An Introduction' in M. De Bruijn, R. Van Dijk, and D. Foeken (eds) *Mobile Africa: Changing Patterns of Movement in Africa and Beyond* (Leiden, Boston and Köln: Brill), 1–7.

Dieterlen, G., and Sylla, D. (1992) *L'Empire de Ghana: Le Wagadou et la Tradition de Yéréré* (Paris: Karthala/Arsan).

Donà, G., and Veale, A. (2011) 'Divergent Discourses, Children and Forced Migration', *Journal of Ethnic and Migration Studies*, 37(8), 1273–1289.

Einarsdóttir, J. (2006) 'Relocation of Children: Fosterage and Child Death in Biombo, Guinea-Bissau' in C. Christiansen, M. Utas, and H. E. Vigh (eds) *Navigating Youth, Generating Adulthood: Social Becoming in an African Context* (Uppsala: Nordic Africa Institute), 183–200.

Ensor, M. O., and Gozdziak, E. M. (eds) (2010) *Children and Migration: At the Crossroads of Resiliency and Vulnerability* (Hampshire: Palgrave Macmillan).

Evers, S., Notermans, C., and Van Ommering, E. (eds) (2011) *Not Just a Victim: The Child as Catalyst and Witness of Contemporary Africa* (Leiden: Brill Academic Publishers).

Fainzang, S. (1994) 'L'Objet Construit et la Méthode Choisie: L'Indéfectible Lien', *Terrain*, 23, 161–172.

Faist, T. (1998) 'Transnational Social Spaces of International Migration: Evolution, Significance, and Future Prospects', *Archives Européennes de Sociologie*, 39(2), 213–247.

Fassin, D., Morice, A., and Quiminal, C. (eds) (1997) *Les Lois de l'Inhospitalité: La Politique de l'Immigration à l'Épreuve des sans Papiers* (Paris: La Découverte).

Gasparetti, F. (2011) 'Relying on Teranga: Senegalese Migrants to Italy and Their Children Left Behind' in É. Razy and V. Baby-Collin (eds) *Autrepart* (La Famille Transnationale dans Tous Ses États), 57, 215–232.

Godelier, M. (2004) *Les Métamorphoses de la Parenté* (Paris: Fayard).

Godelier, M. (2007) *Au Fondement des Sociétés Humaines: Ce Que Nous Apprend l'Anthropologie* (Paris: Albin Michel).

Goody, E. N. (1982) *Parenthood and Social Reproduction: Fostering and Occupational Roles in West Africa* (Cambridge: Cambridge University Press).

Grier, B. (2004) 'Child Labor and Africanist Scholarship: A Critical Overview', *African Studies Review*, 47(2), 1–25.

Grillo, R., and Mazzucato, V. (2008) 'Africa-Europe: A Double Engagement, African-European Linkages', *Journal of Ethnic and Migration Studies*, 34(2), 199–217.

Guillermet, É. (2010) *Constructions de l'Orphelin au Niger: Anthropologie d'une Enfance Globalisée* (Sarrebruck: Éditions Universitaires Européennes).

Hannerz, U. (1996) *Transnational Connexions: Culture, People, Places* (London: Routledge).

Hashim, I., and Thorsen, D. (2011) *Child Migration in Africa* (London: Zedbooks, The Nordic Africa Institute).

Kuczynski, L., and Razy, É. (2009) 'Anthropologie et Migrations Africaines en France: Une Généalogie des Recherches', *Revue Européenne des Migrations Internationales*, 25(3), 79–100.

Lallemand, S. (1976) 'Génitrices et Educatrices Mossi', *L'Homme*, 16(1), 109–124.

Lallemand, S. (1988) 'Adoption, Fosterage et Alliance', *Anthropologie et Sociétés*, 12(2), 25–40.

Lallemand, S. (1993) *La Circulation des Enfants en Société Traditionnelle: Prêt, Don, Échange* (Paris: L'Harmattan).

Lancy, D. F. (2008) *The Anthropology of Childhood: Cherubs, Chattel, Changelings* (New York: Cambridge University Press).

Lancy, D. F. (2012) 'Unmasking Children's Agency', *AnthropoChildren: Perspectives ethnographiques sur les enfants and l'enfance/Ethnographic Perspectives in Children and Childhood*, 2. <http://popups.ulg.ac.be/AnthropoChildren/document. php?id=1253>. Accessed November 30, 2012.

Lange, M. F. (ed) (2003) 'Enseignements', *Cahiers d'Études Africaines*, 1–2, 169–170.

Le Gall, J. (2005) 'Familles Transnationales: Bilan des Recherches et Nouvelles Perspectives', *Diversité Urbaine*, 5(1), 29–42.

Lefeuvre-Déotte, M. (1997) *L'Excision en Procès: un Différend Culturel* (Paris: Éditions L'Harmattan).

Levitt, P., and Glick-Schiller, N. (2004) 'Conceptualizing Simultaneity: A Transnational Social Field Perspective on Society', *International Migration Review*, 38(3), 1002–1039.

Levitt, P., and Waters, M. (eds) (2006) *The Changing Face of Home: The Transnational Lives of the Second Generation* (New York: Russell Sage Publication).

Lord, J. (2011) 'Child Labor in the Gold Coast: The Economics of Work, Education, and the Family in Late-Colonial African Childhoods, c. 1940–57', *The Journal of the History of Childhood and Youth*, 4(1), 88–115.

Manchuelle, F. (1997) *Willing Migrants: Soninke Labor Diasporas, 1848–1960* (Athens, OH: Ohio: University Press).

Marcus, E. G. (1995) 'Ethnography in/of the World System: The Emergence of Multi-sited Ethnography', *Annual Review of Anthropology*, 24, 95–117.

210   *Élodie Razy*

Marcus, E. G. (1998) 'Ethnography in/of the World System: The Emergence of Multi-sited Ethnography' in *Ethnography through Thick and Thin* (Princeton: Princeton University Press), 79–104.

Marfaing, L., and Wippel, S. (eds) (2004), *Les Relations Transsahariennes à l'Époque Contemporaine: Un Espace en Constante Mutation* (Paris: Karthala-ZMO).

Marie, A. (1997) 'Avatars de la Dette Communautaire: Crise des Solidarités, Sorcellerie et Procès d'Individualisation (Itinéraires Abidjanais)' in A. Marie (ed) *L'Afrique des Individus: Itinéraires Citadins dans l'Afrique Contemporaine* (Abidjan, Bamako, Dakar, Niamey) (Paris: Karthala), 249–328.

Mazzucato, V., and Schans, D. (2011) 'Transnational Families and the Well-Being of Children: Conceptual and Methodological Challenges', *Journal of Marriage and the Family*, 73(4), 704–712.

Meillassoux, C., Doucouré, L., and Simagha, D. (1967) *Légende de la Dispersion des Kusa: Epopée Soninké* (Dakar: IFAN).

Nicollet, A. (1992) *Femmes d'Afrique Noire en France: La Vie Partagée* (Paris: L'Harmattan).

Olwig, K. F. (2007) *Caribbean Journeys: An Ethnography of Migration and Home in Three Family Networks* (Durham, NC: Duke University Press).

Parreñas, R. S. (2005) *Children of Global Migration: Transnational Families and Gendered Woes* (Stanford: Stanford University Press).

Poiret, C. (1996) *Familles Africaines en France* (Paris: L'Harmattan).

Pollet, É., and Winter, G. (1971) *La Société Soninké* (Dyahunu, Mali) (Bruxelles: Éditions de l'Université de Bruxelles).

Pradelles de Latour, Ch.-H. (2001) 'Clivages et Dérapages', *L'Homme*, 157, 151–166.

Pries, L. (1999) *Migration and Transnational Social Spaces* (Ashgate: Dansk Center For Migration Og Etniske Studier).

Quiminal, C. (1991) *Gens d'Ici, Gens D'ailleurs* (Paris: Christian Bourgeois Éditeur).

Quiminal, C. (1995) 'La Famille Soninké en France', *Hommes et Migrations*, 1185, 26–31.

Quiminal, C. (2002) 'Retours Contraints, Retours Construits des Emigrés Maliens', *Hommes et Migrations*, 1236, 35–43.

Quiminal, C., and Bodin, C. (1993) 'Mode de Constitution des Ménages Polygames et Vécu de la Polygamie en France', *Migrations Études*, 41, 1–8.

Quiminal, C., Timera, M., Fall, B., and Diarra, H. (1997) 'Les Jeunes Filles d'Origine Africaine en France: Parcours Scolaires, Accès au Travail et Destin Social', *Migrations Études*, 78, 1–18.

Rabain, J. (1994) *L'Enfant du Lignage: Du Sevrage à la Classe d'Âge* (Paris: Payot).

Rabain, J. (2000) 'De l'Anthropologie à la Clinique: De l'Usage des Représentations Culturelles', *L'Autre*, 1, 127–143.

Razy, É. (2006) 'De Quelques "Retours Soninké" aux Différents Âges de la Vie: Circulations entre la France et le Mali', *Journal des Anthropologues*, 106–107, 337–354.

Razy, É. (2007a) *Naître et Devenir: Anthropologie de la Petite Enfance en Pays Soninké* (Mali) (Nanterre: Société d'Ethnologie, Collection Sociétés Africaines).

Razy, É. (2007b) 'Les "Réfugiées de l'Intérieur": Excision et Mariage Précoce Contraint entre la France et le Mali' in J. Freedman and J. Valluy (eds) *Persécutions des Femmes: Savoirs, Mobilisations, Protections* (Paris: Éditions Du Croquant, Collection TERRA), 189–204.

Razy, É. (2007c) 'Les "Sens Contraires" de la Migration: La Circulation des Jeunes Filles d'Origine Soninké entre la France et le Mali', *Journal des Africanistes*, 77(2), 19–43.

Razy, É. (2010) 'La Famille Dispersée: Une Configuration Pluriparentale Oubliée?', *L'Autre*, 11(3), 331–339.

Razy, É., and Baby-Collin, V. (2011) 'Introduction' (La Famille Transnationale dans Tous Ses États), *Autrepart*, 57/58, 7–22.

Razy, É., and Rodet, M. (2012) 'Les Migrations Africaines dans L'Enfance, des Parcours Individuels entre Institutions Locales et Institutions Globales' (Migration dans l'Enfance, Migrations de l'Enfance: Regards Pluridisciplinaires), *Journal des Africanistes*, 81(2), 5–48.

Rezkallah, N., and Epelboin, A. (1997) *Chroniques du Saturnisme Infantile, 1989– 1994* (Paris: L'Harmattan).

Rich, J. (2010) 'Searching for Success: Boys, Family Aspirations, and Opportunities in Gabon, ca. 1900–1940', *Journal of Family History*, 35(1), 7–24.

Rodet, M. (2009) *Les Migrantes Ignorées du Haut-Sénégal* (1900–1946) (Paris: Karthala).

Rouse, R. (2002) 'Mexican Migration and the Social Space of Postmodernism' in J. X. Inda and R. Rosaldo (eds) *The Anthropology of Globalization: A Reader* (Blackwell Publishers: Oxford), 157–171.

Scheper-Hughes, N., and Sargent, C. (1999) *Small Wars: The Cultural Politics of Childhood* (Berkeley: University of California Press).

Semin, J. (2009) 'L'Ethnologue dans les Réseaux Économiques des Femmes Migrantes: Modes de Présence Simultanée entre la France et l'Afrique', *Revue Européenne des Migrations Internationales*, 25(3). <http://remi.revues.org/4989>. Accessed November 30, 2012.

Szulc, A., Hecht, A. C., Pía Leavy, M. C. H., Varela, M., Verón, L., and Finchelstein, I. (2012) 'Naturalism, Agency and Ethics in Ethnographic Research with Children: Suggestions for Debate', *AnthropoChildren: Perspectives Ethnographiques sur les Enfants and l'Enfance/Ethnographic Perspectives in Children and Childhood*, 2. <http://popups.ulg.ac.be/AnthropoChildren/document.php?id=1270>. Accessed November 30, 2012.

Thorsen, D. (2007) ' "If Only I Get Enough Money for a Bicycle!" A Study of Childhoods, Migration and Adolescent aspirations against a Backdrop of Exploitation and Trafficking in Burkina Faso', *Working Paper T21*, (Brighton, Development Research Centre on Migration, Globalisation and Poverty).

Timera, M. (1996) *Les Soninké en France: D'une Histoire à l'Autre* (Paris: Karthala).

Timera, M. (1999) 'Logiques Familiales, Communautaires et Scolarisation des Jeunes Filles d'Origine Africaine Noire en France', *Formation Emploi*, 65, 57–75.

Timera, M. (2001) 'Les Migrations des Jeunes Sahéliens: Affirmation de Soi et Émancipation' (Les Jeunes, Hantise de l'Espace Public dans les Sociétés du Sud?), *Autrepart*, 18, 37–49.

Ungruhe, C. (2010) 'Symbols of Success: Youth, Peer Pressure and the Role of Adulthood among Juvenile Male Return Migrants in Ghana', *Childhood*, 17, 259–271.

Van Djik, R. (2002) 'Religion, Reciprocity and Restructuring Family Responsibility in the Ghanaian Pentecostal Diaspora' in D. Bryceson and U. Vuorela (eds) *The Transnational Family: New European Frontiers and Global Networks* (Oxford: Berg Publishers), 173–196.

Vuorela, U. (2002) 'Transnational Families: Imagined and Real Communities' in D. Bryceson and U. Vuorela (eds) *The Transnational Family: New European Frontiers and Global Networks* (Oxford: Berg Publishers), 63–82.

Whitehouse, B. (2009) 'Transnational Childrearing and the Preservation of Transnational Identity in Brazzaville, Congo', *Global Networks*, 9(1), 82–99.

10
Protecting Children or Pandering to Politics? A Critical Analysis of Anti-Child Trafficking Discourse, Policy and Practice
Neil Howard

Introduction

Although child labor had long been a focus of international attention, child trafficking began to emerge as *the* major child protection issue across the Majority World at the start of the last decade (Castle and Diarra 2003; Hashim 2003; Hashim and Thorsen 2011; Huijsmans and Baker 2012; O'Connell Davidson 2011; Thorsen 2007). This was no more apparent than in Benin, where two high-profile events saw child trafficking catapulted to the status of number one social policy challenge. The first of these was the interception of a Nigerian trawler bringing Beninese adolescents to work in Gabon. The second was the high-profile 'rescue' of Beninese teenage labor migrants who were working in the artisanal quarries of Abeokuta, Nigeria. Both episodes saw young workers identified as 'slaves', and both led to Benin's being tarred as the new 'epicenter' of the international traffic in children (Alber 2011; Feneyrol and Terre des Hommes 2005; Howard 2011, 2012a; Morganti 2007, 2011).

It was in this context that I first arrived in Benin, in 2005, as a young intern for a nationally prominent child rights nongovernmental organization (NGO). Though previously aware of Benin's child 'trafficking problem', my subsequent work with young labor migrants who were defined by child protection actors such as the United Nations Children's Fund (UNICEF) as 'trafficked' quickly revealed the disjuncture between the dominant representations of child trafficking and the lived realities of those migrants who were represented as trafficked. Policy also seemed to mirror that disjuncture, as many early anti-child trafficking efforts focused on preemptively preventing youth labor migration, even as youth labor migrants experienced their migration as unproblematic (Alber 2003, 2011; Morganti 2011).

It was in order to explore these tensions that I began my research in 2007. First, I wished to ascertain whether anti-child trafficking discourse and policy were really as problematic as they had initially appeared. Second, I wished to delve *inside* the anti-child trafficking field in order to understand why exactly this was the case. For the purposes of this research, I defined the 'anti-child trafficking field' as all those institutional actors involved in the creation and spread of anti-child trafficking discourse and policy. These institutions included UNICEF and the International Labour Organization (ILO), from among the core UN agencies; the US Department of Labor and the US Agency for International Development (USAID), Danish Aid, the European Union (EU) and France, from the donor community; the Family and Justice Ministries, from within the Beninese government; and a collection of national and international NGOs. I decided that the most sensible strategy would be to conduct fieldwork that would allow me to access both those upon whom discourse and policy (attempt to) act and those responsible for the constitution of this discourse and policy. This meant working not only with young migrants (constructed by the anti-child trafficking and child protection community as 'victims of trafficking') and their communities but also with discourse and policymakers in each of the various institutions central to anti-child trafficking in Benin.

In terms of the former, I decided to examine what had been widely depicted within the national and international media as one of the Benin's most notorious examples of child trafficking – that of (mainly male) teenagers moving from the Zou region in the south of the country to the artisanal quarries of Abeokuta, Nigeria. In concert with my research assistant, who was from the Zou and had previously worked for an NGO engaged in the anti-child trafficking field, I selected four case study villages from the Zou 'sending region', and in these villages I purposively sampled current and former migrants to the quarries, those involved in the migrant labor network linking the region to the quarries, and village authorities. I chose these villages because they had experienced significant anti-child trafficking interventions and were known to my research assistant. This research took place over six months, between February and July 2010. It was later buttressed by a short period of targeted fieldwork in February 2012, during which I spent time in and around the 'receiving region' of Abeokuta's quarries, in Nigeria. This fieldwork involved (1) observing the living and working conditions in the quarries, and (2) interviewing 18 representatives of the key actors engaged in the quarry economy, including labor leaders, gravel purchasers, traders and transporters, landowners, and 20 Beninese adolescent migrant quarry workers from villages across the Zou region, including two whom formed my original case studies.

In terms of those responsible for discourse and policy – in other words, the anti-child trafficking field – I focused specifically on those bodies named above that are most active in forming and implementing anti-child trafficking policy in Benin and internationally. I identified these actors in a number of ways. First, I drew on my preexisting contacts in the field and snowballed relevant information and interviewees across it. Second, I examined publicly available funding records to see which bodies provided funding for anti-child trafficking efforts. Third, I engaged in extensive participant observation with one UN agency and one significant international NGO active in the field, in order to further develop both an 'insider's perspective' and an overview of precisely which bodies were important actors in the field. Importantly, I paid attention both to the internal and external dynamics of the relevant institutions, interviewing actors placed at different levels within each bureaucratic hierarchy. I interviewed over 100 anti-child trafficking actors.

In total, I spent almost a year engaged with these institutions throughout 2009 and 2010. This included an extended period of participant observation in the headquarters of one UN agency and in the field office of one major INGO. It also involved gathering a wide variety of relevant internal and published documentation and conducting interviews with over 100 people at almost all levels of the institutional chain – ranging from donor politicians to local NGO staff active in my case study villages.

The rest of this chapter is divided into three parts. In the first, I offer an overview of dominant anti-child trafficking discourse and policy as it manifests in Benin within the institutional settings named above. In the second, I contrast the heavy antimigratory emphasis prevalent in these with the empirics I have gathered with young labor migrants from Benin to Nigeria. In the paper's third and final segment, I turn my lens inside the policy system in order to offer the beginnings of an account for why the difference between official narrative and ground-level experience manifests and persists. This chapter captures the experiences of adolescents who engage in outmigration and circular and return migration, independently of the adult members of their families, as they transition from childhood to adulthood, and their juxtaposition with local and global discourses of migration, mobility, trafficking and childhood.

Discourse and policy

Discourse

The nature of the dominant discourse around trafficking in Benin is well
captured in the following *Agence France Press* article extract.

> *Benin's Child Slaves Working Nigeria's Quarries*
>
> Irenee, a skinny Beninese girl of 15, points to three mounds of
> earth: *the graves of her friends who died of exhaustion* here in the gravel
> quarries of Abeokuta, in south-western Nigeria.
>
> UNICEF says about 5,000 children from neighboring Benin are
> laboring here, eight hours a day, six days a week.
>
> In the sweltering heat and in the lashing rain, Irenee crushes
> chunks of granite rock, naked to the waist, her skin coated in a thick
> layer of grime. Failure to produce her quota, whatever the weather
> conditions, brings with it the risk of being beaten up.
>
> In September 2003, when she was just 11, Irenee and 260 other
> children were freed by the Nigerian police and sent home, after a
> dispute between two rival trafficking gangs. *But their parents sold them
> again to traffickers* and they ended up back in Abeokuta, some 100
> kilometers (62 miles) north of Lagos.
>
> The idea is that the child is *sold into bonded labor for a fixed term* –
> normally two or three years. At the end of the term he gets a bicycle
> and 100 or 200 dollars (68 to 136 euros). If he completes three terms
> his master may build a new hut for the child's family.
>
> *Many of the families who sell their children into slavery are unapolo-
> getic.* "How do you expect me to keep 37 children here when I have
> no income?" shrugged Luc Gbogbohoundada, an octogenarian with
> eight wives. Gbogbohoundada lives in Za-Kpota, a village across the
> border in Benin about 150 kilometres from Abeokuta. *Za-Kpota is
> notorious as the child-trafficking capital of the region.*
>
> The land here can no longer support the huge families that have
> sprung up from generations of polygamous marriages. In spite of the
> children who bring home bicycles and money to smarten up huts
> Za'Kpota looks just as wretched as any other poor village.
>
> Child trafficking in Benin has risen sharply in the past few years. A
> law cracking down on the practice was voted in January 2006 but has
> never been promulgated. *'Clearly, as long as this law is not put into prac-
> tice, some villages carry on with this trafficking without fear'*, said Philipe
> Duhamelle, the head of UNICEF, the United Nations Children's Fund,
> in Benin. ... UNICEF estimates that some 7,000 children from Benin
> are currently working in Nigeria after being sold. Of that number,
> 5,000 are estimated to be in the quarries of Abeokuta.

Statistics published in June by the Juvenile Protection Police of Cotonou indicate that more than 10,000 children *destined to be sold* outside the country are intercepted and turned back every year at Benin's borders'.[1]

This extract focuses on the work of Beninese 'child slaves' in Abeokuta. It features a number of characteristic tropes, including the concept of 'slavery', the sale of children, and their violent exploitation at the workplace. It is notable that the piece draws on respected UN and police sources to build its narrative, and in doing so it reflects the way that the media, state and supra-state actors intertwine in their shared depiction of the migration-trafficking phenomenon in Benin. Significantly, as has been the case elsewhere, the labor migratory departure from the family home is cast here as somehow 'pathological', representing the consequence of unwilled, extraneous cause factors such as poverty, criminal trickery, parental naivety or profligacy (Howard 2008, 2011, 2012a, b; see also Hashim 2003; see De Lange 2007; Huijsmans and Baker 2012; O'Connell Davidson and Farrow 2007; Riisøen et al. 2004; and Whitehead et al. 2007). As the italicized text makes clear, the narrative of 'child sale' permeates this piece. It is paralleled by the depiction of working conditions as brutal, exhausting and exploitative. Clearly, within this understanding, the Benin-Abeokuta migrant flow is a clear context of child trafficking, as is underlined by UNICEF's spokesperson. This picture should be borne in mind when we return below to Abeokuta's quarries.

Policy

In light of the prevailing discourse such as that documented above, it should come as little surprise that anti-child trafficking policy as pursued by the Beninese state and its international partners works fundamentally to protect children by keeping them 'at home' and away from 'slavery-like' work such as that depicted above. The dominant line of force running across the Beninese anti-child trafficking spectrum is, therefore, firmly against the independent mobility of minors, with emphasis placed on 'preemptive protection' through sedentarization (see Howard 2012b and 2013 for a detailed discussion).

This can be illustrated most clearly by discussing the three major elements of the Beninese anti-child trafficking framework, as formulated and operationalized by the Beninese state, its partners and the donor agencies so central to their work. The first of these is the national anti-child trafficking law (LOI N 2006–04), the second is the Memorandum of Understanding with Nigeria regarding anti-child trafficking strategy, and the third are the widely hailed Village Anti-Child Trafficking Committees. I will discuss each in turn.

Benin's anti-child trafficking law is formally entitled the *Law Regulating the Movement of Minors and Suppressing the Traffic in Children*. Building on the ILO's global anti-child labor framework, it defines children as all those under 18 and makes illegal all work seen to harm their 'health, safety or morals', including any work in sectors such as mining, quarrying, building, commercial agriculture or transport. As the law's title suggests, however, it does not merely outlaw certain kinds of work or the 'trafficking' seen to equate therewith; rather, it also regulates the conditions under which minors may legally migrate. What does this regulation entail?

Article 7 establishes that children cannot legally be displaced within the borders of the country unless accompanied either by a direct parent or guardian or with the consent of a local government official. The law thus empowers state agents to directly implicate themselves in personal and familial labor mobility decisions. The law and its related decrees go on to explain that state consent for that (labor) mobility will only be forthcoming if a number of conditions are met. First, a family 'placing' a child must have all the child's papers in order. Second, they must have enough money to pay for the child's return. And third, they must be able to demonstrate that the child's relocation is for the purpose of school attendance or for an official apprenticeship in a state-sanctioned sector, rather than work. Article 4 establishes that relocation for labor 'exploitation' constitutes trafficking and is thus illegal, irrespective of any consent offered. When I asked Deg, a senior government official, whether this law could be considered a little heavy-handed, he replied that it was, but that that was its purpose, since 'you cannot tell the difference between placement, movement and trafficking' and thus you need 'to ban it all' (Interview, March 10, 2010).

Intricately related to the promulgation of the anti-child trafficking law was the signing and operationalizing of the Memorandum of Understanding (MoU) between Benin and Nigeria. Phil, at the time country representative for one of the UN agencies central to Benin's anti-child trafficking field, explained:

> Nigeria was a big issue for us, because we realized that Nigeria was the major destination for Beninese kids. We therefore needed to establish a partnership with them. Our agency convinced both governments to get together and have regular meetings on trafficking. We wanted to develop an MoU on the issue, which we eventually did. ... It is a

very good document, stating the multilevel cooperation that is to take place between the countries, from police, to border officials to NAPTIP and the BPM.[2] Each country also developed concrete joint and separate plans of action, including border sensitization. ... Ministers and our staff go to border villages in the Zou and tell people that the law has changed and that behavior must therefore also change [i.e., that child (under 18 years) mobility must stop]. They tell people there are severe punishments for transgression, including 25 years in jail if they are found accompanying any [non-kin] kids to Nigeria. Some people have in fact now been arrested. (Interview, November 9, 2011)

Further interviews and documentary analysis confirm this picture. Indeed, one interviewee explained that the MoU is precisely about harmonizing institutional responses at the political level, providing support for the expansion of national border controls and persuading border communities to desist from the teenage (labor) mobility that the discourse constructs as so problematic.

This is paralleled in the final component of Beninese anti-child trafficking policy to be discussed here – the village committees. These were developed shortly after trafficking exploded as an issue in Benin by UNICEF, a collection of donors and the Child and Family Ministry, to be the state's arm at the village level (Interviews, March 10, 2010 and April 7, 2010). Although state officials claim a wide variety of tasks performed, and goals worked for, by the village committees, interviews with their founders, with committee members in my case study villages, and myriad unpublished material, including internal committee documentation and UN agency reports relating to their work, suggest otherwise. Indeed, it seems that their major objective is to preemptively protect minors by thwarting their movement. For instance, an important, confidential UN document I obtained reveals that the emphasis in activities is squarely placed on 'community surveillance [regarding movement]' (p. 3), while a consultant's report on the work of the committees offered precisely the same conclusion, arguing that most of the work they do is 'anti-movement' (Botte and UNICEF 2005: 16). Such an assessment is echoed in one report that documents committee plans of action. In this publication, we learn that committee goals are to 'watch over suspicious movements', to 'denounce and dissuade', and to provide 'social surveillance' (MFPSS and UNICEF Benin 2006), all actions confirmed as important by committee members interviewed in my case study villages.

Youth labor mobility

In this section, I will contrast the dominant discursive and political paradigm around child trafficking in Benin with empirical data gathered from current and former youth labor migrants involved in what the *Agence France Presse* newspaper article excerpted above identified as trafficking – the migrant labor of teenage boys from Za-Kpota to the artisanal gravel pits of Abeokuta, Nigeria. This section will dispute that claim. It will do so, first, by describing the nature of life and work in Abeokuta's gravel pits, as witnessed as part of my research and recounted to me by those working in this environment. Subsequently, it will address the importance of money and social transition in the conscious choices young migrants make to move to Nigeria. Finally, the section will offer brief reflections on the alternative policies young migrants and their communities would like to see pursued *instead of* anti-child migratory efforts.

Work in Abeokuta

The Abeokutan quarry economy is a well-organized social and economic world that is highly structured along class lines. First, absentee Nigerian landlords own and rent out patches of land that is rich in the gravel that is ideal for use in the construction industry. Second, female Nigerian gravel dealers lease this land from those landlords and have contracts with them that date back two or three generations. They have come together to form a gravel dealers union and contract with a third class – lorry owners/drivers, who themselves operate under the auspices of a union – in order to have the extracted gravel transported to a fourth class, the gravel purchasers in Lagos. Gravel prices and prices for the services rendered by each of the links in this chain are predominantly set through negotiation between the unions representing these latter three classes. The gravel dealers also contract with a fifth group, however – Beninese 'bosses' who provide the (migrant) labor used to extract that gravel. These bosses are all men from Benin's Zou region encompassing my case study 'sending region'. They have themselves all worked six-year 'apprenticeships' under their own bosses until eventually they were 'liberated' and given the freedom by the hierarchy of the Beninese expatriate community that provides and manages the labor force in Abeokuta to hire their own gangs of laborers, for whom the task is to work according to the directions of these bosses in extracting the gravel.

The teenage migrant laborers identified as 'trafficked' in the *Agence France Presse* piece and in anti-child trafficking documentation from my case study region are precisely the young men who constitute these gangs of laborers. Each individual is hired on a two-year contract, and is expected to work six days a week for his *patron*, who in return houses, clothes and feeds the young worker and ultimately pays him 140,000 FCFA (about $250) or an equivalent sum in material terms (for instance a motorbike) on completion of the contract. The boys are free to work on their own account on their day off or when they have already loaded the lorry that is their day's work for their boss.

Although the work is hard, they work in groups of three, with the biggest and strongest pickaxing the ground, the second biggest and strongest shoveling the gravel, and the smallest sifting it through a filter. They rest when they need to, share the load of work among them, and are often helped by the *patron*, who is in many ways dependent on them. This dependence is not only intrinsic to the employer–employee relationship; however, it is also reflected in the fact that each *patron* relies on his reputation as a good employer in order to attract the laborers whose surplus he will ultimately extract, such that he has an interest in treating each of his charges sufficiently well that they will not tarnish his image when they return to Benin.

It is notable that, of the 20 quarry-working adolescents I interviewed, only one claimed that his work was too difficult or that he had been lied to regarding the nature of the work he was to expect. This was Placide, who said that he had originally been told that he would be working in a shop in Nigeria, only to find later that he was to work in the quarries (Interview, May 10, 2010). For the majority, however, Jack's experience

Figure 10.1 Teenagers working in Abeokuta
Source: Author.

and his assessment were representative. When I met him in Abeokuta, Jack was 15 years old. He is from a village on the border between Za-Kpota *commune* and the *commune* of Bohicon, in Benin. He came to Abeokuta a year before we met and planned to stay to work in the quarries for a further year, in order to complete the standard two-year contract. In return for his labor, he was to be bought a motorbike at the end of his two years, which was the price agreed between him, his parents and his *patron*. On top of this, Jack also worked in his free time and 'on his own account'. He said that he was able to earn around 2000 Naira (about $12) every week by doing this. His relationship with his boss was also always very good – he was never mistreated, was 'never shouted at' and was consistently 'well fed'.

Jack was saving his money week by week and aiming to return to Benin in order to set himself up in a trade. When I asked him why he came to Nigeria, he was very clear and explained simply that his goal was 'to earn money'. 'Work here is much better than it is at home', he stated, because in Abeokuta he 'can earn a lot and also keep' what he earns. Although the work can be difficult, Jack contended, the fact that he earns money makes it all worthwhile. He was also very clear that *working on the family farm is much more physically demanding than work in the gravel pits*, even though the former is legal while the latter is not. Jack stated that he strongly opposed any laws that say that young people such as him should not be able to migrate to Nigeria for this kind of work (Interview, February 4, 2012).

'We move for the money'

Although the trafficking discourse in Benin has predominantly constructed labor mobility to places like Abeokuta as an unwilled and highly exploitative experience, my research with current and former teenage labor migrants to Abeokuta's quarries suggests otherwise. For most migrants, as for their wider communities, the chance or need to access the money that is essential to any life project in Benin represents *the* major motivation for moving and mobility's major justification.

This was underlined consistently across the interviews I conducted in Abeokuta and with those in Benin who have returned from Abeokuta. Zeze is an illustrative example of this (Interview, February 2, 2012). Zeze is 17. He is from a village in the heartland of Benin's Zou region, and first came to Abeokuta with relatives after his parents passed away. This was when he was 11. Zeze has since completed two and is now finishing his third consecutive two-year labor contract. After the first two years, he earned enough money to return and build himself a dwelling in his home village. His earnings from the second two years gave him enough money to equip that house. Now, with the money he earns from this third contract, he intends to buy a motorbike. For Zeze, work in Abeoluta is not a challenge. 'I grew up working in the fields', he explained, which more than prepares a young man for the lesser rigors of life in the gravel pits. Since he will soon have performed the six years necessary to finish with his 'apprenticeship', he will soon be 'free' either to work entirely for himself and 'on his own account', or to hire other young laborers to work under him. His plan, however, is to return to Benin to see whether he can set himself up in business, although he is very frank that if he is unsuccessful, *he will simply keep returning to Abeokuta to earn money*. Money is, for Zeze, the single primary motivation for his work. When I asked him why people come to Abeokuta, *'akwe'*, or 'money', was his simple, one word answer. When I asked him what he made of the antimigratory anti-child trafficking message, he was very disdainful. 'If you want to make something of your life', he says, 'move to Abeokuta'.

Relationships and transitions

Although earning money is crucial and underpins all labor migration to Abeokuta, we should not see that labor migration as a one-dimensional, money-only phenomenon. In my interviews with current or former youth labor migrants to the quarries, a number of other socially important factors emerged. One of these involved young males fulfilling their social responsibilities by providing for their families. This was underlined particularly clearly in the refrain 'I went to Abeokuta in order to put a roof on my father's house', as young migrants returned from their two-year contracts to give their fathers their money.

Individual social transitions, however, are also significant. These transitions can involve acquiring respect and status, or acquiring the material resources necessary to marry. In terms of social respect, it is significant that one of the major motifs I heard when reflecting with interviewees on the value of migration was that, if successful, it can offer the chance for an individual to become 'considered'. To be 'considered' (or 'known') in this part of Southern Benin means to be well-thought-of, respected, seen as an important or successful person. It is an essential goal for many people, and successful migration is a principal means of achieving it. Numerous interviewees in fact explained that returning from Abeokuta with material goods such as a motorbike, clothes or a generator represented evidence of an individual's successful migration, and thus constituted a material path to their being 'considered' by those around them upon their return.

This is of course related to social manhood and to the marriage that this is seen to inevitably prefigure. My village interviews revealed that the understanding predominant in this region of when and how one transitions from the status of 'boy' or 'youth' to 'man' is neither fixed nor universally attributed to biological age, but contingent upon the attainment of economic independence. In one group interview with a collection of adolescents in one of my Zou commune case study villages, for instance, an adolescent explained with the agreement of his peers that one is a man in his community when 'he works and eats without the help of his parents (Interview, May 14, 2010), while his assessment was echoed by another young man, who declared that to be a man in his village is 'to farm, to have a big harvest, and to be able to sell your crops' (Interview, May 10, 2010). As many youth lamented to me, however, this transition and the related transition to marriage are now more difficult than ever. Where being self-sufficient through successfully farming lots of land had, historically, been the major indicator that one was a 'man', with declining soil fertility, the decreasing size of landholdings as a result of titling and population growth, and the increasing importance of the monetized economy, more and more teenage boys are finding their path to the material independence that underpins one's status as a man – and thus as a potential husband – blocked. In Sommers' (2012) terms, these youth are 'stuck' (2012), and thus need new strategies for self-articulation. Crucially, as is increasingly the case across the region (De Lange 2007; Imorou 2008; Thorsen 2007), it is often independent labor migration that represents their go-to strategy.

What should be done?

Perhaps unsurprisingly, the kinds of policies that young migrants and their communities would like to see deployed in an effort to 'protect' them or to improve their living conditions differ radically from those adopted as part of the dominant anti-child trafficking strategy. Indeed, when I asked people what they would want to see, two clear trends emerged in the responses I received. The first can be summarized as the provision of economic alternatives to labor migration. 'Give us jobs', 'promote development', 'bring industry here', 'pay us more for our crops', 'give us what you have', and 'train us in skills' were all refrains I heard. The second major trend was similarly widespread, and is summarized in the phrase 'improve our working conditions'. Since very few see quarry work as exploitative, it is extremely rare to find anyone who would like to see that work illegalized. At best, people desire improved labor relations, with 'pay us more wages' representing the central demand. Importantly, since these alternatives are not pursued as part of the mainstream anti-child trafficking strategy, the young migrants I interviewed and their communities admitted that they treat anti-child trafficking initiatives as little more than an obstacle to be navigated, like any ordinary border guard. The dominant village analysis of anti-child trafficking strategy (and, by implication, its success) can thus be summarized in the following exchange I had with two elder women in one of my case study villages:

> *Neil*: What do you think of the message that young people shouldn't leave the village?
>
> *Woman1*: Those who tell us this are those who hold back the development of the village! It is a terrible message! And they give us nothing in return. They come here, but they bring nothing with them!
>
> *Neil*: Why do NGOs and the government do this and say these things?
>
> *Woman2*: They don't want people to leave the village because they don't want to see us go and develop elsewhere instead of here. That's fair enough, but their words are useless to us, because they bring us nothing'. (Interview, April 28, 2010)

Why the divergence?

The contrast between the ground-level realities of the youth labor migrants I have researched and the official anti-child trafficking discourse and policy as presented above could not be more apparent. In light of this, the question that necessarily poses itself, and that my research has largely been designed to answer, is why? What factors prevent the anti-child trafficking field from better representing and responding to phenomena such as the labor migration of young males to Nigeria? Which forces underpin this state of affairs? In this section, the chapter will draw on data gathered from *inside* the anti-child trafficking system in order to offer tentative explanatory answers to these questions.

Lack of understanding

At the most basic, yet highly significant, level, my data suggest that a major factor explaining the divergence between the world of discourse and policy and the world of youth labor migration in Benin is the sheer lack of understanding that predominates within the former. In this regard, it should be noted that in my Beninese 'sending communities',

I was applauded for being the first person ever to ask villagers how they understood the labor migration that has so often been depicted as trafficking. When I related this experience to the more senior Benin-based anti-child trafficking actors I subsequently interviewed, in particular those in head offices in Cotonou, none were surprised, as none had *ever* visited their 'field sites'.

This is paralleled by the insignificant role that detailed qualitative research seems to play in the formation of discourse and policy. Abidi[3], for instance, is a UN employee who was central to the early evolution of the anti-child trafficking field in Benin. When I questioned him on the information gap and the role of research, he declared: 'We didn't have to work too hard to have a good idea of what was going on before establishing our interventions in Benin' (Interview, January 12, 2010). Mitch and Yaya, who have responsibility for designing and implementing research projects at the headquarters of their UN agency, explained similarly with reference to their organization's work on trafficking: 'With mining/quarrying kids, it doesn't matter if they've been trafficked or not, we know they shouldn't be there, so we just take them out before research even begins' (Interview, June 3, 2009). Likewise, when I asked Carl, a senior figure responsible for donor relations and project financing for a UN agency, whether research plays a role in his organization's project and policy work, he simply replied, 'It never really happens that way. This isn't a ground-up thing' (Interview, June 9, 2009). Similarly with Martin, an international NGO employee who formerly occupied a senior position within the donor hierarchy of one powerful donor government, I had the following exchange:

> *Neil*: Did your new approach take a long while to develop?
> *Martin*: Yes. Most people don't have an in-depth understanding of what we're dealing with. There's a lack of conceptual clarity as well as information sharing. There are huge battles between various organizations over intelligence. We need a better understanding across the board, and we need some coordination in what we do.
> *Neil*: Do people have on-the-ground understandings?
> *Martin*: No. Zero. There is a major problem, data-wise, with where people get their information in this field. Look at the example of the *Global Report on Human Trafficking*. It's awful, but people believe it because 'the UN says so'. (Interview, June 8, 2009)

What this informational gap leads to is a perpetuation of received understandings. Anti-child trafficking discourse and anti-child trafficking policy tend to feed on themselves, failing to break the cycle of misinformation with genuine empirics.

The politics of silence

The lack of ground-level understanding that I experienced in my field-work is not, however, the whole story. Indeed, my interviews, participant observation and documentary analysis suggest that other serious factors plague this field. The first is what I term the 'politics of silence'. What do I mean by this? In Benin, although poverty is frequently decried as *the* underlying 'cause' of child trafficking (see, for instance, MFE and ILO 2008:13), engagement with what causes that poverty is almost nonexistent. Indeed, in all my work and research with(in) Benin's anti-child trafficking field, never have I come across any single instance of an individual or an agency addressing or even mentioning the political economic causation of poverty.[4] Why the silence?

Sometimes this silence is *self-imposed*. When I asked one UN employee working at organizational headquarters and with ample responsibility, for instance, whether she had the freedom to speak out over things like EU trade tariffs or US cotton subsidies (which studies suggest affect Beninese peasant income in areas such as those in which I conducted my research; Minot and Daniels 2005; OXFAM 2002; Sumner 2007) she said, after a long pause,

> Look, it depends. Generally speaking, of course you can say what you want, but you'll be blasted left and right and bullied by countries if you do. Some people criticize us for not being critical enough...but we take a long-term view because we don't want to endanger long-er-term collaboration and cooperation with the states. (Interview, September 24, 2009)

Another UN employee said,

> In our agency, you have to be diplomatic. Often that's just an organizational culture thing, where there isn't always even any direct political pressure. It can often just be staff overcompensating and trying not to alienate states by saying things they think they won't want to hear. (Interview, June 6, 2009)

Sometimes, however, this silence is *imposed from above*. As part of my research, I interviewed various people within the US Trafficking in Persons Bureau (which is part of the Department of State) hierarchy, and

I asked them whether they, at the top of the anti-child trafficking tree, could bring issues like subsidies into the trafficking debate, given the understanding that trafficking is caused by poverty and that poverty in Benin is arguably related to Minority World subsidies. These were two of the responses I received:

> No way could I mention this! We're constrained by US interests and that means we're restricted to corridor discussions. (Interview, October 29, 2009)

> Listen, I can try and raise this in our meetings, but the chances of success or of public discussion are slim-to-none, because there are very big interests to fight. (Interview, September 16, 2009)

Even more telling were the words of two EU officials I spoke to in Benin's de facto capital, Cotonou. We had previously discussed political economy and had even privately reflected on the role that EU or US policies play in perpetuating global conditions of poverty. I therefore asked whether they could consider including, if not in their policies, then at least in their discourse, mention of things like subsidies. These were their responses:

> We can take account of the effects of these things at ground level – people being poor in Benin and such. But we can't talk about the top level. Our last reference is the national level, the Beninese government. *The Westerners who work here know that their policies cause poverty and trafficking. Many of them would even like to change it, but they can't.* (Interview, February 17, 2010)

> We simply cannot talk about this, Neil. This is a national structure, it's a national delegation. *We structurally cannot go beyond borders.* If we want to do something like this regarding EU or US subsidies, we need to have a formal political position sent down to us from Brussels. *Otherwise we can't mention it.* (Interview, April 2, 2010)

The politics of representation

The politics of silence ties in to what I argue is the overarching and highly problematic *politics of representation*. What do I mean by this? As has been documented in a number of similar contexts (Bierschenk 2008; Easterly 2002; Lecomte and Naudet 2000; Olivier de Sardan 1998, 2008), most of the agencies active in the anti-child trafficking field depend on funding for their operations, be that from donor governments, international bodies or multilateral institutions. This funding is almost always conditional upon recipients' being able to report on 'successes', to demonstrate 'outputs', and to show that limited resources have been well spent. It is also conditional upon recipients' refraining from stepping outside of the boundaries of what it is acceptable to their donors for them to say or do. Thus, as Alexia, an international nongovernmental organization (INGO) operative working in Benin, explained to me: 'Neil, in child protection, you have to be fashionable to attract funding' (Interview, September 2, 2007). Or, in the words of Nina, a UN agency employee who had worked on trafficking projects for the better part of a decade: 'It's all about being "sexy", trafficking is sexy, so trafficking is the way we have to go. Plus, you must remember that suffering sells in Africa' (Interview, May 28, 2009).

Instead of engaging the political economy of poverty-causation as part of anti-child trafficking discourse and policymaking, and instead of addressing the murky reality that working conditions might be poor, but better than nothing, institutions involved in this field must necessarily reproduce the simplistic stories featured in the newspaper article above and the reductive projects that focus attention on 'slavery', since nothing else will be politically acceptable.

Moreover, since donor pressure to produce representable 'outputs' is severe, anti- child trafficking actors must perpetuate problematic policies and simplistic narratives even when they aware of their problems, simply because 'the money needs to get spent'. Indeed, should they stop doing so, donor money – and with it their jobs, livelihoods and the wages on which their families depend – will dry up. As one former Organization for Security and Co-operation in Europe (OSCE) Special Representative on Trafficking tellingly admitted,

> The reality [in this field] is that not much happens; people just produce papers – they cut and paste, cut and paste, cut and paste. Or, it's seminar, seminar, seminar, conference. *We have to do something to justify our money. Otherwise, the gravy train will stop rolling.* (Interview, September 23, 2009; emphasis added)

In like fashion, Martin, himself a former donor government employee, complained:

> The problem is that [we] have to demonstrate results and this creates issues for project work. The results-driven framework is one of the reasons why there are so many conferences and workshops – *people*

have to do something to show some form of tangible outcome. (Interview, June 8, 2009)

Conclusion

The research underpinning this paper began with a desire to explore the tension between representation and reality when it came to 'child trafficking' in Benin. It expanded to examine the anti-child trafficking field itself and sought to use this examination to formulate explanations for the existence and persistence of this tension. The data now presented offer clear insights into that tension and into what underpins it.

First, as was initially suspected, the data suggest that anti-child trafficking discourse and policy are indeed fundamentally flawed. Where, in the case of discourse, the language of 'slavery', 'coercion' and 'abuse' is current, for those young migrant laborers putatively identified as 'victims' of coercion or abuse, labor migration to places like Abeokuta seems to represent a conscious, purposive response to life's immediate circumstances. Anti-child trafficking discourse would appear, therefore, to be intrinsically reductive and misrepresentative.

What of policy? While its major emphasis lies in preemptively protecting those young migrants who, upon migration, are assumed to inevitably end up in situations of exploitation and trafficking, little evidence suggests that this is appropriate with respect to the cases represented in my research. Indeed, among the current or former young labor migrants documented here, only one was tricked, and the rest either consented to or sought out their migrant labor opportunities. What this implies of course is that a policy predicated on preventing them from accessing those opportunities through migration runs directly contrary to their interests as they perceive them.

Why this disjuncture? The latter third of this paper has advanced two major explanatory hypotheses. The first is that many actors in the anti-child trafficking field (and thus constituting the major part of anti-child trafficking discourse and policy) remain so divorced from ground-level empirics that they formulate discourse and policy on the shoddiest of empirical foundations. They therefore often reproduce received ideas without critical empirical challenge.

The second hypothesis is, perhaps, even more troubling. It points to a deeply antipolitical core at the heart of the anti-child trafficking field. As has also been made painfully clear by the literature on the politics of development and the ethnography of aid (Lecomte and Naudet 2000; Mosse 2005; Mosse and Lewis 2000; Shore and Wright 1997), it suggests that discourse and policy are molded more by the contours of donor desire and financial pressure than by the interests of those vulnerable migrants whose welfare nominally justifies their existence. Pandering to politics, therefore, seems to trump protecting young people. The question, of course, is with what consequences?

Notes

1. http://www.oijj.org/en/news/general-news/benins-child-slaves-working-nigerias-quarries. International Juvenile Justice Observatory website. Accessedd 14 April 2014.
2. The Nigerian Anti-trafficking Agency and Benin's special child police unit, the Brigade de Protection des Mineurs.
3. All names have been changed to protect the identity of research participants.
4. NotesFor a truly classic example of the failure to engage in any political economic thinking, see the representative ILO and Beninese Child and Family Ministry 'National Child Trafficking Study' (MFE and ILO 2008).

References

Alber, E. (2003) 'Denying Biological Parenthood: Fosterage in Northern Benin', *Ethnos*, 68(4), 487–506.

Alber, E. (2011) 'Child Trafficking in West Africa' in A. M. Gonzalez, L. de Rose, and F. Oloo (eds) *Frontiers of Globalization: Kinship and Family Structure in Africa* (London: Africa World Press), 71–93.

Bierschenk, T. (2008) 'Anthropology and Development: An Historicizing and Localizing Approach', *Working Papers 87* (Department of Anthropology and African Studies, University of Mainz).

Botte, R., and UNICEF (2005) *Documentation des Stratégies et Activités de Prévention et de Réinsertion Mises en Place par des Comités de Village dans le Cadre de la Lutte contre la Traite des Enfants* (Dakar: UNICEF).

Castle, S., and Diarra, A. (2003) 'The International Migration of Young Malians: Tradition, Necessity or Rite of Passage?', *Research Report* (London: School of Hygiene and Tropical Medicine).

De Lange, A. (2007) 'Child Labour Migration and Trafficking in Rural Burkina Faso', *International Migration*, 45(2), 147–167.

Easterly, W. (2002) 'The Cartel of Good Intentions: Bureaucracy versus Markets in Foreign Aid', *Working Paper No. 4* (Washington, DC: Center for Global Development).

Feneyrol, O., and Fondation Terre des Hommes (TdH) (2005) *Les Petites Mains des Carrières: Enquête sur un Trafic d'Enfant entre le Bénin et le Nigéria* (Lausanne: Terre des Hommes).

Hashim, I. M. (2003) 'Child Migration: Pathological or Positive?', *International Workshop on Migration and Poverty in West Africa* (Brighton: University of Sussex).

Hashim, I., and Thorsen , D. (2011) *Child Migration in Africa, Uppsala* (The Nordic Africa Institute and London: Zed Books).

232   *Neil Howard*

Howard, N. P. (2008) *Independent Child Migration in Southern Benin: An Ethnographic Challenge to the 'Pathological' Paradigm* (Saarbrucken: VDM Verlag).

Howard, N. P. (2011) 'Is "Child Placement" Trafficking? Questioning the Validity of an Accepted Discourse', *Anthropology Today*, 27(6), 3–8.

Howard, N. P. (2012a) 'Protecting Children from Trafficking in Benin: In Need of Politics and Participation', *Development in Practice*, 22(4), 460–472.

Howard, N. P. (2012b) 'Accountable to Whom? Accountable to What? Understanding Anti-child Trafficking Discourse and Policy in Southern Benin', *Anti-child Trafficking Review*, 1(1), 43–59.

Howard, N. P. (2013) 'Promoting "Healthy Childhoods" and Keeping Children "At Home": Beninese Anti-trafficking Policy in Times of Neoliberalism', *International Migration*, 51(4), 87–102.

Huijsmans, R., and Baker, S. (2012) 'Child Trafficking: "Worst Form" of Child Labour, or Worst Approach to Young Migrants?', *Development and Change*, 43(4), 919–946.

Imorou, A. B. (2008) *Le Coton et la Mobilité: Les Implications d'une Culture de Rente sur les Trajectoires Sociales des Jeunes et Enfants au Nord-Bénin* (Cotonou: Plan-Waro, TdH, Lasdel-Bénin).

Lecomte, B. J., and Naudet, J. D. (eds) (2000) *Survivre Grace à ... Réussir Malgré ... l'Aide, Autrepart*, (13), Editions de l'Aube, IRD.

LOI N 2006–04 du 05 avril (2006) *Portant Répression des Auteurs de Traite et Conditions de Déplacement des Mineurs en République du Bénin* (Cotonou: Présidence de la République).

Ministère de la Famille et de la Protection Sociale (MFPSS) and UNICEF Benin (2006) *Appui au Renforcement des Capacités du MFPSS, des CPS et CLs dans le Cadre de la Lutte Contre le Trafic des Enfants* (Elaboration de plans d'actions des CLs, de plans d'appui des CPS aux CLs et de plans de suivi des CPS des actions des CLs) (Cotonou: MFPSS and UNICEF).

Ministère de la Famille et de l'Enfant (MFE) and ILO (2008) *Plan D'action National De Lutte Contre La Traite Des Enfants A Des Fins D'exploitation e Leur Travail* (Cotonou: MFE and ILO).

Minot, N., and Daniels, L. (2005) 'Impact of Global Cotton Markets on Rural Poverty in Benin', *Agricultural Economics*, 33(Supplement), 453–466.

Morganti, S. (2007) 'Il Lavoro dei Bambini in Bénin', in P.G. Solinas (ed), *La Vita in Prestito: Debito, lavoro, dipendenza* (Lecce: Argo), 75–104.

Morganti, S. (2011) 'La Mobilità dei Minori in Benin: Migrazione o Tratta ?' in A. Bellagamba (eds) *Migrazioni: Dal Lato dell'Africa* (Padova: Edizioni Altravista), 127–156.

Mosse, D. (2005) *Cultivating Development: An Ethnography of Aid and Practice* (London: Pluto Press).

Mosse, D., and Lewis, D. (2000) *The Aid Effect: Giving and Governing in International Development* (London: Pluto Press).

O'Connell Davidson, J. (2011) 'Moving Children? Child Trafficking, Child Migration, and Child Rights', *Critical Social Policy*, 31(3), 454–477.

O'Connell Davidson, J., and Farrow, C. (2007) *Child Migration and the Construction of Vulnerability* (Gothenburg, Sweden: Save the Children).

Olivier de Sardan, J. P. (1998) 'Peasant Logics and Development Project Logics', *Sociologia Ruralis*, 28(2/3), 216–226.

Olivier de Sardan, J. P. (2008) 'Le Développement comme Champ Politique Local', *Le Bulletin de l'APAD*, Numéro 6. <http://apad.revues.org/document2473.html>. Accessed April 14, 2014.

OXFAM (2002) 'Cultivating Poverty: The Impact of US Cotton Subsidies on Africa', *Oxfam Briefing Paper* (OXFAM: Oxford).

Riisøen, K. H., Hatløy, A., and Bjerkan, L. (2004) 'Travel to Uncertainty: A Study of Child Relocation in Burkina Faso, Ghana and Mali', *Fafo Report No. 440* (Oslo: Fafo).

Shore, C. and Wright, S. (eds) (1997) *Anthropology of Policy: Critical Perspectives on Governance and Power* (London: Routledge).

Sommers, M. (2012) *Stuck: Rwandan Youth and the Struggle for Adulthood* (Athens and London: University of Georgia Press).

Sumner, D. A. (2007) 'U.S. Farm Programs and African Cotton', *IPC Issue Brief 22* (Washington DC: International Food and Agricultural Trade Policy Council).

Thorsen, D. (2007) ' "If Only I Get Enough Money for a Bicycle!" A Study of Child Migration Against a Backdrop of Exploitation and Trafficking in Burkina Faso', *Occasional Paper*, (University of Copenhagen: Centre for African Studies).

Whitehead, A., Hashim, I. M., and Iversen, V. (2007) 'Child Migration, Child Agency and Inter-generational Relations in Africa and South Asia', *Working Paper T24* (University of Sussex Working Paper Series, Migration DRC).

11
Mobility-in-Migration in an Era of Globalization: Key Themes and Future Directions

Giorgia Donà and Angela Veale

Introduction

This book brought to the fore the complexity, multidirectionality and dynamism of children's and young people's movements in the contemporary world. As a result of globalization, individual migratory trajectories have shifted from being long-term, bidirectional, permanent and somewhat static to being characterized by multiple journeys, short, circular or seasonal migrations, holiday and pleasure mobilities that are dynamic and often ongoing into the future.

We introduced the concept 'mobility-in-migration' to capture the underlying thread of this edited collection that explains the ways in which across the life span, individuals engage in different kinds of movements within a larger individual or family migratory arc, much in response to the challenges, barriers, creative adaptation and changes brought about by globalization.

Bringing together the interdisciplinary fields of migration, mobility and childhood studies, the book showed how individuals' mobility-in-migration is embedded in family lives and community histories. Children and young people are mobile. Their migratory trajectories are often connected to and represent a continuation of preceding migration waves. Even when they are not migrants themselves, children's lives are impacted by the migration of others. Rather than construing child and youth migration as a separate kind of migration that takes place in isolation from the broader context, contributors to the edited collection examined the connections that exist between children's and young people's movements and those of others around them, and the contexts in which they take place.

The book shared a methodological framework for the study of migration, which can be summarized as being multisited and/or multitemporal. This general approach enabled contributors to unravel and reveal multiple kinds of movements as they take place across individual life spans: children move with their families or on their own; as they grow up to become adolescents they engage in seasonal, circular, holiday or return migration; and as young migrants they form new families and become parents to children whose lives are shaped by migratory experiences. The adoption of a longer time frame than that usually adopted in mono-sited one-off studies was instrumental in shifting current perspectives on child and youth migration. The book suggested that child and youth mobility-in-migration should not be subordinated to or kept separate from that of adults, but rather that it represents one of potentially many movements across an individual's life span. We suggest that child and youth migration should be reconceptualized as migration across the life span and mainstreamed in textbooks on general migration.

This concluding chapter summarizes the innovative contribution of this edited collection to the existing literature on child migration and migration more generally. It identifies existing gaps and limitations, and it makes recommendations for future research. The first part of the chapter summarizes the underlying themes of the book, namely the concept of mobility-in-migration and the developmental continuities in child and youth migration. The middle section identifies specific topics highlighted by contributors that as editors we thought deserved special attention because of their relevance, novelty or innovation. They are gender dynamics, work and consumption and changing transnational families. The last part of the chapter examines limitations and future directions for research.

Mobility-in-migration: an underresearched kind of movement

The chapters contained in the edited collection capture the multidirectionality of contemporary movements and their dynamism. The book moves away from analyses of south to north/west migrations that continue to dominate the literature on international migration to capture multidirectional, regional, continental and intercontinental movements across the globe. Punch describes cross-border regional migration in Latin America, from Bolivia to Argentina, while Carpena-Méndez writes about intercontinental movements from Latin to North America, specifically from Mexico to the United States. Howard describes transnational migration of young people within Africa, who are 'trafficked' from Benin for Nigeria, while Thorsen captures rural–urban migration as she follows young people who migrate from the southeastern region of Burkina Faso to the capital Ouagadougou or to Abidjan, the capital Côte d'Ivoire.

Veale and Andres show how conventional countries of exit migration, like Ireland, have become countries of immigration for Nigerian migrants, while Donà identifies multiple destination countries for Rwandan forced migrants who spend time in Togo, the UK and Belgium. Razy's chapter highlights 'reverse' mobility from Europe to Africa, with children of Malian migrants being sent 'back' from France to Mali to be socialized into Malian society. Lakshman, Perera and Sangasumana examine the impact of parental migration from Asia to the Middle East on the children who are left behind in Sri Lanka, while Yeh examines the pleasure mobility of young Asian migrants and British-born children of Asian migrant families. Taken together, these examples of child and youth migration indicate that contemporary movements are multidirectional and global. In the book, we used the word 'migration' to refer to broad migratory movements, and we introduce the term 'mobility-in-migration' to highlight the multiple mobilities that take place within broader migratory waves.

While migration is generally understood as long-term mass movement, such as international migration, rural–urban migration, or return migration, mobility usually refers to daily trips, short-term holidays and journeys, and short-distance movements that usually take place in rooted environments. Children and young are growing up in an increasingly mobile world (Urry 2007), and settled individuals too can lead 'mobile lives'. In this book, we use the term 'mobility-in-migration' to describe multidirectional and multitemporal movements that occur within individual, family and community migratory 'arcs'.

The book focuses on forms of mobility that take place within broad migration waves. Yeh, for instance, writes about pleasure mobility to refer to trips that young Asian migrants as well as UK-born children of Asian migrants undertake to participate in 'Oriental nights', while Punch shows the use of 'ongoing mobilities' that take place within international labor migration as an adaptive response to the neoliberal economic crisis in Argentina, where young Bolivians who migrated to Argentina continue to move as they look for seasonal work across the country. As a result of the crisis, there are also changes in the frequency and duration of short-term mobilities, with visits to family and friends in Bolivia becoming shorter and return trips less frequent. Overall, contributors show that return mobilities fulfill important functions for these young migrants. Thorsen, for instance, writes about the meaning that commodity gifts have as a status symbol of being a successful migrant.

Donà examines the collective function of return trips for young Rwandans who grew up in the diaspora and who return during their holidays to participate in solidarity camps, where they learn about Rwanda culture, values and norms and strengthen their national identity. Razy's describes the community functions of such short return trips not only for the children involved but also for the community at large. French-Malian children are sent back to learn the culturally appropriate gender-based social skills that are valued in Mali. These trips fulfill a broader compensatory function, and they compensate for what Razy refers to as 'migratory debt'. Children are sent back to compensate for the departure of their parents, and through this type of child mobility, intercontinental kinship and community ties are maintained.

Thus, this edited collection's contribution to the existing literature on the migration of children and young people lies in the identification, description and analysis of different forms of mobility-in-migration. This specific type of movement is still an underresearched area of investigation, and we hope that this book has contributed to giving visibility to this phenomenon, highlighted the significant functions it fulfills and showed how it is embedded in family and community lives.

Migrant child and family life trajectories

As contributors followed the movements made by children, young people and their families over time, it became apparent that a strict distinction between children, adolescents and adults was difficult to maintain, as some of those who first moved as children continued to do so while growing up, and other young migrant adults gave birth to new generations of children whose lives are shaped by intergenerational migrant lives. A distinctive feature of this edited collection is that it brings to the fore the complex relationship that exists between migration and child development. Contributors show that migration takes place across the life span, and the movements of children and young people are ongoing or on-and-off arrangements that are embedded in individual, kin and community lives.

Lakshman, Perera and Sangasumana analyze the educational impact of parental migration on young children left behind, while Veale and

Andres examine transnational families and the long-distance relationships among parents and their children and among siblings abroad and those who stayed behind. Both chapters situate the experiences of children left behind in relation to those of other family members of different ages, including siblings. Thorsen and Howard explore the work and consumption practices of older children and adolescent migrants, and their relationships to other children and family members during their holiday trips. Punch, Carpena-Méndez and Donà describe the different kinds of mobility-in-migration that children of different ages engage in as they grow up. Carpena-Méndez goes further to follow adolescents into adulthood and writes about the challenges of young Mexican migrant girls who become single mothers in Philadelphia. The edited collection gives a sense of the passing of time for children and young people, and it shows the relationship between migration and developmental trajectories. Migration and mobility-in-migration are dynamic and adaptive responses to globalization.

The book offers insights into the developmental and migrant trajectories of children and young people in general. Additionally, it brings to the fore contemporary issues that are relevant to specific groups. For instance, Howard problematizes discourses on 'trafficked children' and compares them to the realities of their working lives. Carpena-Méndez clearly describes the challenges encountered by young undocumented Mexican migrants in the United States, and Donà examines the impact of war and genocide on internally displaced and refugee children and young people. Contributions by Lakshman, Perera and Sangasumana and by Veale and Andres help us understand the developmental impact of parental migration on children left behind, while Yeh and Razy add an intergenerational dimension to the understanding of mobility-in-migration by writing about children from migrant families.

Children's and young people's movements are embedded in intergenerational and historic migrations. Carpena-Méndez shows the historic connections between youth migration from Mexico to the United States and previous generations of Mexicans who have crossed the border. The gifts brought back by successful young migrants, described by Thorsen, become pull factors to migrate for children and young people living in the rural communities of southeastern Burkina Faso from where migration originated. These examples indicate that child and youth migration is embedded in family and community lives, and they show how migration can be used to fulfill multiple purposes that are both individual and collective.

The book situates micro-level analysis of individual and family mobility-in-migration within macro-level processes of globalization.

Punch describes regional and internal migrations in the context of the Argentinian economic crisis; Lakshman, Perera and Sangasumana examine the impact of parental migration on children in a postconflict context of poverty and development. Howard examines contemporary global discourses on trafficking that take place at the policy level nationally and internationally. Yeh discusses the power and influence of global youth cultures on the lives and mobilities of young people. The book brings to the fore the connections that exist between individuals and contexts, and it shows how child and youth migration are embedded in globalized sociopolitical and sociocultural contexts.

In addition to the key thematic threads of the book described above, a number of subthemes emerged in the different chapters. In the following sections we explore in greater depth three of them: gendered migrations, consumption and self-representation, and changing transnational families. Gender is an underexamined dimension of child and youth migration, while consumption is an emerging research topic in migration studies, and changes in transnational families are worth exploring in greater depth.

Children's and young people's gendered migrations

In contrast to adult migration literature in which gender dynamics and the impact of gender on migration is considered, child and youth migration is often perceived to be gender neutral. Crawley (2011), for instance, criticizes the view of asylum-seeking children in the UK as 'asexual beings'. A number of contributors to this book examine the intersection of gender and migration. Carpena-Méndez illustrates the ways in which gender dynamics in rural Mexico influence migration patterns: a division between boys' and girls' *bandas* is replicated in the separate migration of boys and girls who move with other male or female members of their gangs and rely on one another for support in Philadelphia. In the new country, Mexican boys, who live in same-sex dwellings with other banda members, learn to perform tasks traditionally done by women, most notably cooking. Young male migrants show adaptability to the new environment but also readiness to revert to old gender roles models upon return. Through return migration migrant youth adapt and revert gender roles. This shift captures how gender roles are dynamic and shaped by context.

Lakshman, Perera and Sangasumana show that the education-related benefits for children left behind are gender nuanced. They compare the impact of mother- versus father-migration on the education of children left behind, a distinction that has not been sufficiently examined in the literature on transnational families, which tends to focus on the mother's migration. The authors show that households with migrant mothers spend a lower proportion of funds on education than those with migrant fathers. The reasons for this difference are attributed to the contexts and backgrounds of these families. The majority of migrant mothers come from poor backgrounds and had to resort to working as housemaids in the Middle East as a survival strategy. In many cases the spouses of migrant women had low educational qualifications and were in low-paying jobs or unemployed. The extended family was also involved in the care of the children left behind, and remittances sent home by migrant mothers had become the main income for the whole family. The migration of fathers had a positive influence on children's school enrolment and educational outcomes, and this difference was attributed to social factors and motivations, with fathers migrating for higher wages or higher status, leaving their spouses behind to look after the family and children.

Razy's description of gendered mobilities of French-born Malian children brings to the fore the intersection between gender, migration and child development. These visits take place so that boys and girls learn to conform to traditional values and prepare to fulfill culturally appropriate gender roles. Young girls, usually between the ages of seven and nine, are sent 'back home' to Mali, and the purpose of their stay is to learn the skills associated with being good wives and mothers. Razy's work reveals the developmental function of these trips, which take place not for marriage, as described in the literature on child brides, but to learn the skills that will prepare them for marriage when they are older. Boys' trips fulfill different functions. In addition to socializing them into adult roles, the visits also serve to reeducate 'problem boys'.

The examples given highlight the gendered nature of child and adolescent migration and the need to study this subject systematically in future research.

Migrant workers and migrant consumers: migration, consumption and self-representation

A number of chapters in this edited collection show the connections that exist between migration, work and consumption. Globalization turns citizens into consumers of global goods. Thorsen and Howard show how young migrants work in order to be able to buy cheap products that enhance their status as successful migrants. Yeh describes the 'pleasure consumption' of British-born Chinese through their participation in 'Oriental nights' and more broadly in global youth cultures.

As young people move to find work or to find better or regular work, they become migrant workers. Differently from adult migrants or from older generations who may have saved to buy houses or invested in long-term products, the young people described in this book move in order to work to partake in a youth and consumption-oriented, cash-based economy. Their migration is not only carried out for survival but also for consumption. Adolescents use their earnings to buy status-symbol goods or to experience pleasure, and in this process they shift from being migrant workers to becoming migrant consumers.

Work and consumption are part of growing up in the era of globalization. Children's and adolescents' consumption of global goods fulfills developmental and social functions. Young people undergo individuation as they move and make consumerist choices to express their migrant selves. The ability to work and to buy signals their transition from being dependent children to becoming independent adults. Migration increases their opportunities to become consumers of global goods and to show their purchasing power. This fulfills a social function of enhancing their status as successful migrants in the eyes of their communities and strengthens their positive self-representation. As Howard indicates, an individual's returning from Abeokuta to rural Benin with material goods such as a motorbike, clothes or a generator represented evidence of his successful migration and thus constituted a material path to his being 'considered' by those around him upon his return.

However, the link between migration, work and consumption is not always straightforward. Carpena-Méndez shows the subaltern economic integration of young Mexican migrants to the United States in the context of the segmentation between protected and unprotected labor that makes it difficult for them to find jobs and simultaneously forces them to keep several low-paid jobs. Their subjection to capitalist discipline produces feelings of exhaustion and disorientation in many of the youth, showing the negative impact of globalization.

Punch also reveals the negative impact of the neoliberal crisis on young Bolivian migrants living in Argentina, who had to change their consumption practices to adjust to the huge reduction in the exchange rate and high levels of inflation. For some of them, that meant eating less as well as eating cheaper foodstuffs. These young migrants and migrant consumers are subjected to the appeal of consumerism. And yet they also convey a sense of disillusionment that comes from their inability to fully access some of anticipated benefits of being a migrant consumer. They live at the peripheries of global centers of power and are located at the margins of globalization.

Transnational families and communities: living together at a distance

While research on transnational families has expanded to include individual, family and community levels of analysis (Falicov 2007; Graham and Jordan 2011), as well as to explore transnational family dynamics (Åkesson et al. 2012; Reynolds 2009), the literature is dominated by a conceptual model that is bilocated, or 'here and there', whereby family members live in different countries. The practice of children following migrant adults, described by Orellana et al. (2001), as 'the immigrant sent for his wife and children' (p. 578) is often described as a once-off mobility to a final destination point. Only rarely has the literature noted the cross-border comings and goings of children in migrant households. One notable exception is that of Boehm (2008), who captured the mobility of transnational children, ranging in age from infants to adolescents, between the United States and Mexico. Taken together as a collection, the chapters in this book have extended the understanding of transnational families beyond bilocated homes to look at the 'in-between' spaces, such as when children move to and fro for short or longer periods, as we saw in Razy's chapter, in which she interrogates the function of this movement for the collective group. The chapters add an extra dimension to our understanding of the complexity of transnational family dynamics, through extending the focus from the nuclear family, in which one or both parents migrate and children are left behind, to the mobility of different actors and the implications for the family as a whole; to the impact on children when mothers rather than fathers migrate (Lakshman, Perera and Sangasumana); to the impact on grandparents when young migrants have children in another country (Punch); to the impact on siblings when they are separated from their siblings who live elsewhere (Veale and Andres). The book captures new transnational structures, such as when children, teens and young people move and it is parents who are left behind, creating other forms of transnational families (Punch, Carpena-Méndez).

Conclusion

This edited collection has highlighted the complexity of contemporary migration as it is undertaken by and impacts upon children and youth. The book adopted a child-and-youth-centered approach, privileging the use of empirical research that was for most part psychological, sociological and anthropological. Future research on child and youth migration would benefit from an examination of the implications of the interconnections between childhood and lifespan trajectories, mobility and migration, which are brought to the fore in this volume, for child and migration policies.

The multisited and multitemporal methodological approach that is shared across chapters helped us to think about and make connections across contexts, and it was instrumental in revealing the dynamism of contemporary movements. It also helped problematize existing distinctions between child, adolescent and adult migrant trajectories, recommending that future research investigate migration across the life span and across generations. We asked the contributors to think about the connections across the contexts in which they had conducted their research, and the contributors did so retrospectively. In future research we recommend that a multisited, multitemporal methodological lens be adopted from the beginning of the project, if possible, as it would help strengthen the depth of analysis.

The book has shown the need to track child and youth mobility-in-migration more systematically and to conceptualize the centrality of understanding child and youth migration within the field of migration studies in general because it fulfills multiple functions for the group and society. The connection between child and youth migration and globalization is an area that requires further study; we are aware that we have only 'scratched the surface'.

Castles and Miller (2009)'s classic book *The Age of Migration* showed the global nature of migration. To fully capture the changing nature of global migration, there is a need to examine its new manifestations, and that includes not only corporeal but also 'virtual' movements. Information and communication technologies are an important dimension of globalization, and as children and young people grow up in the digital age, there is a need to explore how young migrants engage with social media. There is an increased interest in e-diasporas (Diminescu 2012; Fortunati et al. 2012; Wilding and Gifford 2013), but these recent studies have examined the role of information and communication technologies in the lives of adult migrants. In this edited collection, Yeh and Donà described some of ways in which young mobile people engage with virtuality, and there is much scope to study young e-diasporas.

References

Åkesson, L., Carling, J., and Drotbohm, H. (2012) 'Mobility, Moralities and Motherhood: Navigating the Contingencies of Cape Verdean Lives', *Journal of Ethnic and Migration Studies*, 38(2), 237–260.

Boehm, D. (2008) '"For My Children:" Constructing Family and Navigating the State in the U.S.-Mexico Transnation', *Anthropological Quarterly*, 81(4), 777–802.

Castles, S., and Miller, M. (2009) *The Age of Migration: International Population Movements in the Modern World*, 4th ed (Basingstoke: Palgrave Macmillan).

Crawley, H. (2011) 'Asexual, Apolitical Beings': The Interpretation of Children's Identities and Experiences in the UK Asylum System', *Journal of Ethnic and Migration Studies*, 37, 1171–1184.

Diminescu, D. (2012) Digital Methods for the Exploration, Analysis and Mapping of E-Diasporas, *Social Science Information*, 51, 451–458 (Special Issue: Diaspora on the Web).

Falicov, C. (2007) 'Working with Transnational Immigrants: Expanding Meanings of Family, Community and Culture', *Family Process*, 46(2), 157–171.

Fortunati, L., Pertierra, R., and Vincent, J. (eds) (2012) *Migration, Diaspora and Information Technology in Global Societies* (London: Routledge).

Graham, E., and Jordan, L. (2011) 'Migrant Parents and the Psychological Well-Being of Left-Behind Children in Southeast Asia', *Journal of Marriage and Family*, 73, 763–787.

Orellana, M., Thorne, B., Chee, A., and Lam, W. (2001) 'Transnational Childhoods: The Participation of Children in Processes of Family Migration', *Social Problems*, 48(4), 572–591.

Urry, J. (2007) *Mobilities* (Cambridge: Polity Press).

Reynolds, T. (2009) 'Transnational Family Relationships, Social Networks and Return Migration among British-Caribbean Young People', *Ethnic and Racial Studies*, 33(5), 797–815.

Wilding, R., and Gifford, S. M. (2013) 'Special Issue: Forced Displacement, Refugees and ICTs: Transformations of Place, Power and Social Ties', *Journal of Refugee Studies*, 26(4), 495–504.

Index

Printed and bound by CPI Group (UK) Ltd, Croydon, CR0 4YY